Anne **Vallayer-Coster**

KELSEY BROSNAN

GETTY PUBLICATIONS
LOS ANGELES

Published in the United States of America by Getty Publications, Los Angeles
1200 Getty Center Drive, Suite 500
Los Angeles, California 90049-1682
getty.edu/publications

Distributed in the United States and Canada by the University of Chicago Press

Printed in Bosnia and Herzegovina

A catalogue record for this book is available from the Library of Congress
ISBN 979-8-88712-010-2

Published simultaneously in the United Kingdom by Lund Humphries
Originated by Lund Humphries
Second Home Spitalfields
60-80 Hanbury Street
London E1 5JH
UK
lundhumphries.com

Copy edited by Julie Gunz
Project managed and designed by Crow Books
Set in Adobe Caslon Pro

Front cover: Anne Vallayer-Coster, *Still Life with Seashells and Coral* (detail), 1769, oil on canvas, 130 × 97 cm (51⅛ × 38¼ in.), Musée du Louvre, Paris

Back cover: Anne Vallayer-Coster, *Still Life with Flowers in an Alabaster Vase and Fruit*, 1783, oil on canvas, 108.5 × 89.5 cm (42¾ × 35¼ in.), National Gallery of Art, Washington, DC

With generous support from the Tavolozza Foundation

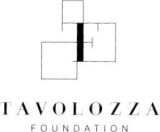

TAVOLOZZA
FOUNDATION

MIX
Paper | Supporting responsible forestry
FSC® C118234

Contents

Series Foreword

Illuminating Women Artists: The Eighteenth Century was conceptualized at a moment of reinvigorated interest in contemporary culture about women artmakers and their contributions to the visual arts. A burgeoning awareness of the implications of structural bias as it relates to gender, race and sexual identity simultaneously infused new perspectives into academic research, museum exhibitions and acquisitions of art, both public and private. Books in Illuminating Women Artists engage with insights of these related cultural initiatives to advance a feminist enterprise through the study of their subjects. The volumes investigate the lives and contributions of women of the eighteenth century, embedding them into their specific social and historical contexts. Accounting for diverse identities and experiences, they make evident various ways that early modern women negotiated, and sometimes resisted, structural constraints in the sphere of the visual arts.

The series is indebted to feminist art-historical studies that were first produced in the 1970s in response to the broader women's rights movements of that time. This foundational scholarship aimed to disrupt the traditional academic focus on early modern male artists by writing their female counterparts into the discipline of art history. Since then, feminist scholarship has investigated gender norms that created different conditions for women and men who sought to practice art as professionals or amateurs. That scholarship has demonstrated that women were ambitious, successful and fully embedded in artistic practice on a variety of levels, and were not merely marginal to the story of masculine creation and triumph that has yet to be seriously decentered in art history. This work also began to make clear the challenges of the category of the 'woman' artist, pointing toward a certain fluidity in gender and sexual identities with which some current scholarship is concerned. Certainly, the term 'artist' is also fraught in gendered terms, given that early modern women sometimes worked in media that were undervalued in later centuries and thus were obscured in the scholarship.

Illuminating Women Artists: The Eighteenth Century considers women artists within their social, cultural, temporal and geographic contexts. In particular it shows how women in Europe worked under a variety of challenging conditions from the late seventeenth century into the early nineteenth. This 'long eighteenth century' was an era defined by radical transformations in thought, culture, society and politics brought about by the philosophical movement known as the Enlightenment, the rise (and sometimes the fall) of expansionist ambitions of colonialism and empire, wars and revolutions. Questions about the nature and ideal role of women in society were at the heart of the most pressing cultural, philosophical, political and social debates of this period. Women authors and artists played a key role in those debates and challenged normative structures in important ways. They were also products of the social structures of their place and time, such as gender, class and race. These structures contributed to the formation of women's identities and to their conceptions about others. Thus acculturated into dominant cultural attitudes, women artists were complicit in supporting social hierarchies of class and race. They themselves derived from a spectrum of social classes – artisan, merchant, professional or patrician. So far, none has come to light that can be identified as anything other than racially white.

Societal limitations disadvantaged most women who aspired to a life in the visual arts. For example, women were excluded from the formal training open to male artists through art academies or guilds, and therefore they sought private instruction elsewhere, often from relatives, both male and female, but also in the private studios of established artists. Marriage and motherhood could contribute to a lapse in artistic production. Presumably for this reason, some women did not marry until they were fully established as professional artists, or they did not marry at all. Being unmarried presented challenges of its own, as women in this period had virtually no civil or political rights, and they generally needed a supportive male relative to act on their behalf in legal and business matters. Some men did train, and/or supportively promote their daughters or wives as artists, which also aggrandized the family and improved its financial standing through patronage and sales.

Women who were professionally successful and their artistic production critically acclaimed, were nonetheless often evaluated according to gender stereotypes. Yet, certain women independently challenged, and circumvented or broke, restrictive gender protocols to enable prolific art production. In the process, they revised those protocols and influenced the history of art. Some established their own professional studios, publicly exhibited their works and trained pupils, both female and male, who in turn established themselves as professionals in studios of their own. Some produced images for prestigious European courts and churches. Others were involved with scientific enquiry, producing illustrations for research and publications in the fields of natural history, medicine or entomology. Women held official posts as royal botanical illustrators, court portraitists or drawing teachers. Some were members of art academies or guilds. Many more – hundreds by the end of the eighteenth century – had no official affiliations, but availed themselves of expanding opportunities to exhibit their work at public exhibitions and commercial venues. Thanks to a burgeoning art market and a taste for collecting art, women were able to produce work for patrons and customers across a broad social spectrum, from the most elite classes (kings, queens, aristocrats) to the more middling sorts. These women in the aggregate produced works that varied widely in artistic media and in subject and genre, including narrative subjects from history, mythology and literature, as well as sacred themes, portraiture and still life.

Five decades of sustained research have transformed our understanding of early modern women artists. *Illuminating Women Artists: The Eighteenth Century* takes stock of this work through books that offer state-of-the-question analyses of their subjects. These peer-reviewed volumes variously interweave established conclusions with new discoveries investigated through emerging modes of analysis to reframe our understanding of the lives, artistic production and works of art by European women. Books in this series make a substantive case for women's presence in aesthetic culture, and trace the complex circumstances that conditioned their making of art, their careers and their lives. Together they reveal the varied ways in which women of the long eighteenth century skillfully and often successfully navigated restricting gender norms to stake out productive lives as artmakers and develop innovative approaches to the works they produced. The volumes offer an unprecedented contextualization of the lives and works of their subjects, to whom in some cases a monograph has not previously been dedicated.

Marilyn Dunn, Loyola University Chicago
Melissa Hyde, University of Florida

Acknowledgements

My sincere thanks go to Erika Gaffney, the sage steward of this project, who offered much guidance and encouragement. The editors of this series, Melissa Hyde and Marilyn Dunn, provided essential critical feedback; it was a privilege to have my writing interrogated and improved by these scholars. I thank Julie Gunz for her sharp edits, as well as the two anonymous peer reviewers for their generous evaluations of the manuscript. Thank you to the team at Lund Humphries, especially Lucie Ewin, Sarah Thorowgood and Rebeccah Williams.

I thank my colleagues at museums across the United States, United Kingdom and France for sharing their extensive knowledge and images with me. I remain indebted to Aaron Wile, Associate Curator of seventeenth- and eighteenth-century French paintings, who enabled me to visit his recent Vallayer-Coster acquisition in the conservation studio of the National Gallery of Art in Washington, DC. I must also acknowledge Galerie Eric Coatalem, Taylor Alessio at Christie's and Zola Hoehn at Sotheby's, all of whom provided me with access to images of works in private collections.

This project was informed by my doctoral research on Anne Vallayer-Coster, undertaken at Rutgers University. My graduate advisor, Professor Susan Sidlauskas, provided vital support throughout the writing process. In its final stage, my dissertation was further shaped by comments from Professors Catherine Puglisi, Sarah McHam and Jennifer Jones. My writing on this artist has also benefited from editing by Brigid Boyle, Franchesca Fee and Virginia McBride of the *Rutgers Art Review*, as well as Arlene Weis and Kacie Willis, the editors of *Women and the Art and Science of Collecting in Eighteenth-Century Europe*. I am thankful for the opportunities to present my ideas on this artist at the College Art Association (CAA) Annual Conference in 2022, in a panel on eighteenth-century women organized by Melissa Hyde and Paris Spies-Gans, as well as the American Society for Eighteenth-Century Studies (ASECS) Annual Meetings in 2019 and 2018. My work was also supported by the History of Art and Design Department at the Pratt Institute.

I could not have finished this book without the kind support and childcare provided by the Coriell family: thank you Carol, Brian and Michelle. I am especially grateful to my own family, including my beloved siblings, Ally and Ryan Brosnan. My parents, Marianne and Timothy Brosnan, have loved me all my life in a way that I only now fully understand. I hope that I have made you all proud. Finally, to David Coriell and our daughters, Violet, Ophelia and Cleopatra: it is all thanks to you and it is all for you.

Introduction

Anne Vallayer-Coster (1744–1818) was 25 years old when she was accepted into the Académie royale de peinture et de sculpture (French Royal Academy of Painting and Sculpture) in Paris in July 1770 (fig.1) – one of only 15 women artists admitted to the Académie in its history. Between 1771 and 1817, Vallayer-Coster exhibited regularly at the biennial Salon, a public exhibition sponsored by the Académie. Her bold, complex and sensual still-life paintings elicited ample praise from critics, and she soon earned the patronage of Queen Marie Antoinette and other members of the French court.[1] Vallayer-Coster is today known by her hyphenated name, which she used to sign her work after her marriage in 1781 – as did her fellow *académiciennes* (female academicians), the royal portraitists Adélaïde Labille-Guiard (1749–1803) and Élisabeth Vigée Le Brun (1755–1842).[2]

Despite her professional success, Vallayer-Coster has received relatively little scholarly attention. This is due in part to her subject matter: she primarily painted still lifes, considered to be the least important and least interesting genre of painting in the eighteenth century and beyond.[3] Yet Vallayer-Coster has also been marginalized in comparison with the most esteemed French still-life artist, Jean Siméon Chardin (1699–1779). The philosopher and art critic Denis Diderot (1713–84), for example, directly compared Chardin and Vallayer-Coster when they both exhibited at the Salon of 1771, when he was 71 years old and she 26. Diderot described Vallayer-Coster's work as 'excellent, vigorous, harmonious; it's not Chardin, however, but if it's less good than this master, it's far above what is to be expected of a woman . . .'.[4] Vallayer-Coster exceeded Diderot's low expectations for women artists (who were more often discussed in relation to one another), even if he believed she did not equal Chardin.

Since the eighteenth century, much of the modern scholarship on still lifes has been dedicated to Chardin, and his name remains practically synonymous with the genre.[5] Chardin eclipsed Vallayer-Coster until 2002, when the first major exhibition devoted to this *académicienne* traveled from the National Gallery of Art in Washington, DC to the Dallas Museum of Art and the Frick Collection in New York. The accompanying exhibition catalogue, *Anne Vallayer-Coster: Painter to the Court of Marie-Antoinette*, was the first monograph in English dedicated to this artist. The catalogue included a biographical summary by Marianne Roland Michel, author of the 1970 French catalogue raisonné. Eik Kahng, then Curator at the Dallas Museum of Art, contrasted the paintings of Chardin and Vallayer-Coster. Colin Bailey, then Chief Curator of the Frick Collection, outlined Vallayer-Coster's patronage network, and

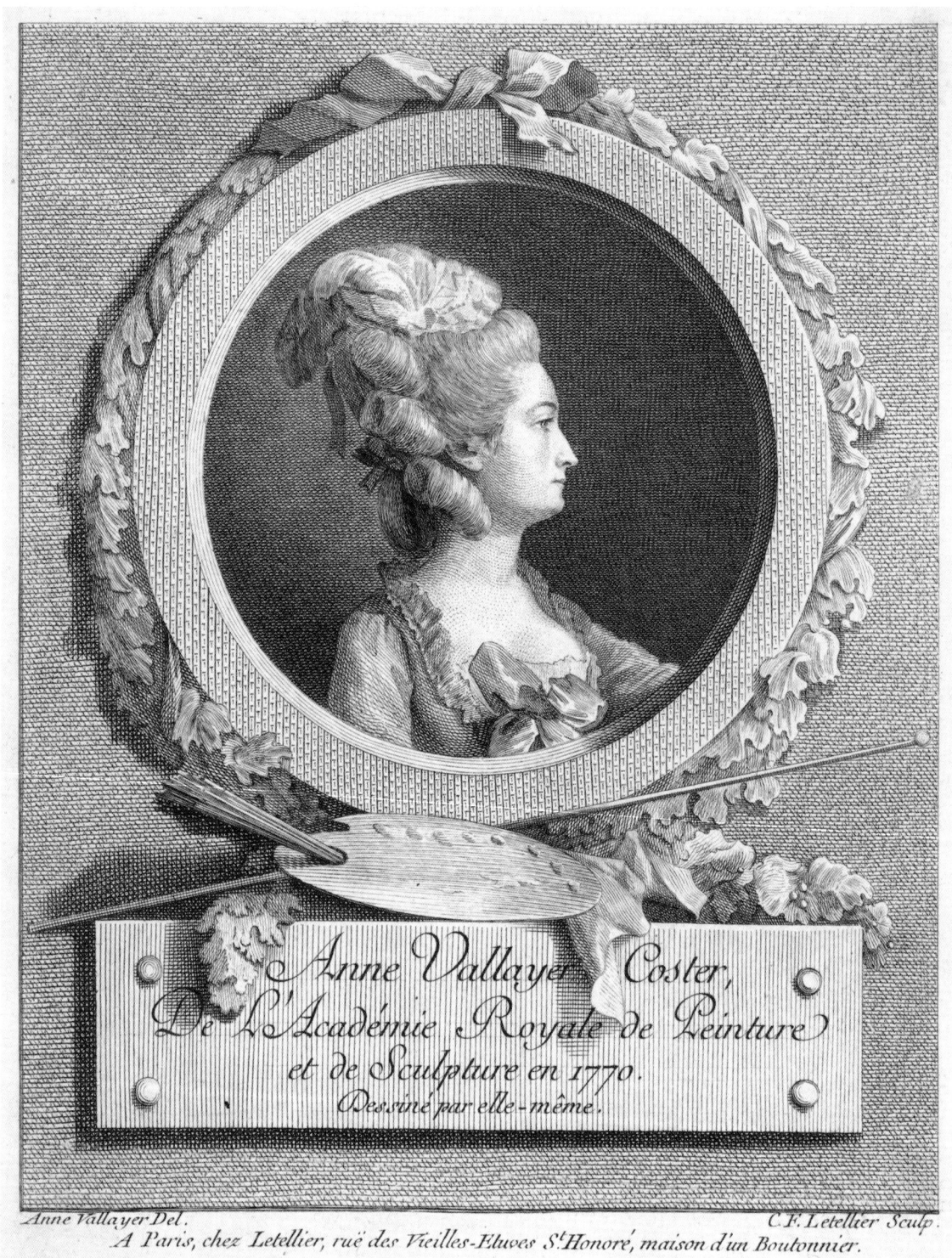

1 Charles Francois Le Tellier after Anne Vallayer-Coster, *Anne Vallayer-Coster, Académicienne*, after 1781, etching and engraving, 23.4 × 18.6 cm (9 ¼ × 7 ⅜ in), National Gallery of Art, Washington, DC

Melissa Hyde described the professional landscape for female artists in eighteenth-century Paris. Claire Barry, then Director of Conservation at the Kimbell Museum of Art, analyzed the technique and materiality of Vallayer-Coster's paintings. The catalogue concluded with a checklist of 137 extant oil paintings and 22 works in other media (including tapestries and works on paper).[6]

The present book, the first dedicated to this artist in more than 20 years, builds upon the major scholarly contributions of the 1970 catalogue raisonné and 2002 exhibition catalogue, but offers a fresh, feminist re-evaluation of Vallayer-Coster's life and work. My analysis is indebted to several art historians who have provided compelling models for writing about women artists: notably, Mary Sheriff's groundbreaking feminist study of Vigée Le Brun,[7] Melissa Hyde's substantial body of writings on many of Vallayer-Coster's female peers[8] and Paris Spies-Gans's data-driven macro-history of French and British women artists during the revolutionary era.[9]

This text proposes a new conceptual framework for looking at Vallayer-Coster's still-life paintings. Her canvases convey a wide range of different textures, which are directly inspired by the embodied acts of looking, touching, smelling and tasting. Her paintings in turn elicit a range of somatic responses: visual, tactile, olfactory and gustatory. Accordingly, Vallayer-Coster's works are here placed in dialogue with the eighteenth-century philosophical discourse on the senses.[10]

During Vallayer-Coster's lifetime, French philosophers sought to understand sensory experience.[11] In *Traité des sensations* (*Treatise on Sensations*, 1754), Étienne Bonnot de Condillac maintained that subjectivity was developed through the total integration of all the senses.[12] Diderot also wrote extensively on this topic, musing 'nothing is real but our sensations, the void of space, and even the solid mass of bodies may contain nothing but what we feel . . .'.[13] He went on to rank the senses as

follows: 'sight is the most superficial, hearing the most arrogant, smell the most voluptuous, taste the most superstitious and the least faithful, touch the most profound and the most philosophical'.[14]

These *philosophes* seem to define a universal human condition, but their descriptions of sensory experience were undeniably gendered. Men and women were believed to feel and respond to sights, sounds, tastes and smells differently – much as they were understood to think and paint in different ways. In his 1772 essay, 'On Women', Diderot wrote that women are often overwhelmed by physical sensations – because they are 'less in control of their senses than we [men] are'.[15] The physician Pierre Roussel concurred, writing of a woman's 'difficulty in shedding the tyranny of her sensations that constantly binds her to the immediate causes which produced them'.[16] For Roussel, this had direct consequences for a woman artist, who was 'more capable of sensing than of creating, she receives more easily in her mind the image of objects that she cannot reproduce'.[17]

Women were considered vulnerable to sensory whims, but men could also be led astray – especially in close proximity to women. As Jean-Jacques Rousseau's tutor warned his pupil in *Émile, ou De l'Éducation* (*Emile, or, On Education*, 1762): 'You do not know the fury with which the senses, by the lure of pleasure, drag young men like you into the abyss of the vices.'[18] The risk of temptation informed debates about women across French society, including women artists in the Académie. In 1790, the Secretary of the Académie, Antoine Renou (1731–1806), wrote of male and female artists: 'It is said that Talent has no sex but those who possess it have one, and when it is feminine, it must be kept away from the masculine because of its inevitable influence.'[19] Renou argued that *académiciennes* might distract or use their feminine charms to sway male artists and critics: 'One knows how heavily women weigh in the balance of judgment and how even judges with the most integrity risk being seduced by them. The centuries of antiquity, like ours, give a thousand examples of seduction of this kind.'[20]

The theme of seduction also emerges in the eighteenth-century criticism of Vallayer-Coster's art. Her contemporaries debated the seductive qualities in her work, while emphasizing the artist's own modesty. M. Guichard declared in the *Mercure de France* in September 1770: 'The disadvantages of her sex notwithstanding, she has taken the difficult art of rendering nature to a degree of perfection that enchants and surprises us.'[21] After her work appeared at the Salon of 1775, art critic Gabriel Bouquier praised the artist herself: 'This Demoiselle combines in her person all the graces of her sex.'[22] An anonymous enthusiast concurred in 1777, writing: 'Ah! I admire her character / Even more than her talent / She knows how decently / to combine agreeable pleasure / Candor and prudence / Intelligence and feeling. The common-place art of seduction / Has ever been foreign to her heart; / She pleases as she breathes / Without effort or reflection.'[23] Conversely, others hailed the 'seductive color, and the refined and vigorous touch' of her paintings.[24] Another simply exclaimed 'Superb! Truly superb! Observe how very truthful and seductive!'[25]

These eighteenth-century critics characterized Vallayer-Coster and her work as either voluptuous or prim, but the idea of seduction is at the heart of their rhetoric. Their hyperbolic language is somewhat typical of the art criticism of that period, particularly of women artists. Yet it has also infiltrated twenty-first-century discussions of Vallayer-Coster. Roland Michel concluded her essay in the 2002 catalogue: 'We are seduced today by this gathering of exceptional works. The contemporaries of Anne Vallayer-Coster were as well . . .'. .[26] In his review of the 2002 exhibition, Mario Naves of *The New York Observer* noted that Vallayer-Coster's paintings are 'sensual and hedonistic' and 'suffused with a languid opulence' – though 'one can't quite work up a passion for Vallayer-Coster's art', which warrants only 'polite admiration'.[27] In a *Washington Post* article entitled 'Sensual Still Lifes: Built to Lust?', Blake Gopnik wrote that this 'modest little still-life exhibition' included paintings that at first 'seemed chaste and mild-mannered enough for any lady-in-waiting'; soon, however, Gopnik 'began to feel a little overheated'; he goes on to describe the depicted surfaces in salivating detail.[28]

There is no denying that Vallayer-Coster delighted in painting a diversity of textures – smooth, rough, spongy, silky, scaly, furry, fleshy, sticky-ripe – that provoke strong sensory responses. Accordingly, this book is organized around the various surfaces that occupied the artist throughout her career. The first chapter summarizes the facts of Vallayer-Coster's personal and professional life and situates her within the cultural context of late eighteenth-century Paris. The second chapter analyzes Vallayer-Coster's three largest and most ambitious allegorical still lifes, all produced in the first decade of her career. These works glorify the very substance of human life: art, music, nature, nation and war are allegorized through inanimate objects. The third chapter deals with Vallayer-Coster's paintings of food, which are informed by aesthetic and gustatory taste, but also entangled within the broader cultural, economic and philosophic food systems of eighteenth-century Paris.

Vallayer-Coster's paintings of guns and game are the subject of the fourth chapter. Hunting, a masculine and aristocratic sport, had been a popular theme of French painting since the seventeenth century.[29] In her own rather ambiguous representations of the subject, however, Vallayer-Coster emphasized the sensuality of the plumed breasts of felled pheasants and furry underbellies of limp hares, draped over the tools of their slaughter. The fifth chapter discusses the throbbing femininity of Vallayer-Coster's paintings of shells – embodied by slick, fleshy-pink conchs – along with the early modern fashion for collecting 'exotic' natural specimens. The sixth and final chapter is devoted

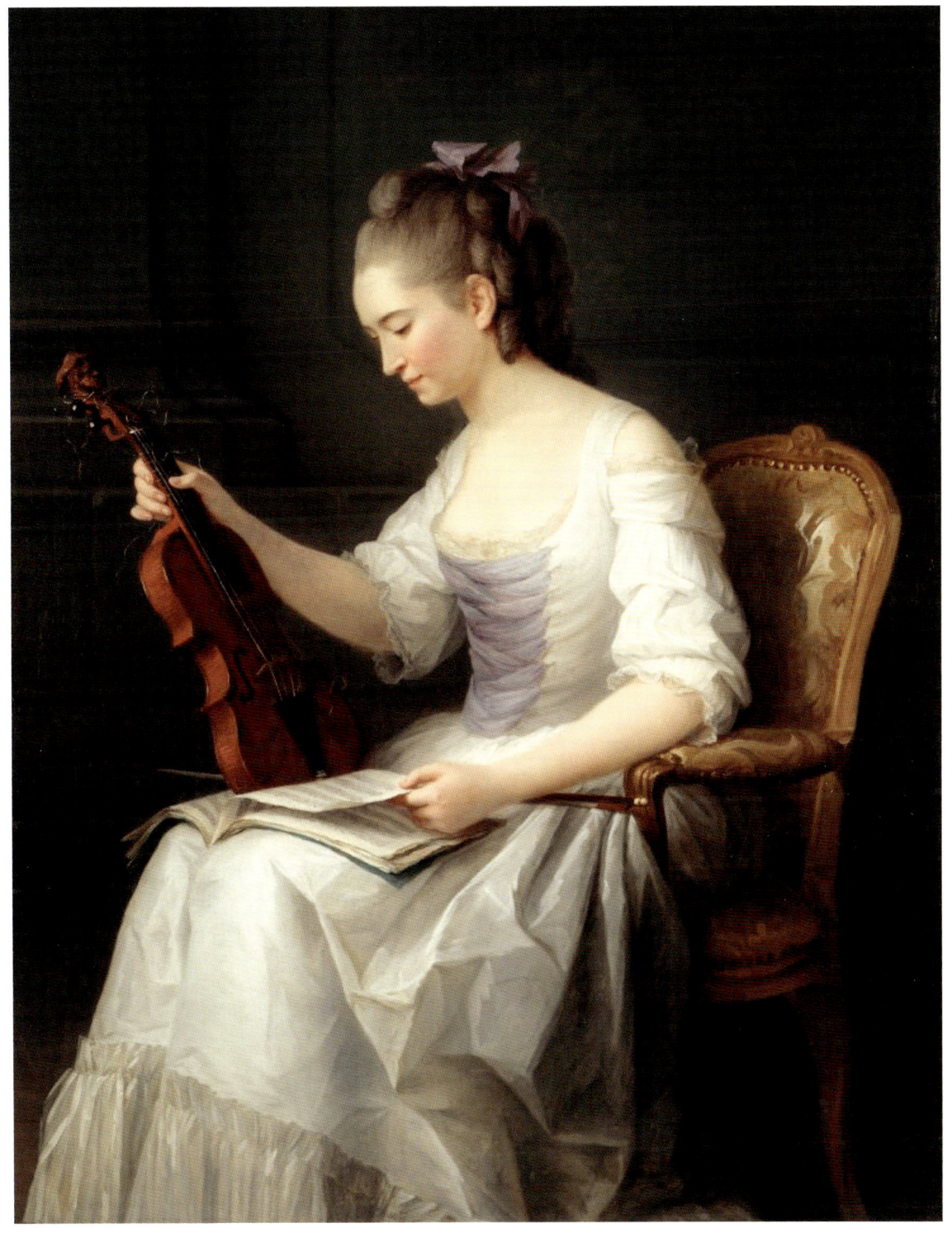

2   Anne Vallayer-Coster, *Portrait of a Violinist*, 1773, oil on canvas, 116 × 96 cm (45 ⅝ × 37 ¾ in), Nationalmuseum, Stockholm

to Vallayer-Coster's representations of flowers, the subject for which she is now best known, and which she painted most frequently in the final decades of her career. This chapter probes the perceived femininity of Vallayer-Coster's subject matter and painting technique, which are so evocative of floral scents.

This text concludes with an Appendix itemizing the paintings that Vallayer-Coster showed at the Salon. As the Appendix reveals, Vallayer-Coster's five-decade-long career was highly productive. Her participation in the Salon was most robust in the nearly two decades between her debut as an *academiciénne* in 1771 and the advent of the French Revolution in 1789, during which time she submitted 64 entries to the Salon. She participated only intermittently thereafter until her death in 1818, showing a total of 23 entries in three decades. In many cases, however, pendants or related groups of works are listed in the *livret* under a single number, thwarting a precise count of the number of artworks that she exhibited. In total, between 1771 and 1817, Vallayer-Coster contributed to 18 Salons. She abstained from eight Salons, beginning in 1791.

This book focuses on Vallayer-Coster's still-life paintings produced during the *ancien régime*. As the Appendix makes clear, however, she painted a significant number of figurative works – mostly depictions of women. In addition to portraits of Queen Marie Antoinette and Mesdames (the daughters of King Louis XV),[30] Vallayer-Coster also painted portraits of female performers: opera singer Madame de Saint-Huberty (National Museum of Women in the Arts, Washington, DC)[31] and an unknown violinist, perhaps modeled by one of the Vallayer sisters (Nationalmuseum, Stockholm; fig.2).[32]

In Vallayer-Coster's lifetime, paintings of people were considered more important than paintings of things. Still, many contemporary critics responded negatively to Vallayer-Coster's figurative work; her still lifes, by contrast, were more warmly received.[33] In this author's opinion, the artist's portraits are no less skilled than her paintings of inanimate objects. However, her still lifes offer twenty-first-century viewers profound insight into philosophical debates about the senses during the Enlightenment. For this reason, Vallayer-Coster's still lifes are the primary subject of this book.

I

Vallayer-Coster, *Académicienne / Citoyenne*

Before looking more closely at her still-life paintings, let us collate what is known of the artist's personal and professional life. Anne Vallayer was the second of four daughters born to Anne de la Fontaine (d.1791) and Louis-Joseph Vallayer (1704–70), a goldsmith of the Gobelins royal manufactory in Paris who initially specialized in luxury snuffboxes. Anne was baptized on 22 December 1744 at the nearby Église Saint-Hippolyte. Ten years later, in 1754, Monsieur Vallayer left Gobelins to establish his own practice, assisted by his wife. The Vallayer family then lived above their workshop on the rue du Roule, two blocks away from the Académie's headquarters at the Louvre (fig.3).[1]

Though she was raised in an artisanal milieu, the facts of Vallayer-Coster's early education are difficult to establish. Excluded from the classes offered to male students of the Académie, aspiring female artists like Vallayer-Coster typically learned to draw and paint through informal study with established artists. Madeleine Françoise Basseporte (1701–80) is often identified as Vallayer-Coster's first teacher. Basseporte became the official *dessinatrice du Jardin du Roi* (draftswoman of the Royal Botanical Gardens in Paris) in 1742 – the first woman to hold this post – and godmother to Vallayer-Coster's oldest sister, Madeleine, in 1743.[2] Given her intimate family connection to this successful female artist, we can assume that Vallayer-Coster admired and sought to

emulate Basseporte, but the extent of her training is unknown. Vallayer-Coster probably also spent some time under the tutelage of landscape painter Joseph Vernet (1714–89), an acquaintance of her father.[3] After her death in 1818, Vallayer-Coster's estate included 27 drawings and three paintings by Vernet, perhaps further evidence of their student-teacher relationship.[4]

Vallayer-Coster was also closely associated with the natural history painter and *académicienne* Marie-Thérèse Reboul (1735–1805). Reboul, who was married to the history painter Joseph-Marie Vien (1716–1809), led her own drawing school for girls; a few contemporaries described Vallayer-Coster as a distinguished student of that school. Importantly, Reboul Vien supported Vallayer-Coster's application to the Académie and personally accompanied her to the meeting at which her candidacy was evaluated in 1770.[5]

Whoever provided Vallayer-Coster's early education in the arts, it was likely with her father's support that she sought membership to the Académie, the elite professional institution for French artists. Sadly, just two days after Vallayer-Coster was received as a member on 28 July 1770, Monsieur Vallayer died at the age of 66.[6] Vallayer-Coster began her tenure as an *académicienne* under the specter of paternal loss.

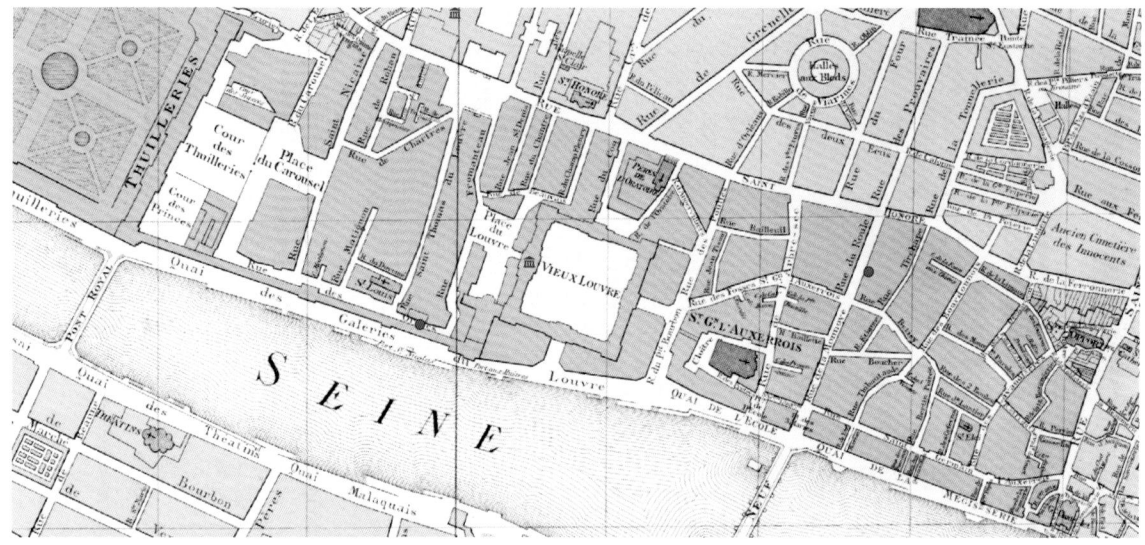

3 Hannah Williams and Chris Sparks, Map of Paris, with Anne Vallayer-Coster's apartments on the rue de Roule (1757–80) and at the Louvre (1780–1806), *Artists in Paris: Mapping the 18th-Century Art World*, at https://www.artistsinparis.org

Vallayer-Coster's success at the July 1770 meeting of the Académie is documented in the institutional records:

The Demoiselle Anne Vallayer, Painter, born in Paris, presented, in view of obtaining provisional membership, several pictures painted in oil, representing scientific and artistic instruments. The Académie, after having taken the usual voice vote and acknowledging her abilities, accepted her presentation, and, there having been among the pictures that she presented and that belonged to her, two paintings, one of a group of musical instruments and the other those of the Arts of Painting and Sculpture, to which the Company took particular satisfaction, the Académie accepted them for her reception. In consequence, the Académie received and receives the Demoiselle Vallayer as *académicienne qualified to sit in its assemblies and enjoy the privileges, prerogatives, and honors accruing to this status*, on the understanding that she is to observe the Statutes and Regulations of the Académie, and *she sat in the assembly in this capacity* [emphasis mine].[7]

As this passage explains, the Académie selected Vallayer-Coster's *The Attributes of Painting, Sculpture and Architecture* and *The Attributes of Music* (see figs 5 and 6) as her *morceaux de réception* (reception pieces). This meant that Vallayer-Coster was *reçue* (received) – the term used to describe full membership to the Académie.

Vallayer-Coster's position as an *academiciénne* was extremely rare and inherently fraught. Just 15 women artists were admitted to the Académie throughout its history of nearly 150 years, a paltry number compared with the total membership of more than 400 artists. Still-life painter Catherine Duchemin Girardon (1630–98) was the first woman admitted in 1663, and six more women soon joined her in rank. Most women accepted to the Académie during this early period benefited from their familial connections to academicians – for example, the Boullogne sisters, Geneviève (1645–1708) and Madeleine (1646–1710; see fig.18), who were both received in 1669, belonged to an impressive artistic lineage.[8]

Like Vallayer-Coster, many of these seventeenth-century *académiciénnes*, including Duchemin Girardon and the Boullogne sisters, were specialists of still life – the lowest-ranking subject within the academic hierarchy of genres, which privileged history painting above all other subjects.[9] By 1706, however, the Académie passed a rule against admitting any additional women, whatever genre they practiced. They briefly suspended the rule to admit two foreign artists in the 1720s: Venetian pastellist Rosalba Carriera (1673–1757) and Dutch still-life painter Margareta Haverman (1693/4–c.1722).[10] There were no others until Reboul Vien, Vallayer-Coster's future drawing teacher, was admitted in 1757. Reboul Vien attended meetings regularly, but by 1767 (the same year the German portraitist Anna Dorothea Therbusch (1721–82) was admitted) she had stopped exhibiting at the Salon, and few works can be securely attributed to her.[11] The pastellist Marie-Suzanne Giroust (1734–72), who is thought to have studied under Vien and was married to the Swedish portraitist Alexandre Roslin (1718–93), joined the Académie a few months after Vallayer-Coster, in October 1770; yet Giroust Roslin died just two years later.[12] Finally, the aforementioned portraitists Adélaïde Labille-Guiard and Élisabeth Vigée Le Brun were both admitted on the same day in 1783, 13 years after Vallayer-Coster.

As with Vallayer-Coster, it was customary for female applicants to be fully received on the same day that they applied to the Académie. By contrast, the majority of male artists were only partially admitted at first, an initial stage of acceptance (*agrément*), and were later fully received after completing reception pieces: paintings or sculptures depicting subjects assigned by the Académie. Most women artists skipped this preliminary step. The precedent was set with the first *académicienne*, Duchemin Girardon, and was maintained throughout the following century: Vallayer-Coster, Giroust Roslin, Labille-Guiard and Vigée Le Brun were all fully received without ever having been partially admitted (although some, like Reboul Vien and Carriera, did produce novel reception pieces later on).[13] Some scholars have suggested that this 'chivalric' custom of fully receiving female candidates was in fact a way to mark them as outsiders and to limit their participation in the official proceedings of the Académie.[14] Yet Vallayer-Coster was present at that July 1770 meeting, during which she agreed to 'observe the Statutes and Regulations of the Académie', and thereby became 'qualified to sit in its assemblies and enjoy the privileges, prerogatives, and honors accruing to this status' of an *académicienne*.

Although the immediate gratification of full membership is often associated with female artists, it should be noted that Jean Siméon Chardin and several other male members of the Académie were also simultaneously admitted and received. The connoisseur Pierre-Jean Mariette (1694–1774) described Chardin's 1728 reception this way: 'M. Chardin having had several of his pictures conveyed to the Académie, all votes cast were in his favor . . . he was received and admitted and, a rare occurrence indeed, two of the works he had presented were allowed to take the place of the reception piece required.'[15] Chardin's example demonstrates that the rules of membership were applied discriminately to both male and female artists throughout the history of the Académie. Vallayer-Coster's concurrent *agrément* and *réception* may be attributed to both her gender and to her exceptional talent as a still-life painter.

We can find visual evidence of Vallayer-Coster's new professional identity in a self-portrait, known today through a 1781 engraving (see fig.1).[16] The artist pictured herself in profile, bearing all the attributes of a fashionable *Parisienne* of the 1770s: a square-necked gown with a ruffled neckline and a towering coif, buttressed by curls and festooned with a bonnet and ribbon. The artist's tools – palette, brushes and mahlstick – rest on a plaque below, which is inscribed with the artist's full married name, the year of her reception at the Académie and the fact that the portrait was originally drawn by the artist herself. This confident, flattering self-portrait gave visual form to Vallayer-Coster's status within the Académie, a major marker of artistic legitimacy.

A few months after Vallayer-Coster was accepted in July 1770, the Académie voted to limit the number of women to four. In September of that year, Jean-Baptiste Pierre (1714–89), the Director of the Académie from 1770 to 1789, explained their reasoning: 'Although [the Académie] is pleased to encourage talent in women by admitting some into our body, nevertheless, these admissions, foreign in some fashion to its constitution, must not be repeated too often. [The Académie] has agreed that it will receive no more than four women.'[17] This rule was still in effect when Labille-Guiard and Vigée Le Brun were admitted 13 years later.

The Académie reiterated its policy in a 1790 document addressed to the National Assembly:

> In fact, the demands of motherhood and a thousand secondary factors prevent women from developing their talents to the height of the Académie, and it is rare that there are four celebrated women in a century. They cannot properly associate with the Academic body . . . They have only rarely attended meetings . . . besides, the decencies of their sex, and the embarrassment of being alone in the midst of a large number of men, have almost always deterred them from attending our assemblies.[18]

Remarkably, Mesdames Vallayer-Coster and Reboul Vien both signed this 1790 statement. It is impossible to know if the artist's signature indicates her full endorsement of this sexist article. She may have simply acquiesced, vastly outnumbered as she was by men, or she may have signed as an expression of her own conservative political leanings.

Whatever Vallayer-Coster's reasons for signing the document, the assumptions therein do not seem to apply to her own life. Vallayer-Coster never had children, so the 'demands of motherhood' did not distract her. She participated in every Salon between 1771 and 1789 and intermittently thereafter until her death in 1818 (see Appendix). Admittedly, Vallayer-Coster's attendance at the monthly meetings of the Académie was inconsistent: she is noted as present only once per year between 1771 and 1776, and not again until 1782 and 1789.[19] Vallayer-Coster's very presence at these meetings at all undermines the axiom that women artists were denied all privileges of institutional membership. Her delinquency could be explained by the 'embarrassment of being alone in the midst of a large number of men' – although many of her male colleagues also declined to attend meetings regularly. In an undated letter preserved at the Morgan Library & Museum in New York, Vallayer-Coster wrote to the miniaturist François Dumont (1751–1831), asking him to accompany her to one such meeting.[20] Does this letter suggest that she felt uncomfortable attending alone – or was this a commonplace platonic gesture? (As a sign of their friendship, Dumont later painted a portrait of Vallayer-Coster in the act of painting a vase of flowers; see fig.63.[21])

It is tempting to imagine the bonds that united the few women artists who became *académiciennes*, given the hurdles they faced. The Reboul Vien and Giroust Roslin couples were friendly, evidenced by a series of portraits exchanged between them, and they likely included Vallayer-Coster in their circle.[22] Publicly, however, Vallayer-Coster was more often linked with Vigée Le Brun and Labille-Guiard. At the Salon of 1783, for example, one critic mused that the three *académiciennes* submitted their paintings for the judgment of contemporary Parisian audiences

– just as Paris, the Trojan prince, judged the beauty of the ancient Greek goddesses Hera, Athena and Aphrodite. This critic similarly imagined the three female artists in competition with one another, rather than with their male peers, and conflated the formal qualities of the women's work with their own physical attributes. As in the Judgment of Paris myth, according to this critic there could only be one winner of the golden apple: 'Mesdames Vallayer and Guiard also display their graces at the Salon; but Paris awards the apple to Madame Le Brun.'[23]

Evidence of personal relationships between these three artists is sparse. However, both Labille-Guiard and Vigée Le Brun mention Vallayer-Coster in their personal writing. In 1783, Labille-Guiard wrote a letter to the comtesse d'Angiviller, wife of the *directeur général des Bâtiments du Roi* (Director of the King's Buildings; see fig.17), complaining of venomous libel that questioned the authenticity of her work and her personal virtue. Labille-Guiard reminded the comtesse 'of the interest that you take in Mme Coster and in your sex in general' – appealing to the comtesse's broad support for women artists.[24]

Vigée Le Brun also named Vallayer-Coster in her memoir, written long after the Revolution. Vigée Le Brun recalled that her colleague, who 'painted flowers perfectly', had already been admitted to the Académie when she herself applied for membership in 1783.[25] Curiously, Vigée Le Brun did not mention Labille-Guiard in her memoir at all. Perhaps she was aware that, unlike Labille-Guiard, Vallayer-Coster signed a 1799 petition in support of the repatriation of Vigée Le Brun, who had been placed on a list of exiled *émigrés* (royalists who escaped France during the Revolution).[26]

Beyond her relationships with fellow artists, Vallayer-Coster's connections to academic leadership can be partially reconstructed. In spring 1779, Vallayer-Coster launched a hard-fought campaign to move into the Louvre, where many academicians and their families resided (see fig.3). By then, the artist had been a member of the Académie for nearly a decade – and yet, as an unmarried woman in her mid-thirties, was still living and working at her mother's home. In March, Queen Marie Antoinette intervened on the artist's behalf, advocating for the transformation of a vacant apartment at the Louvre into lodgings for the artist. On 9 April 1779, the comte d'Angiviller wrote directly to Vallayer-Coster, assuring her that he would procure the lodgings and render them livable for her. The designated room was the former office of the royalist magazine, *Gazette de France*, situated under the Grande Galerie of the Louvre.[27]

Vallayer-Coster toured the proposed space that month, disguising her identity with a bonnet. This incognita visit reassured her that, in the words of one official, she would be able to live and work there 'honorably' and 'comfortably' as a single woman, surrounded by her male colleagues.[28] Vallayer-Coster was certainly bold in pursuing independent lodgings at the Louvre, but she seems to have been quite conscious of maintaining her reputation for modesty in doing so.

Many months later, in a letter to the comte d'Angiviller dated 26 January 1780, Vallayer-Coster expressed profound frustration that the renovations of the apartment were delayed. Though the exact source of her woes is unspecified, Vallayer-Coster's desperation for a room of her own is palpable in this letter.[29] Indeed, the value of having one's own apartment and studio at the Louvre would be difficult to overstate – for the personal prestige, as well as the professional benefits of living in close proximity to other academicians. D'Angiviller responded to Vallayer-Coster's pleas, issuing a work order for the space a few days later. After more than a year of royal intervention and negotiations, Vallayer-Coster finally gained access to the renovated apartment by the end of 1780 – where the artist enjoyed the rare, enviable luxury of her own private bathtub, as Katie Scott has noted.[30]

Remarkably, Vallayer-Coster was the only female artist to earn her own lodgings at the Louvre prior to the Revolution – aside from those living with male academicians, often their fathers, brothers or husbands. Even after Vallayer-Coster moved in, several other women were denied their own rooms. In 1784, the daughter of painter Nicolas Lépicié requested to remain in her father's Louvre apartment after his death. Pierre objected, describing the harassment this woman might encounter in the bawdy fraternal space of the Académie.[31] Labille-Guiard's own repeated requests for lodgings in 1785, 1787 and 1789 were also rejected. D'Angiviller argued that Labille-Guiard's female students might pose a distraction to male students at the Académie – despite the fact that there were already several women who studied unofficially in male artists' studios.[32] These contradictory episodes indicate the internal tensions and personal biases in enforcing academic policies. Vallayer-Coster clearly benefited from her connections to the Queen and institutional leadership in a way that other women did not.

Sometime after Vallayer-Coster moved to the Louvre, Roslin (widower of the *académicienne* Giroust) painted a portrait of his new neighbor, exhibited at the Salon of 1783 (fig.4).[33] This is an alluring image of a mature female artist at work. Vallayer-Coster meets our gaze with an affable expression, her palette and brush in hand. She is dressed in an attractive, if impractical, state of *dishabille:* her milky-white décolletage is framed by blue stays over a lace chemise, which has slipped to reveal her bare shoulders. Her brown bouffant and loose curls are dusted with white powder and adorned with a jade-green ribbon, a casual style popular in the 1780s. When this portrait is viewed in tandem with letters by her own hand, a complex picture of the artist emerges. She was an ambitious and persistent woman in her mid-thirties, confident in her talents and the privileges they afforded her – but also willing to wield 'the graces of her sex' in order to achieve her goals.

Though she had earned the space independently, Vallayer-Coster did not live alone at the Louvre for long. On 21 April 1781, at the age of 36, she married parliamentary lawyer Jean-Pierre Coster in a religious ceremony at Saint-Louis-du-Louvre, a church near the artist's new lodgings. The Costers' legal marriage contract, executed the same day at Versailles, was signed by 16 powerful witnesses, including Marie Antoinette, the comte d'Angiviller and Pierre. According to the marriage contract, the groom brought to the marriage 15,000 *livres* in property, in addition to his income as a lawyer of the *parlement* and *receveur général du tabac* (collector of taxes on tobacco). The bride had a dowry of 20,000 *livres* from her father's estate, in addition to an impressive 14,000 *livres* from her work as an artist.[34] This sum offers us evidence of the viability of Vallayer-Coster's painting practice at this stage of her career.

Little else is known about the Costers' marriage, except for the fact that it remained childless and successfully weathered the revolutionary period. By contrast, the first marriages of Vigée Le Brun and Labille-Guiard both ended in divorce. What enabled Vallayer-Coster and her husband to stay together in Paris throughout the upheaval of the 1790s – unlike Vigée Le Brun, whose reputation was so entangled with her royal patrons that she fled the country with her daughter, leaving her husband behind?[35] There is circumstantial evidence that the Costers also harbored royalist sympathies – particularly in contrast with other women who publicly demonstrated their commitment to the Revolution. On 7 September 1789, two weeks after the Declaration of the Rights of Man and of the Citizen, a group of 21 female artists and artists' wives (Mesdames Vernet and Reboul Vien among them) donated their own jewelry to the newly formed National Assembly. Labille-Guiard later campaigned to remove restrictions on the number of women artists in the revolutionary-era Académie, though her efforts were unsuccessful.[36]

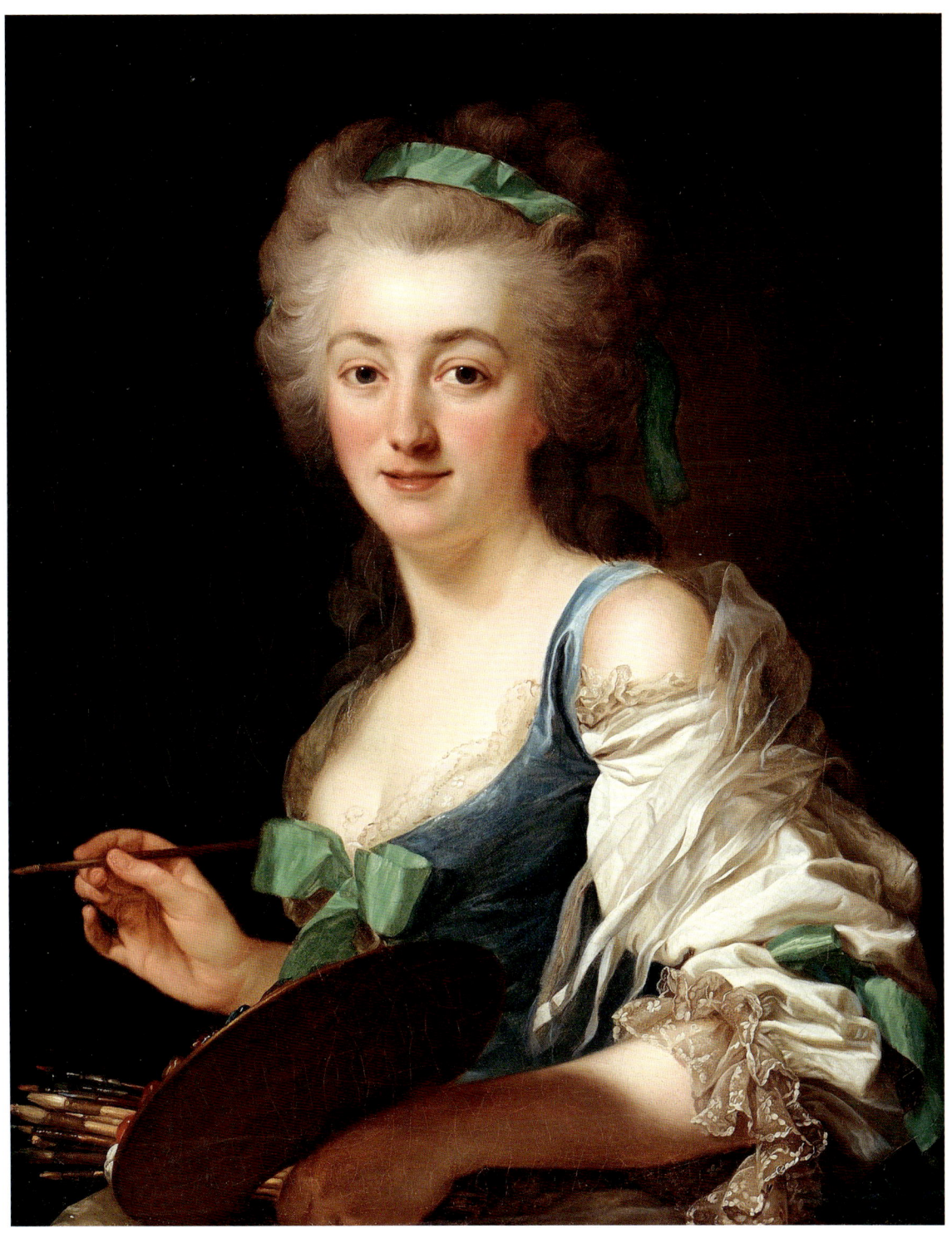

4 Alexandre Roslin, *Portrait of Anne Vallayer-Coster*, c.1783, oil on canvas, 74 × 60 cm (29 ⅛ × 23 ⅝ in), Crocker Art Museum, Sacramento, CA

Vallayer-Coster did not publicly enter the political fray, but she must have felt a personal sense of loyalty to her royal patron. Marie Antoinette had secured her lodging at the Louvre and served as a witness to her marriage – and owned several of her works (including a pastel portrait of the Queen, now in a private collection).[37] Madame Campan, a *femme de chambre* (Lady of the Bedchamber) of Marie Antoinette, recalled that Vallayer-Coster also served as a confidante to the Queen at a critical moment, on the eve of the royal family's attempt to escape arrest in Paris in June 1791:

> The queen told me that she had something precious to entrust to me and that I would have to find some respectable people, financially independent and wholly devoted to their sovereigns, to whom I was to consign a portfolio that she gave me. I had the idea of choosing Madame Vallayer-Coster, painter of the Académie, residing in the galleries in the Louvre, and in whom I found, as in her husband, all of the qualities required by the queen of the persons to be charged with this article. They were as loyal as I had declared them to be.[38]

Though vague, this anecdote characterizes the Costers as discreet, faithful allies of the Crown in its final hours.

Even after the collapse of the monarchy and the dissolution of the Académie royale in 1793, Vallayer-Coster and her husband remained in her lodgings at the Louvre – except for a brief residence in the suburb of Villemomble-en-Montreuil in the early 1790s, at the height of the Reign of Terror. In 1806, Emperor Napoleon evicted all of the academicians of the *ancien régime* from the Louvre; the Costers then moved to an apartment on the rue Neuve de Bons Enfants near the Palais Royal and later to the rue de Coq Héron. There, about 600 meters from her family's former workshop on rue de Roule, the artist died on 28 February 1818 at the age of 73.[39] She had lived nearly her entire life in Paris, the center of the French art world. Monsieur Coster survived his wife by six years. Their collection, which included dozens of works by the artist and her former colleagues at the Académie, was sold at auction after his death in 1824.[40]

One might assume that after the Revolution, Vallayer-Coster's career floundered beyond repair, never recovering from the loss of aristocratic and royal patrons, and that the aging artist simply faded into obscurity. Yet she, like many other former royal academicians, simply adapted to the new economic and political realities. Throughout the revolutionary tumult, public Salons continued to take place at the Louvre, which was converted into a museum known as Musée central des Arts (and later the Musée Napoléon). 'Mlle Vallayer, *Académicienne*' became known as 'Citoyenne Vallayer-Coster' – indicating her status as a citizen of the French Republic, rather than a royal academician of the *ancien régime*. 'Citoyenne Vallayer-Coster' was undeniably less productive than she had been in the 1770s and 1780s. Nevertheless, she persisted in exhibiting her work at the Salon and attracting new patrons, including Empress Josephine, the first wife of Emperor Napoleon. This final phase of Vallayer-Coster's career will be examined in the last chapter.

2

Allegories

On 28 July 1770, Vallayer-Coster presented several paintings to the Académie, including *The Attributes of Painting, Sculpture and Architecture* (fig.5)[1] and *The Attributes of Music* (fig.6).[2] These two large-scale canvases, measuring approximately three by four feet, pleased the academicians; they accepted them as her *morceaux de réception* (reception pieces) and granted her full membership to the Académie that same day. These allegorical pendants demonstrated the scale of Vallayer-Coster's professional ambition, as well as her investment in the ideals of the institution to which she aspired.

The allegorical mode of painting was revered from the very origins of the Académie. In his 1708 text, *Cours de peinture par principes* (*The Principles of Painting*), the connoisseur Roger de Piles defined allegorical painting as the 'choice of objects that serve to represent in a painting, in whole or in part, something other than what they actually are'.[3] In *The Attributes of Painting, Sculpture and Architecture* – as well as two other allegories produced in the first decade of her career (*The Attributes of Hunting and Gardening*, 1774, see fig.11[4] and *Bust of Minerva with Military Attributes*, 1777, see fig.13[5]) – Vallayer-Coster invested inanimate objects with abstract significance, representing the concepts of art, music, nature and nation. These paintings also represent a re-articulation

of the limitations of her genre, beyond the mere imitation of objects and toward deeper meanings.

THE ATTRIBUTES OF PAINTING, SCULPTURE AND ARCHITECTURE, 1769

The allegorical ambitions of Vallayer-Coster's reception pieces, and of still-life paintings in general, have long been underestimated. As one art historian put it, 'In terms of the *morceau de réception* practices, landscape, genre, and still life painters were given no role whatsoever in the glorification' of the Académie, nor were practitioners of these lesser genres able to 'create self-reflexive admission pieces'.[6] Yet Vallayer-Coster's *The Attributes of Painting, Sculpture and Architecture* did exactly that. This painting functioned as a clear artistic statement, demonstrating her knowledge of academic debates about color versus line and ancient versus modern art.

Moreover, with these paintings, Vallayer-Coster courted comparison with Jean Siméon Chardin, the most renowned still-life painter of the eighteenth century, and positioned herself as his successor. She was probably familiar with, and sought to emulate, Chardin's *The Attributes of the Arts and the Rewards Which Are Accorded Them*, of which there are several autograph copies. The Russian Empress Catherine the

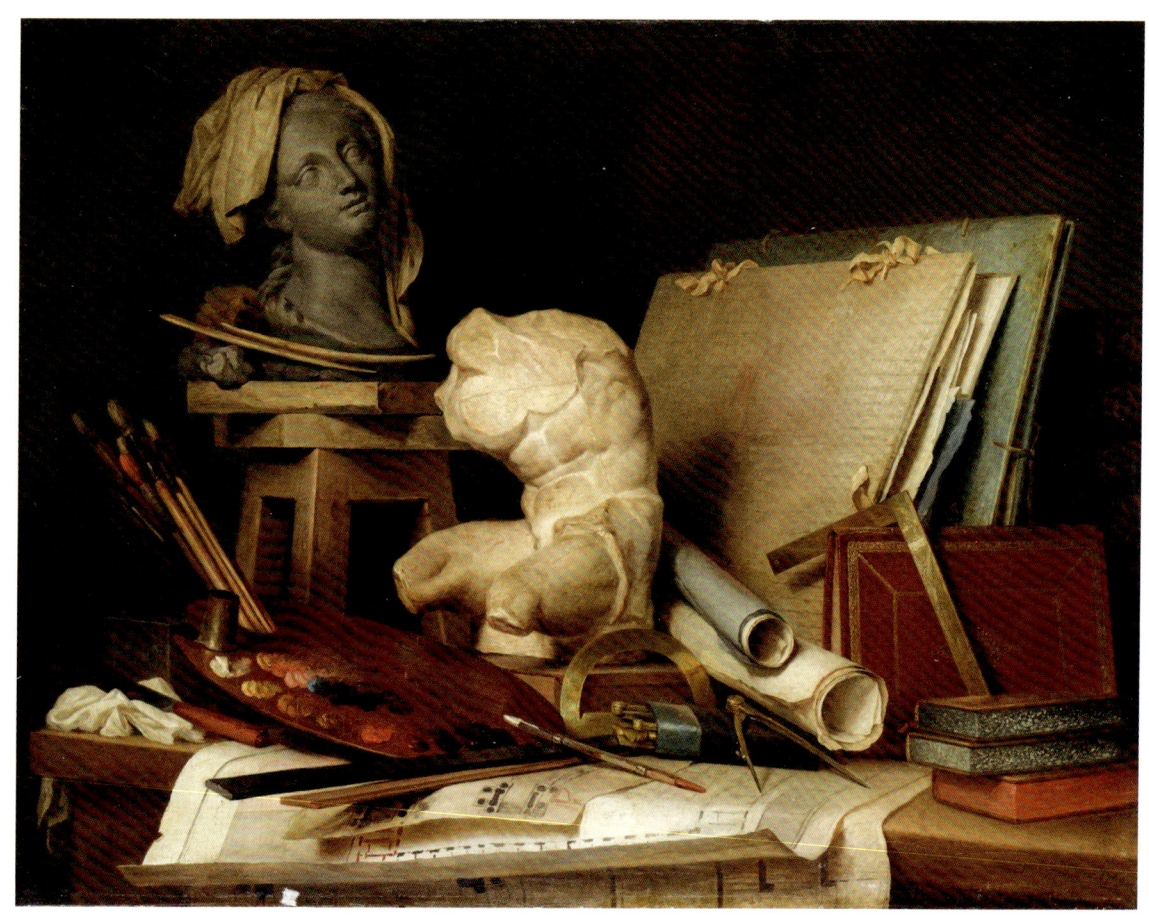

5   Anne Vallayer-Coster, *The Attributes of Painting, Sculpture and Architecture*, 1769, oil on canvas, 90 × 121 cm (35⅜ × 47⅝ in),
Musée du Louvre, Paris

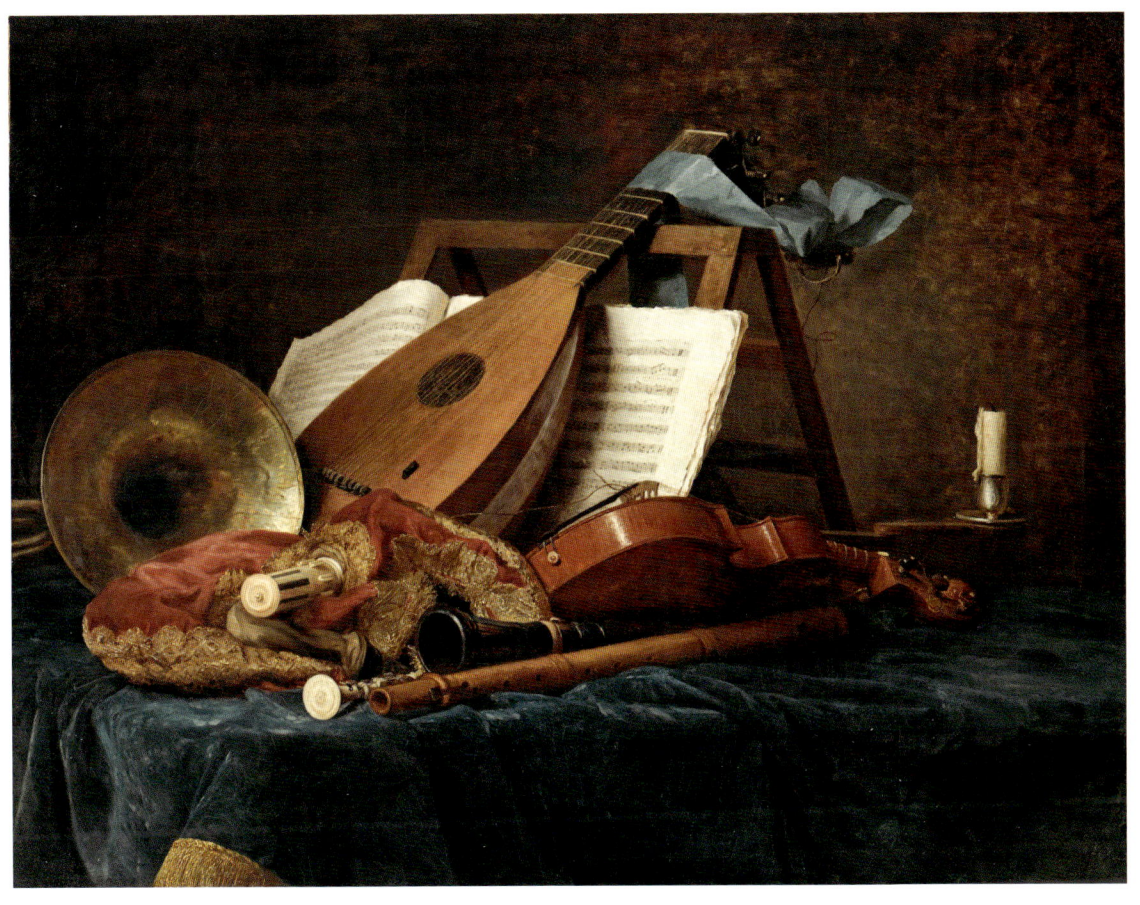

6   Anne Vallayer-Coster, *The Attributes of Music*, 1769, oil on canvas, 88 × 116 cm (34 ⅝ × 45 ⅝ in), Musée du Louvre, Paris

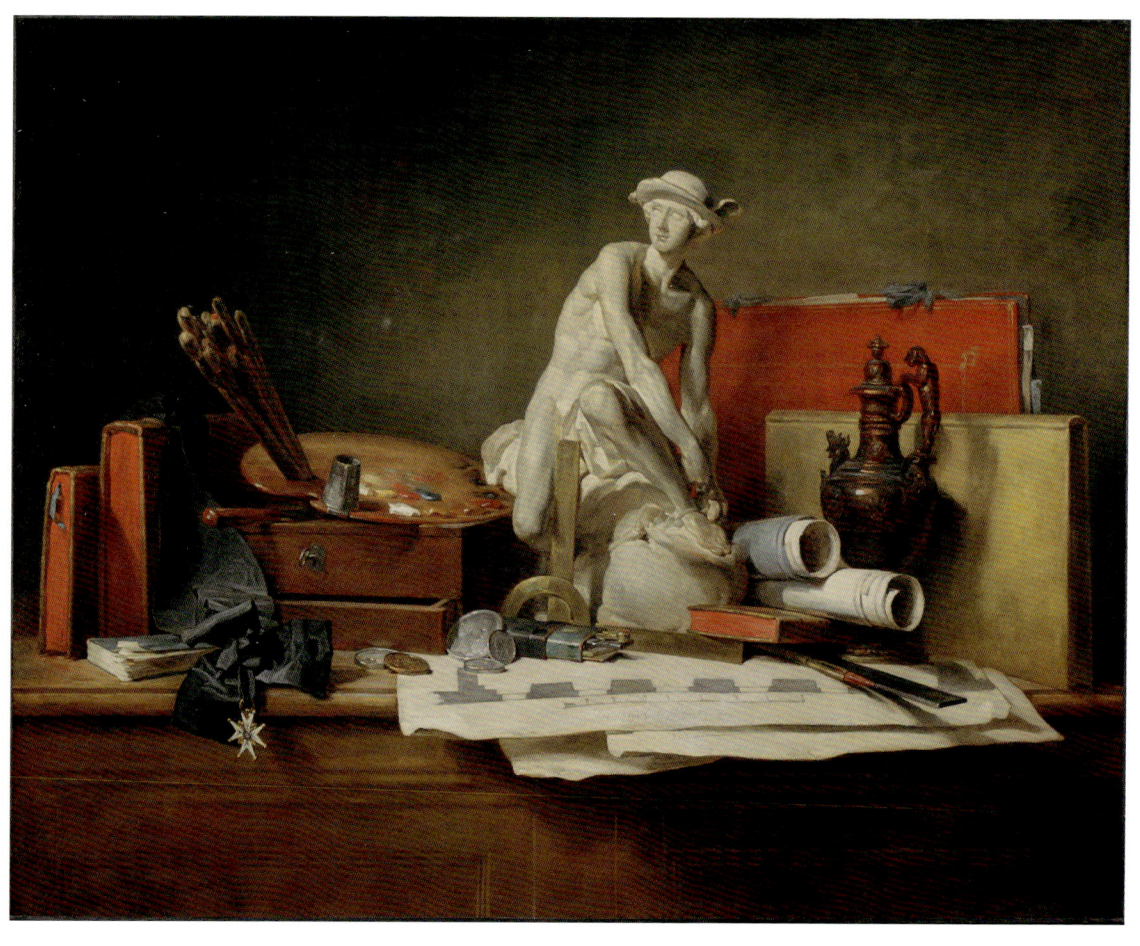

7   Jean Siméon Chardin, *The Attributes of the Arts and the Rewards Which Are Accorded Them*, 1766, oil on canvas, 113 × 145 cm
    (44 ½ × 57 ¼ in), Minneapolis Institute of Art, MN, The William Hood Dunwoody Fund, 52.15

Great commissioned the first for the Saint Petersburg Academy of Fine Arts in 1766. Chardin gifted one copy to his friend, the sculptor Jean-Baptiste Pigalle (fig.7), and displayed another at the Salon of 1769, a year before Vallayer-Coster applied to the Académie.[7]

Far from mere mimicry, Vallayer-Coster's quotation of Chardin was a strategic move. Imitation was baked into the culture and curriculum of the Académie. Students often repeated motifs from the work of older academicians, particularly in their reception pieces, demonstrating their knowledge of the French painting tradition. This was also part of a subtle ritual of flattery, essential to professional success in the Académie.[8] Vallayer-Coster clearly knew the rules of this game and was quite willing to play by them.

Vallayer-Coster's *The Attributes of Painting, Sculpture and Architecture* is populated by many of the same objects that appear in Chardin's composition, highlighting various aspects of academic training: paper, chalk, palette, brushes, plaster models and floor plans represent the arts of drawing, painting, sculpture and architecture, respectively. Heavy tomes, piled in the right corner of the canvas, refer to the biblical, mythological and literary foundations of the visual arts, as well as the liberal aspirations of the Académie itself.[9] Functional tools used in the Académie's classes on geometry and perspective are situated in the foreground: a semicircular protractor and an upright compass leaning on a black-and-blue sheath, a direct quotation from Chardin's work.[10] The legs of Vallayer-Coster's compass point to two architectural floor plans – referring to the Académie royale d'architecture (Royal Academy of Architecture), a separate but parallel institution whose objectives were intertwined with that of painting and sculpture.[11]

Like Chardin's, Vallayer-Coster's painting contains several objects representing drawing, which was considered foundational to both painting and sculpture: scrolls of white and blue paper and a double-ended *porte-crayon* containing sticks of red

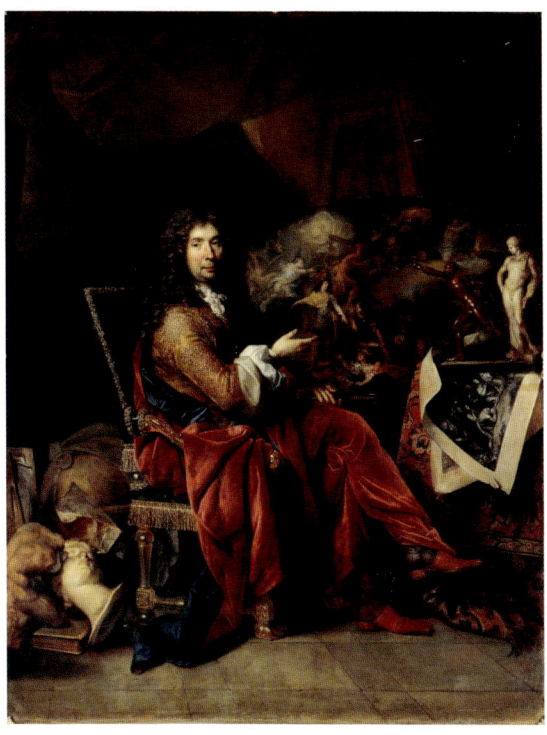

8   Nicolas de Largillière, *Portrait of Charles Le Brun*, 1683, oil on canvas, 232 × 187 cm (91⅜ × 73⅝ in), Musée du Louvre, Paris

and white chalk, the preferred media of eighteenth-century draftsmen.[12] Painters also prepared their canvases with underdrawing of white or red chalk. We can only speculate about Vallayer-Coster's own use of chalk, for there is no evidence of either in infrared scans of her paintings, and independent works on paper play a minor role in her extant oeuvre.[13] Nevertheless, drawing was foundational to academic training and thus an essential component of a painting devoted to its values.

The tools of Vallayer-Coster's own trade, painting, dominate the lower left of her composition. An ovular wooden palette, oriented towards the viewer, bears thick wet blobs of paint. The colorful smears are arranged according to academic convention, as detailed in artist manuals like de Piles's *Les premiers éléments de la peinture pratique* (*The First Elements of the Practice of Painting*, 1684). The outer ring features gradients of yellow, brown and red, culminating in chalky white and inky black; the inner ring is comprised of salmon and powder pinks, as well as dashes of cobalt blue and charcoal. The palette also bears a small pot, known as a *godet*, containing linseed or walnut oil, the liquid vehicle for the artist's ground pigments.[14] The thumbhole of the palette contains a fistful of paintbrushes, similar to the palette in Alexandre Roslin's 1783 portrait of Vallayer-Coster (see fig.4). Here, it appears as if the artist had set down and observed her own tools, before reproducing them on canvas.

The brush, palette, *porte-crayon* and paper function as symbols of painting and drawing. Their juxtaposition also alludes to a theoretical conflict within the Académie: the debate of color versus line. In the late seventeenth century, academicians argued about the relative merits of those formal properties. The artists defined their positions through a series of lectures, summarized in de Piles's *Dialogue sur le coloris* (*Dialogue upon Color*, 1699).[15] Vallayer-Coster demonstrated her awareness of this iconic debate and articulated her own position: she gives painting and drawing equal weight in her composition and even suggests their integral relationship by leaning the draftsman's *porte-crayon* against the edge of the painter's palette. Chardin, by contrast, completely divorced the tools of painting and drawing.

Vallayer-Coster's most obvious departure from Chardin is in her choice of sculpture. Chardin depicted Pigalle's *Mercury Tying His Sandal*, one of the most celebrated three-dimensional works of the eighteenth century.[16] As previously mentioned, Chardin gifted a version of his painting to Pigalle as a sign of their friendship. In her own work, Vallayer-Coster represented the category of sculpture with two figures: a plaster model of an ancient Greek

sculpture known as the *Belvedere Torso* and a clay bust of an anonymous young woman. Vallayer-Coster quoted this combination from the margins of another academic painting: Nicolas de Largillière's 1683 portrait of Charles Le Brun (1619–90), one of the most influential former directors of the Académie (fig.8).[17] The Académie displayed Largillière's portrait of Le Brun in their assembly room at the Louvre – the same room in which Vallayer-Coster was admitted in 1770. In Largillière's portrait, the plaster cast of the *Belvedere Torso* is oriented away from the viewer, but is recognizable by his muscular back. Though headless, the male torso seems poised to kiss or devour an upended female head.

The tussle between these two inanimate objects symbolizes yet another debate that took place within the Académie and beyond: the so-called Quarrel of the Ancients and the Moderns, which pitted classicists against modernists.[18] Vallayer-Coster employed the same combination of the torso and a female head in her *Attributes*, invoking both Largillière's massive, iconic portrait of Le Brun and this theoretical conflict. In her painting, however, Vallayer-Coster inverted Largillière's orientation. Her female bust is raised on a wooden stool, towering above the copy of the ancient male torso. Vallayer-Coster's bust is also rendered in damp clay and has long, fashionably curled hair. A wet white cloth (used by sculptors to smooth the surface of clay) has been left on the bust's head as if in the midst of the work, emphasizing its modernity.

Vallayer-Coster's clay bust is representative of contemporary sculpture, but does not refer to a known eighteenth-century work. As an invention of the artist, the bust has inevitably invited comparisons with images of Vallayer-Coster herself. Marianne Roland Michel wrote of the bust: 'This might be an ideal head, a kind of allegory of timeless beauty . . . but the facial features are not unlike those of Vallayer, and we should not dismiss the possibility that she meant to represent herself in this guise.'[19] Comparing the sculpture to Vallayer-Coster's engraved self-portrait (see fig.1), we find resonance in the high forehead, deep-set eyes, aquiline nose and rosebud lips. It is tempting to imagine that the artist inserted her own likeness, in the form of a clay work-in-progress, into the very painting that launched her academic career.

Vallayer-Coster elevated the contemporary female bust above the severed shoulders of the ancient male torso, yet it is to him that our eyes are first drawn. She arranged her composition around this partial nude, which is oriented so that the torso's left thigh would protect his modesty – whatever there was left to protect. She spared no other detail of his anatomy, carefully observing the interaction of skin, muscle and bone: the bulges at the knees, the linear topography of the thighs, the folds of flesh over the torqued abdomen and the ripple of muscles clinging to the expansive rib cage. With paint, she convincingly rendered the matte surface of the plaster cast, as well as the muscular bulk and tension of the original ancient marble sculpture.

The torso represented an important aspect of the academic curriculum for both painters and sculptors: studying the male body through the art of antiquity. The Académie installed dozens of plaster models of ancient sculpture, including the *Belvedere Torso*, in a studio down the hall from the assembly room at the Louvre.[20] There, young (male) students sketched the plasters, before graduating to drawing live male models.[21] The resulting figure studies are referred to as *academies*, because this practice was considered so fundamental to academic pedagogy.

Vallayer-Coster demonstrated her own formal command over the male anatomy by foregrounding the plaster cast of the *Belvedere Torso* in her *Attributes*. The specificity with which she reproduced it suggests that she observed a three-dimensional model, rather than a two-dimensional print. It is unclear, however, where Vallayer-Coster gained access to such a cast. Female artists were not permitted to enroll in figure classes at the Académie, and were thus officially forbidden from copying the male nude through ancient sculpture, let alone a human model.[22] In a 1783 letter to Louis XVI, the comte d'Angiviller offered justification for excluding women from this training, as well as limiting the number of female artists within the Académie to four: 'This number is sufficient to honor their talent; women cannot be useful to the progress of the arts because the modesty of their sex forbids them from being able to study after nature and in the public school established and founded by your majesty.'[23] Here, d'Angiviller refers to the perceived immodesty of female artists observing the male body alongside their male peers at the Académie.

Where, then, did Vallayer-Coster observe the torso? Might her former teacher Marie-Thérèse Reboul Vien have provided her female drawing students with private access to such models? Interestingly, Vallayer-Coster's estate sale of 1824 included at least 120 drawings of male nudes and heads in red chalk, although their authorship is not indicated in the catalogue.[24] Even if the artist did not produce these *académies* herself, it is still significant that she owned so many examples of these works on paper. She and other female artists during this period clearly gained informal, unsanctioned access to images of male nudes, outside of the Académie curriculum that systematically excluded them.[25]

We know of at least one other eighteenth-century female artist who drew and painted the male body. Angelica Kauffman (1741–1807), a founding member of the Royal Academy in London, was a history painter, a figurative genre that depended on the direct observation of the human body. Yet Kauffman's proximity to the male nude was a delicate matter, which caused some squeamishness among her peers at the Royal Academy.[26] In one early portrait, however, Kauffman is pictured defying social convention, directly observing a plaster model and holding her own sketch after that figure (fig.9).

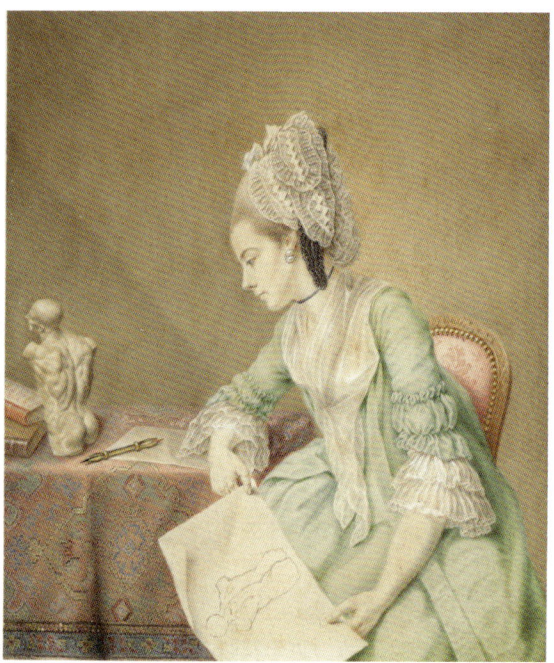

9 Attributed to Nathaniel Dance, *Portrait of Angelica Kauffman*, 1764–6, watercolor on paper, 13.2 × 11.4 cm (5¼ × 4½ in), National Galleries of Scotland, Edinburgh

Johann Georg Wille (1715–1808), for example, noted her unanimous approval at the Académie in his journal: 'This demoiselle, who took her place with the appropriate gratitude, and with skillfully employed modesty, did not have a single vote against her.'[28] The editor Dupont de Nemours wrote, 'Mademoiselle Vallayer unites the grace and timidity of her sex . . . with an enormous talent.'[29] The tenor of this praise recalls Griselda Pollock and Rozsika Parker's assertion in *Old Mistresses: Women, Art and Ideology*: 'A woman artist was acceptable in the eighteenth century . . . only in so far as her person, her public persona conformed to the current notions of Woman, not artist.'[30] Whether or not she was actually 'modest', Vallayer-Coster's ability to perform the role of 'Woman' tempered criticism of her more provocative still-life paintings or her professional aspirations.

After Vallayer-Coster's reception pieces appeared at the Salon of 1771, the Académie retained her paintings for its collection, and they were placed on view in the Gallery of Apollo at the Louvre. This prominent installation suggests that Vallayer-Coster had successfully glorified the institution with her work.[31] Her representation of the torso, in particular, demonstrated her fluency in the patriarchal visual language of the Académie and her understanding of the pedagogical centrality of the male body.

Yet the sculpted bodies represented in her painting also perform another complex gendered dynamic: a radical inversion of the academic norm. The male torso is an icon of classical antiquity and the French artistic tradition, and the female bust is a nameless, contemporary work-in-progress. Both are fragmented, not quite whole – the amputated male body represents a copy of the decay and ruin of the past, while the female head represents the nascent art of Vallayer-Coster's moment. One, blind, mute and deaf, is positioned at the heart of her composition, and the other is positioned above all other attributes of the arts, her eyes gazing upwards – as if to signal her own ambition.

Some years later, between 1778 and 1780, Kauffman painted her own academic thesis statement: a series of four panels intended for the ceiling of the Royal Academy's Somerset House in London. Kauffman imagined the allegorical female figure representing 'Design' drawing the *Belvedere Torso* (fig.10).[27] As in Vallayer-Coster's canvas, Kauffman's torso has been oriented to conceal his (absent) genitals from the female artist and the viewer.

Inanimate, amputated and effectively neutered, the *Belvedere Torso* was perhaps the only nude that was considered acceptable for female academicians like Kauffman and Vallayer-Coster to paint. Far from causing a scandal, Vallayer-Coster was widely praised for her decorum in addition to her talent. Engraver

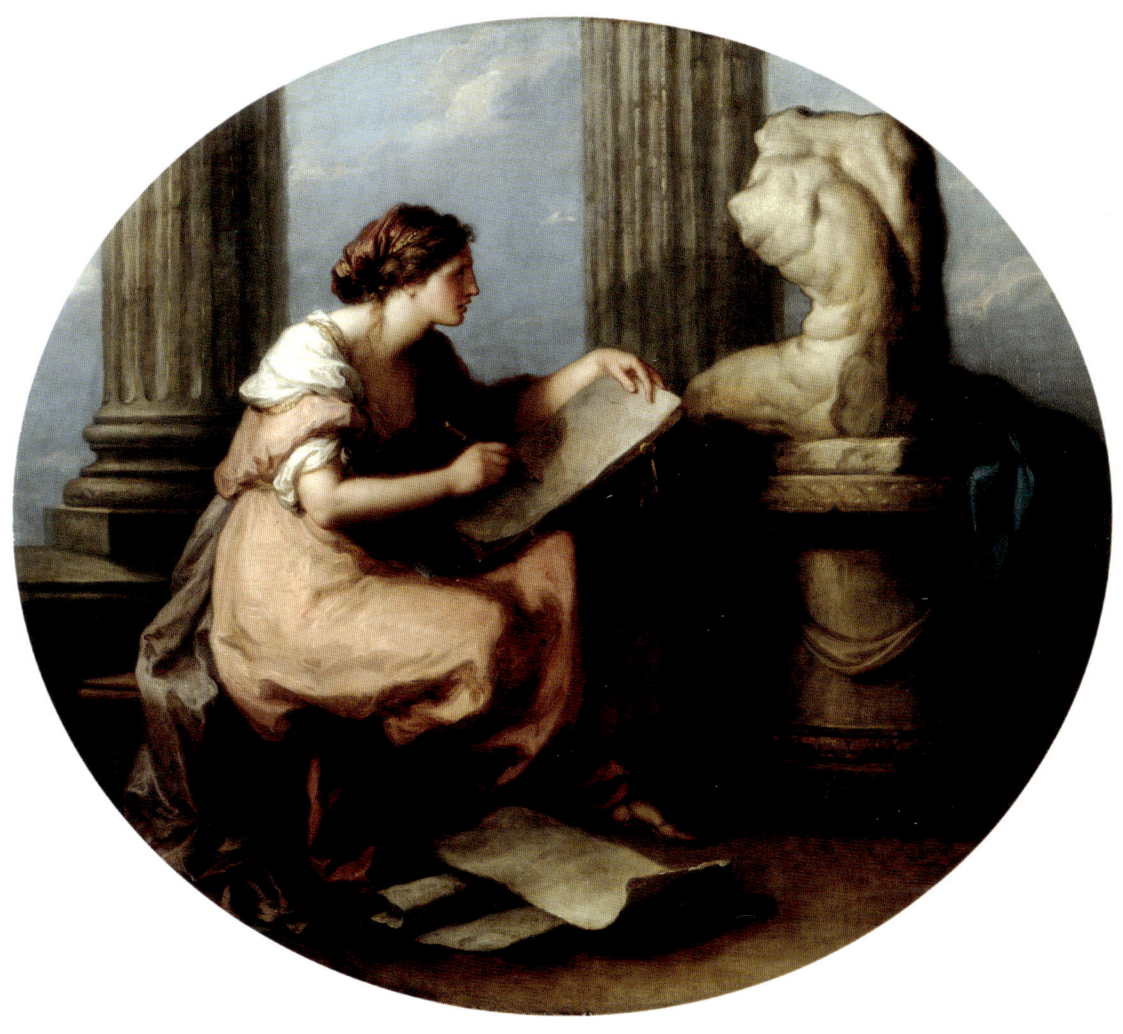

10 Angelica Kauffman, *Design*, 1778–80, oil on canvas, 126 × 148 cm (49 ⅝ × 58 ¼ in), Royal Academy of Arts, London

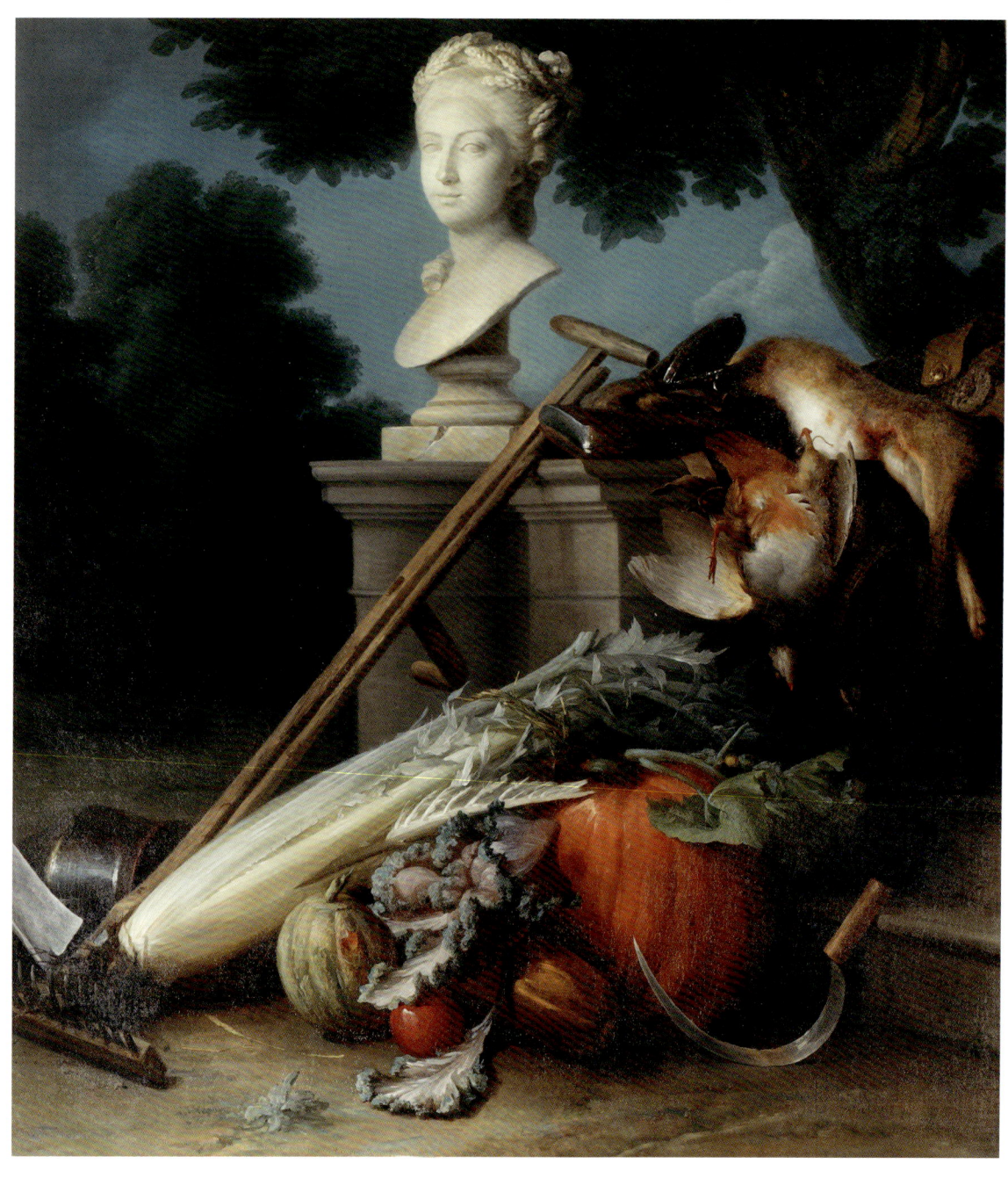

11 Anne Vallayer-Coster, *The Attributes of Hunting and Gardening*, 1774, oil on canvas, 152 × 137 cm (60 × 54 in), National Trust, Basildon Park, Berkshire

The success of Vallayer-Coster's reception pieces led
to the commission of another allegorical painting:
The Attributes of Hunting and Gardening (fig.11). She
exhibited the painting at the Salon of 1775, along with
its pendant (see fig.56).[32] Like her reception pieces,
The Attributes of Hunting and Gardening is a large,
complex composition, measuring approximately five
by four and a half feet, that exalts France itself – in
this case, its natural and agricultural abundance.

This specific theme was also designed to flatter
Vallayer-Coster's patron, the abbé Joseph-Marie
Terray (1715–78). As Louis XV's Controller-General
of Finance from 1768 to 1774, Terray initiated a series
of major economic and agricultural reforms.[33] Terray
began to collect contemporary French art in the early
1770s; he may have commissioned these paintings
from Vallayer-Coster after seeing *The Attributes
of Painting, Sculpture and Architecture* at the Salon
of 1771 or in the Gallery of Apollo in the Louvre
thereafter. He probably came into direct contact with
the artist during his brief tenure as the Director of
the King's Buildings, from July 1773 to August 1774.
We also know that she was present during the 2
October 1773 meeting of the Académie, over which
Terray presided.[34]

Terray may have intended to install Vallayer-
Coster's pendants in his newly renovated hôtel on
the rue Nôtre-Dame-des-Champs in Paris – or
perhaps in his country home, the Château de La
Motte-Tilly, about 80 km south-east of Paris.[35] The
rural landscape of Terray's château may even have
inspired the outdoor setting of Vallayer-Coster's *The
Attributes of Hunting and Gardening*. The fruits of
the forest and the field are piled in front of a regal
stone staircase in the shade of a bent tree. The green
foliage of the forest beyond and the placid blue sky
all evoke summer, the season associated with Ceres,
the Roman goddess of agriculture. Vallayer-Coster

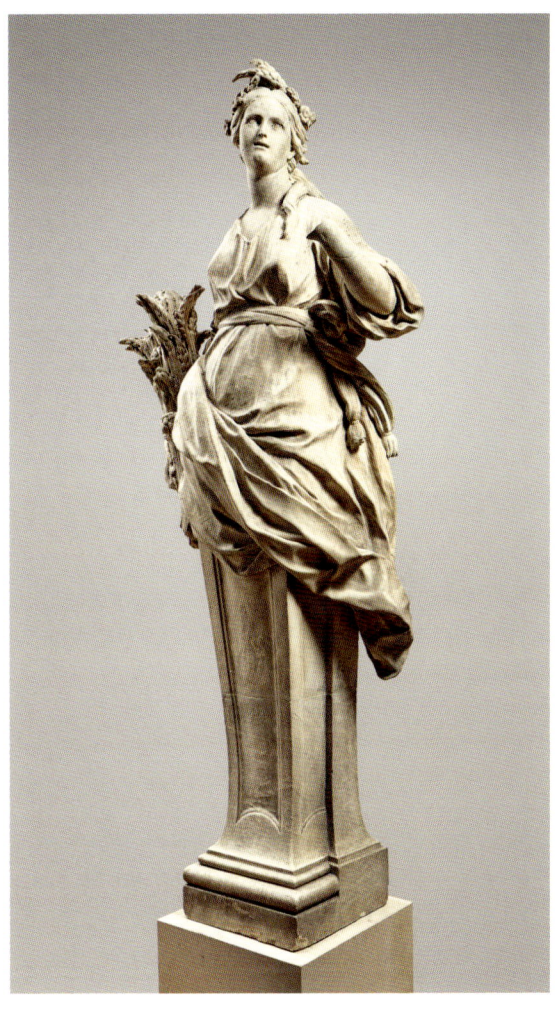

12 Guillaume Coustou I, *Ceres* or *Summer*, c.1735, marble,
312 cm (122 ⅞ in), Musée du Louvre, Paris

positioned a bust of Ceres – recognizable by a crown
of wheat – at the center of her composition. Her
version of Ceres may have been modeled after a real
marble sculpted by Guillaume Coustou (1677–1746)
and installed in the Jardin des Tuileries, a 15-minute
walk from Vallayer-Coster's family home on rue de
Roule (fig.12).

In Vallayer-Coster's canvas, Ceres presides over a cornucopia of recently harvested animals and plants, symbolic of the wealth Terray had hoped to cultivate in France. Vallayer-Coster depicts a spectacular array of colors and textures, including a bulbous pumpkin, a pale orange gourd, a bright red tomato and a leafy green cardoon. A large head of cabbage, comprised of cruciferous pleats with a curly fringe, is formed with strokes, squiggles and dots of violet and turquoise. With paint, the artist also alludes to the brutality of human interactions with nature. The attributes of the hunt are represented by the butt of a rifle, a hunting pouch and the dead bodies of a hare and pheasant. The wound in the belly of the hare, a reference to the practice of field-dressing game, finds an echo in the blemished surface of the green melon on the lower left: a missing chunk in its waxy surface reveals the sweet, ripe orange flesh beneath. The gouged melon and the freshly slaughtered hare invest the painting with a subtle violence, underscored by the presence of a long wooden rake and a scythe, the gleaming blade of which is highlighted with white impasto.

The subject of Vallayer-Coster's *The Attributes of Hunting and Gardening* was likely determined in collaboration with Terray, if not explicitly prescribed by him. There is a clear connection between Terray's political inclinations and the iconography of her painting. Terray was best known for his attempts to stimulate the French agricultural industry, which ultimately failed. Colin Bailey has written that Terray's artistic commissions, including those of Vallayer-Coster, 'reflect nothing of the social upheavals, popular distress or fiercely contested policies concerning the regulation of agriculture and the trade in grain. On the contrary, they celebrate abundance and prosperity . . . Terray's paintings and sculptures function as justifications' of his deeply unpopular and unsuccessful economic initiatives.[36]

Despite Terray's fraught reputation, this commission was displayed at the Salon of 1775,

signaling Vallayer-Coster's precocious talent and ambition to the public. The 30-year-old artist was a junior member of the Académie who had been admitted just four years earlier, yet her star was on the rise. Terray, meanwhile, was not so lucky. He was forced to resign from his position in October 1774 and died four years later. Vallayer-Coster's pendants were sold separately to unknown buyers at Terray's estate sale on 20 January 1779.[37]

BUST OF MINERVA WITH MILITARY ATTRIBUTES, 1777

Vallayer-Coster's next large-scale allegory, *Bust of Minerva with Military Attributes* (fig.13), was owned and lent to the Salon of 1777 by another private patron: Madame Vissitier. This canvas, measuring three and a half by five feet, is also organized around a female bust: Minerva, the Roman goddess of war. This female bust is a reference to a (now lost) sculpture of Minerva by the academic sculptor, Louis-Claude Vassé (1716–72). In a portrait of Vassé by Étienne Aubry, the sculptor is depicted at work on a clay, bust-length version of Minerva (fig.14). Vallayer-Coster probably knew Aubry, who had trained in Joseph-Marie Vien's studio and was admitted at the Académie in 1771. She almost certainly knew Aubry's painting of Vassé, which was his reception piece and was exhibited at the Salon of 1775, for she appropriated the same bust for her own still life two years later.[38] Both Minervas wear the same distinctive helmet, with a laurel wreath and a small bare-breasted sphinx perched on top – though Vallayer-Coster's Minerva appears to be marble or plaster, rather than clay.

Vallayer-Coster's bust of the ancient goddess is surrounded by modern military attributes, symbolic of France and its military prowess. A white standard, embroidered with gold *fleurs-de-lis* and crowned scepters, forms the dominant diagonal line of the composition. The flag is draped over an upended

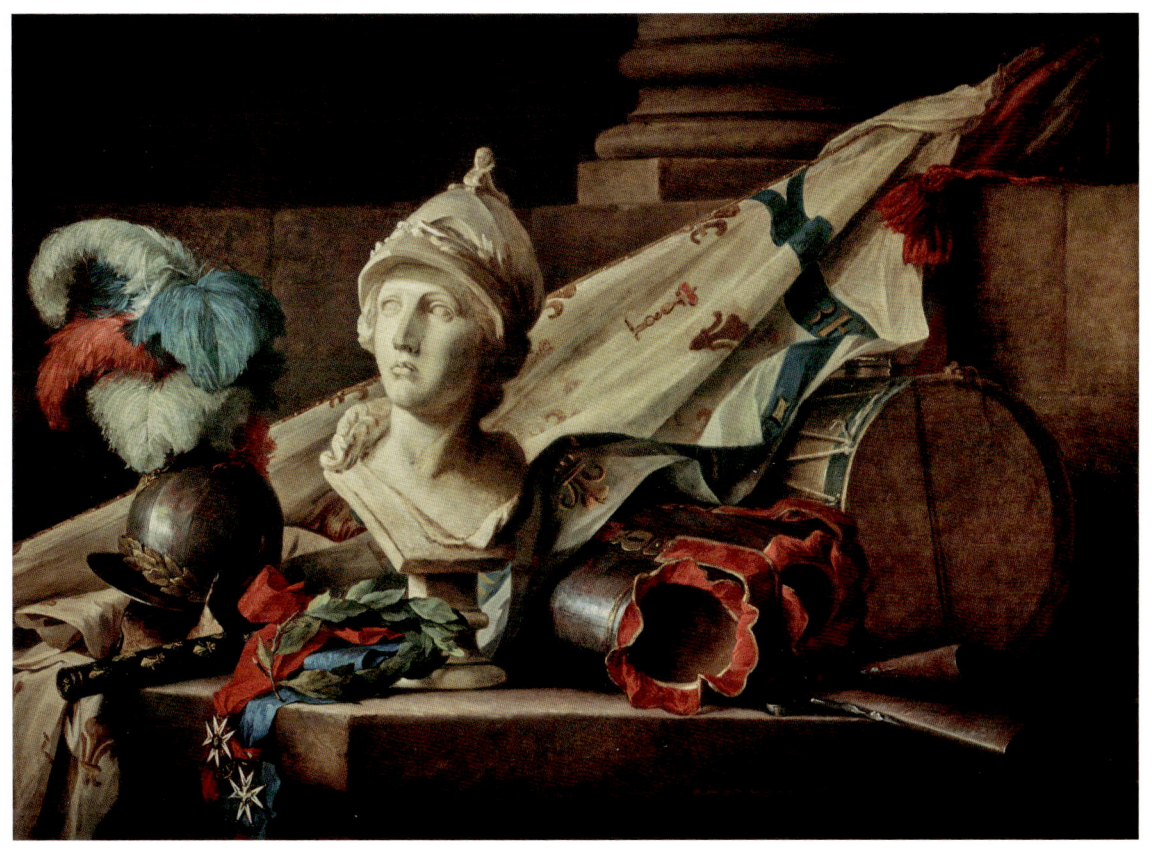

13　Anne Vallayer-Coster, *Bust of Minerva with Military Attributes*, 1777, oil on canvas, 114 × 159 cm (44 ⅞ × 62 ½ in),
Private collection

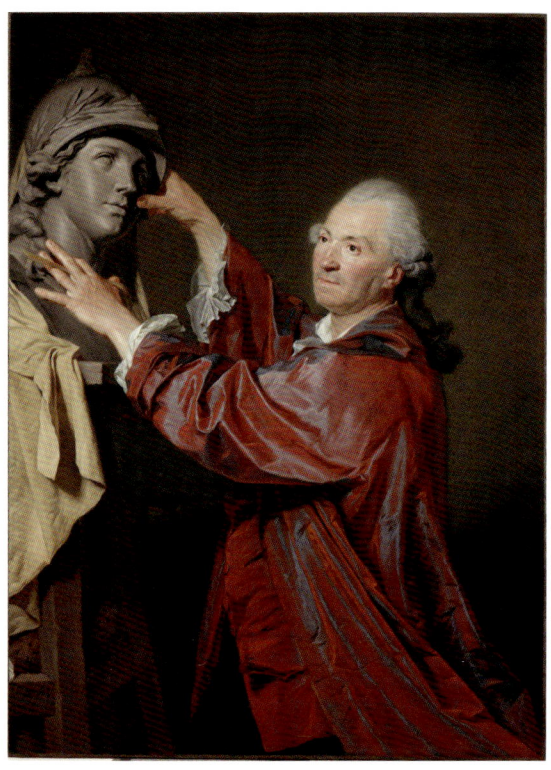

14 Étienne Aubry, *Portrait of Louis-Claude Vassé*, Salon of 1775, oil on canvas, 129 × 97 cm (50¾ × 38¼ in), Musée national des châteaux de Versailles et de Trianon

drum and silk-lined metal cuirass, with two muskets thrust between them. On the left are two ceremonial medals representing the Royal Orders of Saint Louis and Saint Esprit, as well as the blue baton of the Marshal of France and a metal helmet with fluffy feather plumes.

These objects are representative of nation and war, but they also evoke the elite male bodies who formed the upper ranks of the French government and military. These objects were all designed to honor, enhance and protect those bodies – at least, symbolically. Vallayer-Coster's cuirass, for example, is lined with pleated red velvet and bears two gold

buckles on the chest, much like the suit of armor crafted for Louis XIV's five-year-old great-grandson, the Prince of Asturias (1707–24; fig.15). This armor was not a practical uniform for war, but rather a material expression of the wearer's dynastic, masculine identity.[39] Indeed, by the late eighteenth century, armor had been deemed too bulky for the battlefield and was worn primarily as a ceremonial costume in noble portraiture. In several portraits by Largillière, for example, aristocratic male subjects wear armor over velvet coats, while sporting heavy powdered wigs (fig.16). The portraitist probably maintained a set of armor in his studio for clients to don while they posed for him.[40] The cuirass and helmet with tricolor plumes in Vallayer-Coster's *Bust of Minerva with Military Attributes* invoke this tradition of elite male portraiture in the *ancien régime*.

Beyond the cuirass and helmet, the painting contains several other symbols of military and class distinction. The blue baton of a Marshal of France was awarded to distinguished French military leaders – for example, the comte de Saint-Germain (1707–78), who became a Marshal of France a few months before being appointed Secretary of War under Louis XVI in 1775. In this role, the comte initiated a series of reforms to the French military, which he viewed as corrupt and disorderly.[41] In 1777, he commissioned the *Almanach des Chevaliers des Ordres Royaux & Militaires de France*, an inventory of military officers who had been awarded medals by the King, as well as their respective heroic acts and battle wounds.[42] The comte de Saint-Germain's grand ambitions for the French military were initially a source of popular pride (and a possible impetus for Vallayer-Coster's work), but his controversial anti-nepotism policies probably led to his resigning in September 1777, the same month that Vallayer-Coster's painting went on display at the Salon.[43]

In Vallayer-Coster's painting, the Marshal of France baton is accompanied by medals of the Orders of Saint Louis and Saint Esprit, both of which are

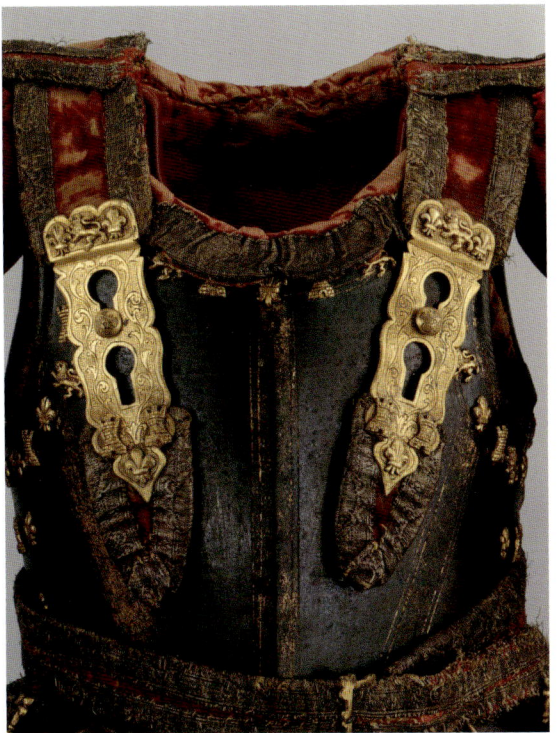

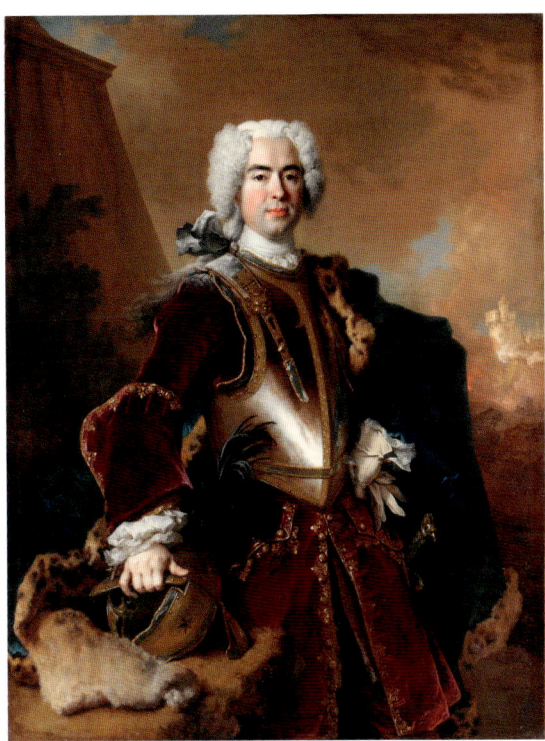

15 Jean Drouart, Armor of Infante Luis, Prince of Asturias, 1712, steel, gold, brass, silk, cotton, metallic yarn and paper, 71.1 cm (28 in), The Metropolitan Museum of Art, New York

16 Nicolas de Largillière, *André François Alloys de Theys d'Herculais*, 1727, oil on canvas, 137.8 × 105.4 cm (54 ¼ × 41 ½ in), The Metropolitan Museum of Art, New York

listed in the comte de Saint-Germain's *Almanach*. The members of the Order of Saint Louis (represented by a gold Maltese cross with an image of Saint Louis at the center, affixed to a red ribbon) were acknowledged for distinguished military service, while the Order of Saint Esprit (a green Maltese cross with a white dove at the center, affixed to a blue ribbon) was a chivalric order for those of noble birth.[44]

Vallayer-Coster's choice to include both of these medals in her *Military Attributes* was intentional. The elite members of these Orders were the very patrons that she hoped to flatter and attract. Like ceremonial armor, these medals were ubiquitous in aristocratic male portraiture. To the Salon of 1779, for example, Vallayer-Coster submitted her own portrait of the comte de Mesnilglaise wearing the Order of Saint Louis.[45] The Orders of Saint Louis and Saint Esprit were also on display in Joseph Duplessis's 1779 portrait of d'Angiviller (fig.17), who was named as Terray's successor as the Director of the King's Buildings in 1774.[46]

Duplessis's portrait conveys d'Angiviller's influence over artistic production during his tenure as Director of the King's Buildings from 1774 through 1789.[47] The

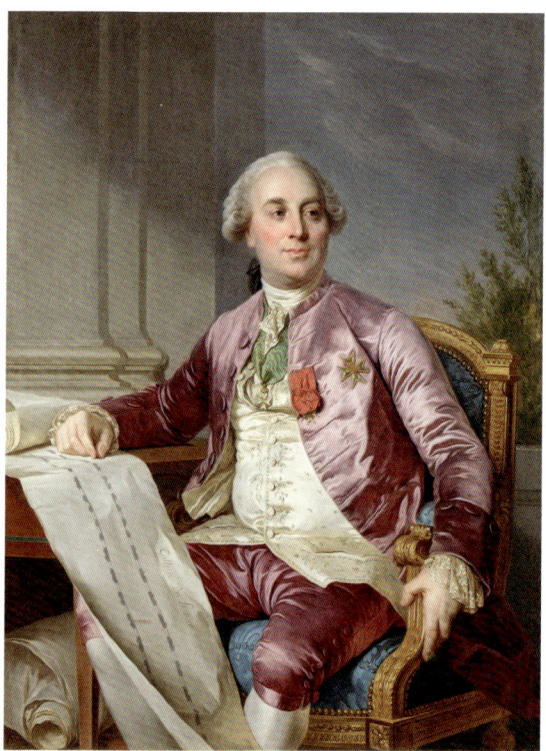

17 Joseph Duplessis, *Charles-Claude Flahaut de la Billarderie, comte d'Angiviller*, 1779, oil on canvas, 144 × 106 cm (56 ¾ × 41 ¾ in), Musée national des châteaux de Versailles et de Trianon

architectural plan of the Louvre that unfurls between d'Angiviller's legs, for example, refers to his plan to establish a museum dedicated to French painting and sculpture.[48] In a 1776 letter to Jean-Baptiste Pierre, then director of the Académie, d'Angiviller articulated his agenda and asserted that contemporary art ought to 'restore virtue and patriotic sentiments' – that is, to glorify France and its monarchy. Between 1774 and 1777, he began to commission history paintings depicting great men of French history – all intended to adorn his new museum, which remained unrealized until after the French Revolution. In this sense, d'Angiviller's cultural mandate has obvious nationalistic parallels with the military agenda of the Secretary of War, the comte de Saint-Germain.[49]

Vallayer-Coster's 1777 painting was not commissioned by d'Angiviller, but her *Bust of Minerva with Military Attributes* belongs to the same patriotic fervor that he inspired in the Académie. This is the only work in her oeuvre that refers so explicitly to France, with symbols of both the French monarchy (the *fleur-de-lis*) and military (instruments of war). After the painting appeared at the Salon of 1777, critics acknowledged this work as more ambitious than her other canvases. Louis Petit de Bachaumont, for example, wrote that her 'sure and faithful brush has submitted all the objects of inanimate nature. But after this triumph she courts something more substantial.'[50] With this painting, Vallayer-Coster challenged the boundaries of her genre, invoking the material trappings of aristocratic male portraiture and history painting.

Though the military medals depicted in Vallayer-Coster's painting connoted upper echelons of male power and prestige, they also held deep personal significance to the artist. In 1754, when she was nine years old, her father opened his own workshop specializing in the production of military medals, including the cross of Saint Louis. After Monsieur Vallayer died in 1770, his wife received legal permission to continue operating her husband's workshop – a widespread practice amongst the widows of craftsmen in the early modern period.[51] It is unsurprising that Vallayer-Coster placed her signature on the stone ledge directly next to the medals, for she was intimately familiar with their iconography, production and social function.

Vallayer-Coster's elegant pile of military attributes, a celebration of masculine power, can thus be read as an expression of patriotic imperative (a response to the policies of d'Angiviller and Saint-Germain) and patriarchal devotion (a reference to her father's craft). After all, as a woman, she could neither join the military nor be personally awarded a military medal.

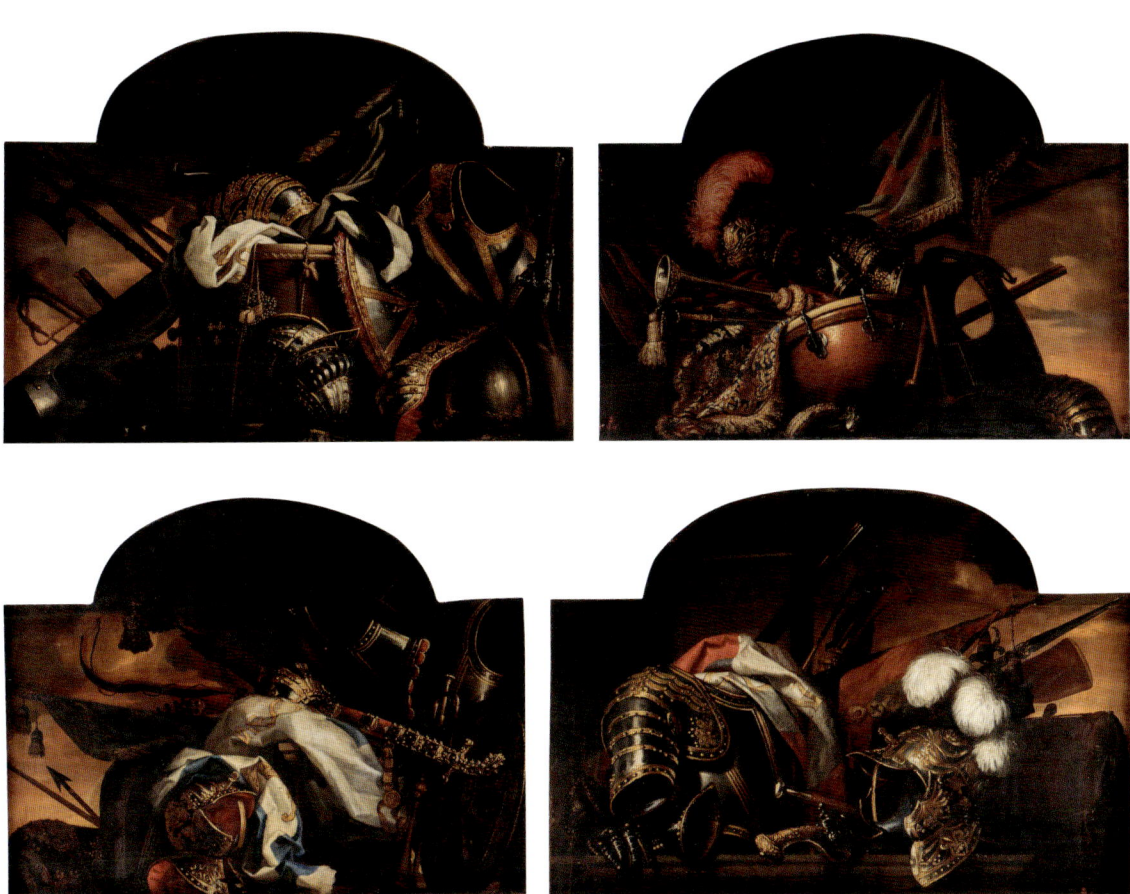

18 Madeleine de Boullogne, *Military Trophies and Instruments*, *c*.1673, oil on canvas, each approximately 114 × 149 cm
(44 ⅞ × 58 ⅔ in), Musée national des châteaux de Versailles et de Trianon

It is ironic, then, that Madame Vissitier – about
whom nothing is now known – owned the work and
lent it to the Salon of 1777.[52] What surrogate pleasure
or pride did Vallayer-Coster's painting offer this
female collector?

Interestingly, the most salient precedent for
Vallayer-Coster's work was that of another female
artist, painted for another female patron. Still-life
painter Madeleine de Boullogne was the daughter
of one of the founders of the Académie. She and her

sister Geneviève were admitted to the institution
in 1669, making them the second and third female
members. At the Salon of 1673, a century before
Vallayer-Coster's own debut, Madeleine exhibited six
of the eight *trophées d'armes* (military trophies) that
she painted as overdoors for the queen's antechamber
at Versailles, then occupied by the first wife of Louis
XIV, Maria Theresa of Spain. Four of those overdoors
remain *in situ* in the palace today (fig.18).[53]

Is it possible that Vallayer-Coster saw Boullogne's

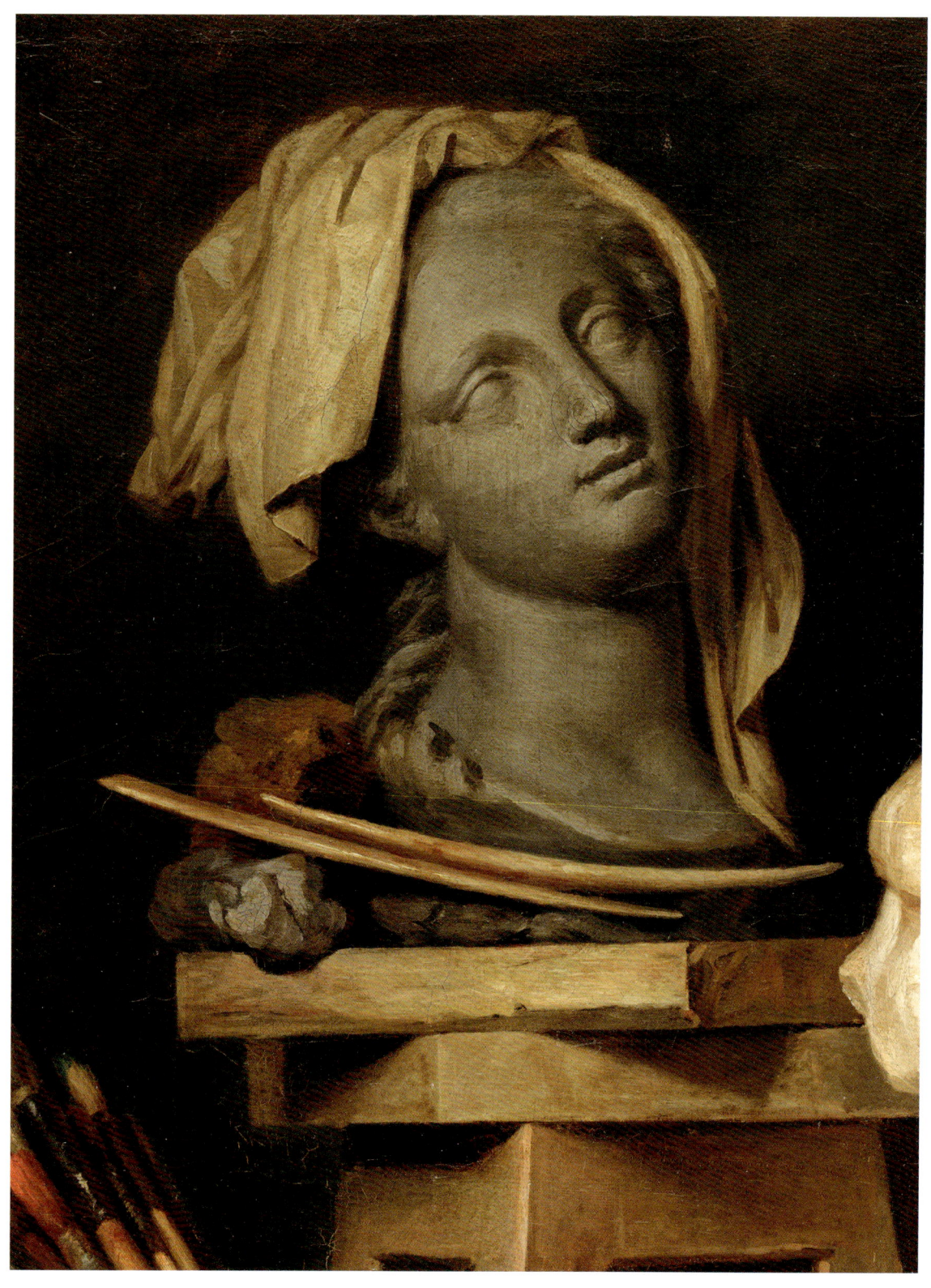

19 Anne Vallayer-Coster, detail of *The Attributes of Painting, Sculpture and Architecture*, 1769, oil on canvas, 90 × 121 cm
(35⅜ × 47⅝ in), Musée du Louvre, Paris

paintings in person at Versailles before 1777? We know that she visited the palace on at least two later occasions: in 1779, to paint Queen Marie Antoinette's portrait, and again to execute her marriage certificate in 1781.[54] In any case, the formal similarities between the works of Boullogne and Vallayer-Coster are too striking to ignore. Boullogne's paintings, like that of Vallayer-Coster, are dominated by a sharp diagonal line formed by a furled banner and are populated with military drums, weapons, vacant armor and plumed helmets.

The objects depicted in Vallayer-Coster's *Bust of Minerva with Military Attributes* connote various male bodies (the decorated French military officer; the *grand hommes* of French history; the Director of the King's Buildings; Vallayer-Coster's own father). Yet they are also linked to one of the first female *académiciennes* (Boullogne) and her most important royal commission for a female patron (overdoors for Queen Maria Theresa's antechamber at Versailles). Like Boullogne's military trophies, Vallayer-Coster's patriotic allegory was painted by a woman and owned by a woman: the mysterious Madame Vissitier. These circumstances distinguish *Bust of Minerva* from Vallayer-Coster's earlier *Attributes*, which were painted for the mostly male members of the Académie and for a powerful minister of the French government. This painting, moreover, would be the last major allegory that she would ever paint. After the patriotic fever dream of 1777, she primarily produced paintings of food, game, shells and flowers.

FEMALE BUSTS

Vallayer-Coster's *The Attributes of Painting, Sculpture and Architecture*; *Hunting and Gardening*; and *Bust of Minerva with Military Attributes* are linked by their large dimensions and allegorical themes. They are all populated by female figures in the form of clay or stone busts, a recurring motif that could be read as a kind of early artistic signature (fig.19). Of course, the presence of the female body in allegorical painting was far from unusual. In early modern art, female bodies (often nude) were considered so neutral that they served as vehicles for a wide range of ideas; they were empty vessels invested with meaning by their male makers.[55] At the Salon of 1775, for example, female figures embodied the following concepts: Fidelity, Sincerity, Truth, Sweetness, Summer, Winter and Wind, to say nothing of the Venuses and Virgins representing beauty and virtue.

Vallayer-Coster's allegorical busts, whether inspired by the works of her contemporaries or her own inventions, each represent the artist's own close engagement with the economy of images and ideas of her time. If not explicitly intended to be self-portraits, these female busts nonetheless serve as visual surrogates for the artist herself.[56] That these heads look so pointedly – upwards, outwards or directly toward the viewer – underscores the fact that they 'perform' Vallayer-Coster's own act of looking and her physical presence before the objects that she painted.

In this sense, the sculptures in Vallayer-Coster's paintings enact a reversal of the Pygmalion myth, told in Ovid's *Metamorphoses* (8 CE). This story was enormously popular in eighteenth-century France and was reimagined in paintings, plays and philosophical treatises as a metaphor for sensation. Pygmalion, a male sculptor, prayed to Venus, the ancient Roman goddess of love and beauty, to transform his own sculpture of a female nude into a living, breathing woman. Venus answered his prayer, animating the object of his erotic desire from marble to flesh. Here, instead, it is as if Vallayer-Coster has used paint to transform woman back into stone or clay – emphasizing her mastery of the still-life genre.[57]

3

Food

Vallayer-Coster's paintings of food are all about the sense of taste. Her work in this category is clearly indebted to her predecessors: she sampled both the rich delicacies of seventeenth-century Dutch still-life artists (lemon, ham and lobster) and the modest foodstuffs favored by Jean Siméon Chardin (pot, knife, fruit and bread). Like Chardin, Vallayer-Coster only loosely approximated their surfaces rather than meticulously reproducing them, evoking the experience of those textures – chunky, pulpy, crisp, scaled, brined – upon the tongue.

The corporeal pleasures of touching, smelling and tasting food are embedded in Vallayer-Coster's work. They appeal to the universal human desire to eat, a daily ritual of desire and satiation. Yet her paintings are also illuminated by culturally specific conditions, customs and systems of knowledge. During Vallayer-Coster's lifetime, several writers imagined the conceptual and material connections between art and food. Vallayer-Coster's paintings are best understood within the context of this eighteenth-century food culture, which linked the philosophers of the French Enlightenment and the fishwives of Les Halles food market.

TASTE

In the eighteenth century, taste was often positioned at the bottom of many philosophical hierarchies of senses, just as still-life painting was often described as the lowest within the academic hierarchy of genres. This is likely due to the association of taste with sinful gluttony and carnal cravings. A few writers, however, defended taste as essential to the human experience. Jean Anthelme Brillat-Savarin (1755–1826), the source of the popular maxim 'you are what you eat', described the synesthetic delights of the tongue in *Physiologie du goût* (*Physiology of Taste*, 1825): '[Taste] mingles with all other pleasures, and even consoles us for their absence.'[1] For Brillat-Savarin, taste was deeply entangled with the other senses: the mild tanginess of bread was inseparable from the yeasty smell, the golden-brown color, the crunchy sound of the crust, or the feel of the warm, spongy interior upon the fingers and lips (see fig.26).

In the eighteenth century, taste referred not only to the physical ability to distinguish between salty and sweet, but also the intellectual ability to evaluate other forms of pleasure: art, literature, music, fashion, and so on. One who had 'good' taste would be able to distinguish between fresh and foul, delicious and bland – but also between beautiful and ugly, elegant and vulgar. In his entry on 'Taste' for Denis Diderot's *Encyclopédie*, for example, baron de Montesquieu (1689–1755) described good taste in vague terms that might equally apply to a painting or a culinary dish.[2]

The famed philosopher Voltaire (1694–1778), who expanded the 'Taste' entry for the 1757 edition of the *Encyclopédie*, sought to understand how good taste developed.[3] Voltaire argued that good taste was stable and enduring, immune from fashionable whims, while bad taste was artificial and fickle. Like Montesquieu, Voltaire believed that taste in both food and art could be good or bad, but suggested two major distinctions between them. Taste for food was subjective and innate, while taste for art required education in light of objective, shared standards. In other words, we might disagree about the deliciousness of a plum, but we need no instruction in order to perceive its sweetness. A painting of a plum, on the other hand, has an objective aesthetic value, but this beauty can only be assessed by the well-trained eye (see figs 21–3).

CUISINE

Much like the French school of painting, French cuisine included various styles, which were documented in a number of culinary treatises, published from the mid-seventeenth to late eighteenth centuries.[4] The most canonical of the early cookbooks was François Pierre de la Varenne's *Le cuisinier françois* (*The French Cook*), which was first published in 1651 and appeared in 61 editions over the following century. La Varenne's book spawned numerous other texts. Some were concerned with the philosophical and physiological nature of taste, while others offered specific recipes and practical cooking advice. While many of these texts were directed toward those professionally responsible for preparing food (that is, domestic servants and cooks), others were addressed to a new audience of *gourmets* – 'foodies' in modern parlance.[5] To these connoisseurs, cuisine and art were both expressions of beauty and knowledge.

Conversations about art and cuisine in the eighteenth century were both organized around another binary: ancient versus modern. Several authors championed modern cuisine, which was simpler and less artificial than the ancient cuisine from the previous century.[6] Modern cuisine highlighted the natural flavors, textures and colors of a few fresh ingredients, with an eye toward seasonal availability, and argued that these whole foods ought to be eaten raw or simply cooked, subtly enhanced with local herbs and butter. Critics of the ancient style believed that fussy, overwrought dishes, associated with the elaborate feasts of the royal court at Versailles, had a negative impact on one's physical and spiritual wellbeing. Chevalier Louis de Jaucourt specifically decried the excessive use of fat, sugar, salt and spice in the ancient cuisine.[7]

The visual arts were subject to similar criticisms of excess and artifice in the mid-eighteenth century. Diderot, for example, assailed the frivolity (and, implicitly, the femininity) of François Boucher's Rococo paintings of cosmetically enhanced nymphs and goddesses. In contrast, Diderot championed the sobriety and truth of Chardin's more naturalistic still lifes.[8] Jaucourt and Diderot thus agreed: the human tongue and eye could be easily seduced by sugar and pink rouge, but thrived on simplicity and close proximity to nature.

Vallayer-Coster's paintings, like Chardin's, represent the modern cuisine. Just as this culinary philosophy prescribed, Vallayer-Coster's paintings highlighted a handful of individual ingredients, juxtaposing raw and cooked materials. Fish still scaled, fowl yet unplucked and fruits and vegetables still attached to their leaves and roots suggest freshness and proximity to the moment of harvest – comparable to Vallayer-Coster's application of paint with a thick, 'raw' facture. Smoother passages with more subtly blended, bright and slick pigments might, in turn, be compared to simply prepared dishes: steaming broths, baked breads and cured hams.

INGREDIENTS

Perhaps the most obvious point of comparison between painting and cooking is their mutual use of natural

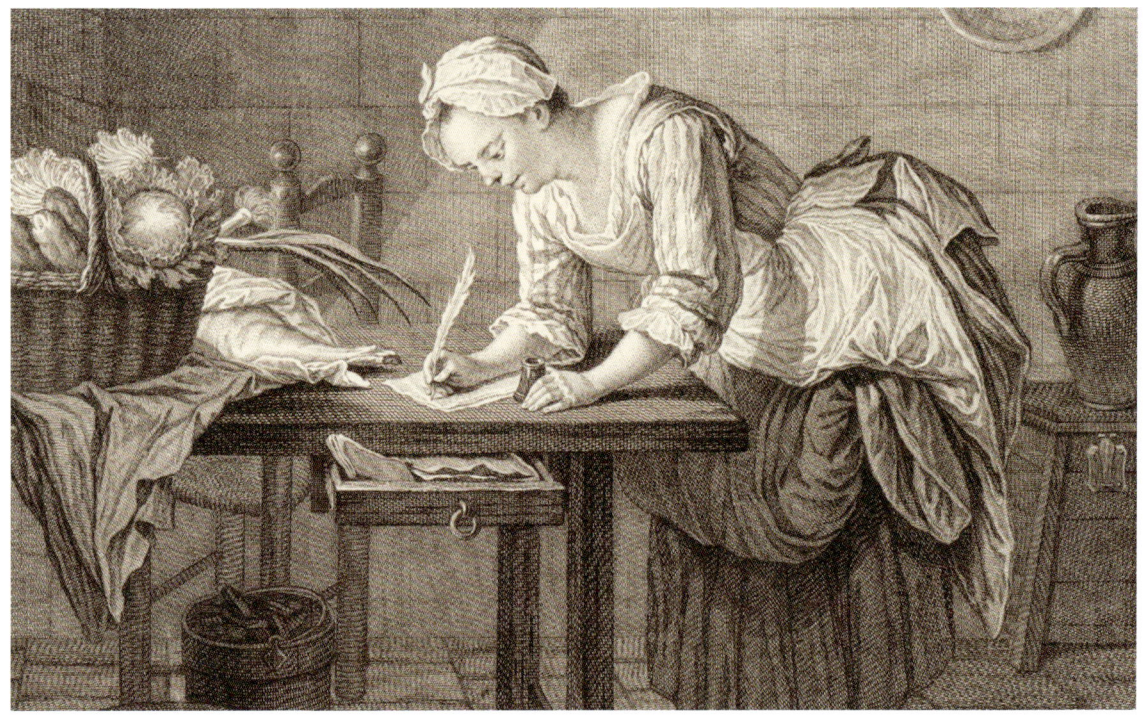

20 Claude Duflos after Pierre-Louis Duménil, detail of *The Female Cook*, c.1762, engraving, 25.3 × 30.5 cm (10 × 12 in), Bibliothèque nationale de France, Paris

ingredients. In *L'art de la cuisine* (*The Art of Cuisine*, 1739), François Marin observed that both the painter and the cook blended organic materials according to specific formulas in order to create sensory pleasure, whether in the form of oil paint or a sauce: 'These ingredients and juices have to be blended and melted, in the same way as the painter blends his colors.'[9]

Vallayer-Coster's food still lifes can be also characterized by her selection of 'ingredients' – that is, her combinations of specific foods and tools in her painted compositions. Some recurring elements were borrowed from Chardin's oeuvre, but others seem to have been culled directly from the artist's own pantry. Tracing these motifs is far from a tidy process. Her canvases are linked across the space of two decades by

repetition, reorientation and recombination – much like a familiar, beloved recipe tweaked and reimagined over time.

This discussion of Vallayer-Coster's paintings takes a cue from the structure of eighteenth-century cookbooks, which were often organized by ingredient. Marin's *L'art de la cuisine*, for example, began with soups, followed by meat, poultry, seafood, vegetables and herbs.[10] The following approximates the chronology of Vallayer-Coster's paintings of food: beginning with her earlier, sweeter representations of fruit and bread, before considering more savory combinations of vegetables, meat and fish.

Far from static objects, the ingredients represented in Vallayer-Coster's paintings were part of a complex network of exchange – from the moment of harvest in the countryside, to their display and sale at an urban food market, to their preparation in the kitchen and consumption at the dining table. As they moved through each of these spaces, ingredients acquired distinct cultural values, which informed the making and meaning of Vallayer-Coster's paintings.

The majority of the goods that she painted could be easily acquired from Les Halles, the principal food market in Paris, located just one block from the Vallayer family workshop on the rue du Roule. The ritual sprawl of food vendors near the church of Saint-Eustache had its origins in the twelfth century and by the eighteenth century had become a central urban spectacle. In *Le tableau de Paris* (*Panorama of Paris*, 1781), Louis-Sébastien Mercier (1740–1814) complained of the noises and smells accompanying the daily influx of thousands of specialized suppliers to Paris, beginning at one in the morning.[11] The market at Les Halles was essential to the economic rhythm of the city, but its riot of color, sound and smell was also integral to its sensory fabric.

Vallayer-Coster would have been familiar with the dynamics of these spaces, given her lifelong proximity to this market, but it is unlikely that she played a major role in acquiring or preparing the food that she consumed. Successful artisan families, like the Vallayers, might have employed at least one or two female servants who were responsible for trips to the market and cooking daily meals. A 1762 print entitled *La cuisinière* (*The Female Cook*; fig.20) represents one such woman presiding over a basket of fresh produce and a hock of ham, and writing an inventory or menu – demonstrating her command over the space of the kitchen, as well as her professional literacy.[12] Some recipe books, like Joseph Menon's *La cuisinière bourgeoise* (1746), catered to this type of domestic worker.[13]

Vallayer-Coster's paintings of food were also predicated upon the physical and intellectual labor

of at least one anonymous woman in the kitchen. There is reason to believe that Vallayer-Coster directly observed this type of labor in her family's household or in her own apartment at the Louvre, which was outfitted with a small '*cuisine sans cheminée*' (kitchen without a hearth).[14] At the Salon of 1783, for example, Vallayer-Coster submitted a now lost painting entitled *Une jeune cuisinière qui écorche une anguille* (*A Young Female Cook Flaying an Eel*).[15] At least once, Vallayer-Coster painted a domestic servant, a genre for which Chardin is now better known.[16]

FRUITS, VEGETABLES AND BREAD

Fruits and vegetables are the most frequent components of Vallayer-Coster's food paintings, just as they were the focus of recipes in many contemporary cookbooks – suggesting their centrality to the French kitchen and diet. While some edible plants might have been grown in private kitchen gardens in Paris, most urban households acquired fresh produce from farmers who grew seasonal crops and sold their wares at food markets like Les Halles.[17]

Just as Vallayer-Coster evaluated the formal qualities of fruits and vegetables in paint, suppliers and buyers at urban markets carefully considered the visual appearance of perishable products. Agricultural manuals like Jean de la Quintinie's *Instruction pour les jardins fruitiers et potagers* (*Instruction for Fruit and Vegetable Gardens*, 1690) tell us that farmers often harvested underripe fruits and privileged specimens with more durable, unblemished complexions. This ensured the viability and desirability of their produce to their connoisseurial customers. Other texts instructed buyers to assess the quality, freshness and taste of perishable materials piled high at food markets simply by looking at their surfaces.[18] Antoine-Joseph Dezallier d'Argenville asserted that other senses could also be called upon: 'Ripeness may also be determined by placing one's thumb gently at the stalk end of each soft fruit: if the flesh gives, the fruit is ripe. With crisp fruit,

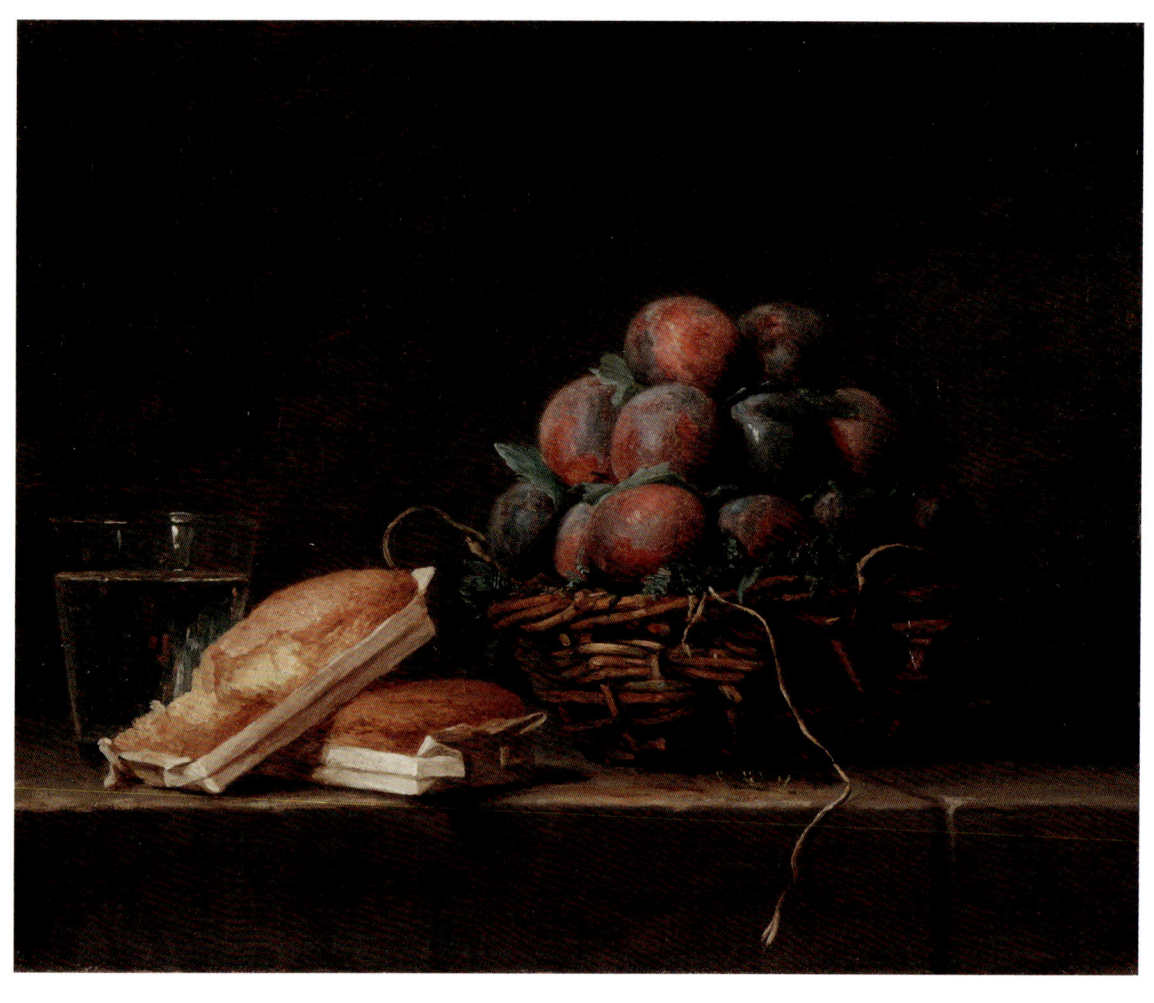

21 Anne Vallayer-Coster, *Basket of Plums*, 1769, oil on canvas, 38 × 46.2 cm (14 ⅞ × 18 ¼ in), The Cleveland Museum of Art, OH

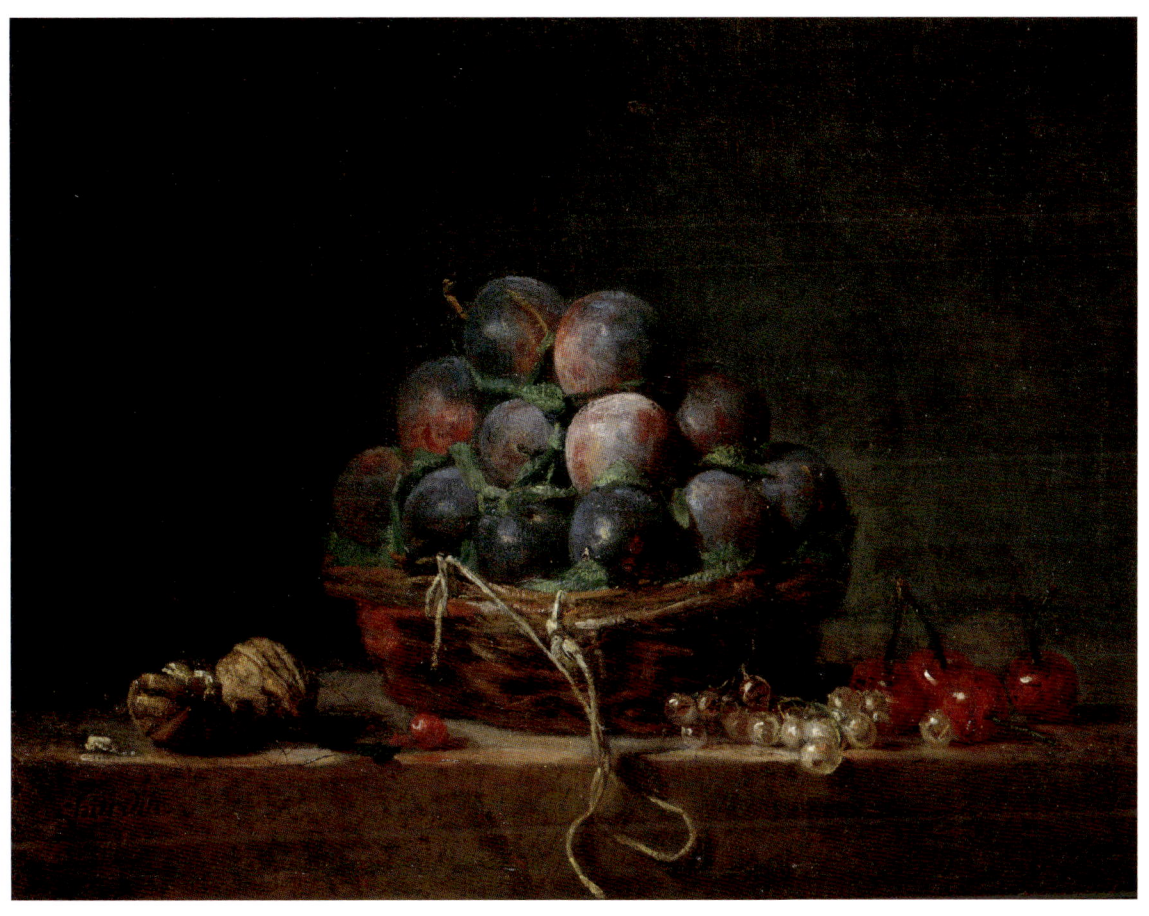

22 Jean Siméon Chardin, *Basket of Plums*, 1765, oil on canvas, 32.4 × 41.9 cm (12 ¾ × 16 ½ in), Chrysler Museum of Art, Norfolk, VA

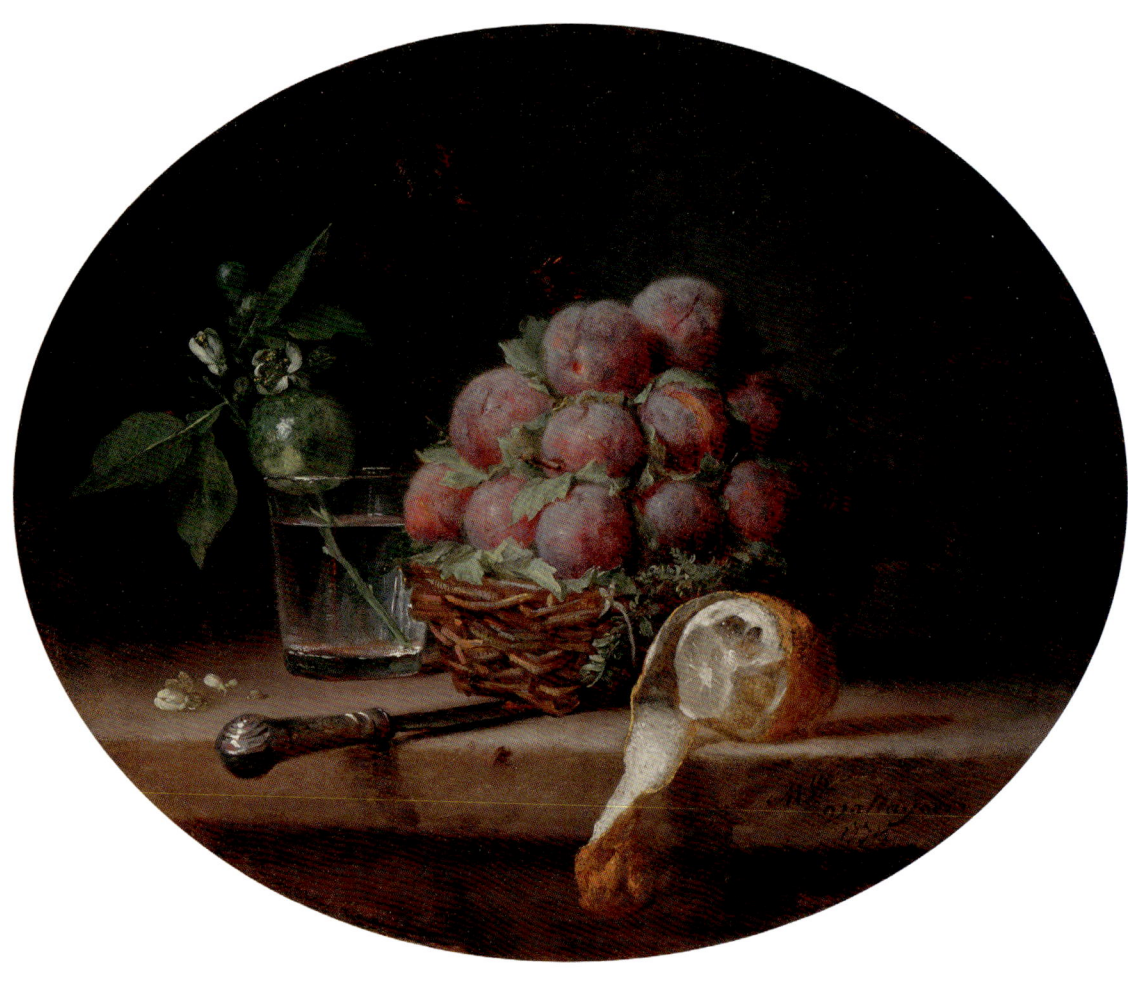

23 Anne Vallayer-Coster, *Still Life with Plums and a Lemon*, 1778, oil on canvas, 41.6 × 47.3 cm (16 ⅜ × 18 ⅝ in), Fine Arts Museums of San Francisco, CA

only the taste decides.'[19] The eyes and fingers might be able to provide a preliminary assessment of ripeness, but final judgment was reserved for the tongue.

Ripe piles of stone fruits with waxy and fuzzy skins – cherries, peaches and plums – populate many of Vallayer-Coster's earliest canvases. In combination with various baked goods, they suggest morning meals; as Brillat-Savarin described contemporary meal patterns in *Physiologie du goût*, 'Ordinarily we breakfast before nine o'clock on bread, cheese, fruit and sometimes cold meats'.[20] Plums, for example, were commonly eaten raw, but could also be baked or preserved.[21] To her first Salon at 1771, Vallayer-Coster likely submitted *Basket of Plums* (fig.21): a pile of ruby and purple plums, still attached to their sage-green leaves.[22] Vallayer-Coster conveyed the glaucous surface of the plums with touches of powdery gray and rich burgundy. The tidy pyramidal arrangement of plums within a loosely woven basket was directly quoted from a 1765 Chardin painting, *Basket of Plums* (fig.22). As observed in the previous chapter, Vallayer-Coster clearly sought to emulate – if not to rival – Chardin at the start of her career.[23]

Vallayer-Coster repeated the same basket of plums in an oval canvas, probably shown at the Salon of 1779 (fig.23).[24] In the later work, Vallayer-Coster replaced the two small cakes with a motif more typical of the Dutch still life (and almost entirely absent from Chardin's oeuvre): the lemon. Here, the lemon is represented in two different states: unripe and ripe. A small round glass filled with water hosts the flowering sprig of the dark green, unripe fruit. The ripe, yellow lemon is partially peeled, revealing the wet pulp and translucent membranes inside. The waxy, pimpled rind, rendered in daubs of marigold, unfurls over the stone ledge, revealing its inner white pith. These fruits provide a contrast in both color and flavor: a lick of the bright and sour citrus would contrast sharply with a sweet, meaty bite of plum.

Totally unique to Vallayer-Coster's 1769 painting of plums are two small cakes, the saccharine sweetness

of which would have paired well with the fresh, juicy plum. This is likely a simple sponge cake, distinguished by its ample use of butter, mixed with flour, sugar and eggs. Vallayer-Coster presents the cakes wrapped in neatly folded *moules de papier* (paper molds). Menon also recommended this technique to domestic bakers as a quick, cheap way to contain the cake batter in the oven: 'For all kinds of cakes, you make a mold with white paper, according to the size you want.'[25] This was also a typical baking vessel in a professional context: a pile of paper molds appears in the *pâtissier* (pastry maker) engraving in the *Encyclopédie*, for example.

Still Life with Brioche, Fruit and Vegetables of 1775 (fig.24) features another rich, leavened dough.[26] The brioche's spiral shape was achieved by kneading and rolling a mixture of egg, butter, flour and yeast into a thick log, then draping the dough into a swirl. Alternately, a *brioche à tête* (brioche with a head) was constructed by placing a smaller ball of dough on top of a larger one, as seen in one of Vallayer-Coster's later works (see fig.30). After the raw dough was given time to rise, the surface was painted with a thin layer of egg wash, rendering it shiny, crisp and golden brown upon baking – a process similar to that of glazing the surface of a finished oil painting with a clear varnish to saturate and preserve the layers of color underneath.[27]

Vallayer-Coster's brioche is accompanied by a shallow glass dish of preserved cherries, fresh peaches in a basket and a cluster of raw radishes. These side fruits and vegetables provide a sense of color harmony: the vivid red of the cherries contrasts with the pale, cool pink of the radishes and the warm orange of the peaches is offset by subtle dabs of pale green, standing for the moss on the peach skin, and the deep emerald of the radish leaves. The painting represents the chromatic, textural and gustatory contrasts between the stone fruits, root vegetable and bread: tart and juicy cherries, sweet and smooth peaches, crunchy and bitter radish, and rich, flaky brioche.

Vallayer-Coster likely borrowed the brioche from Chardin's 1763 painting (fig.25).[28] As did her

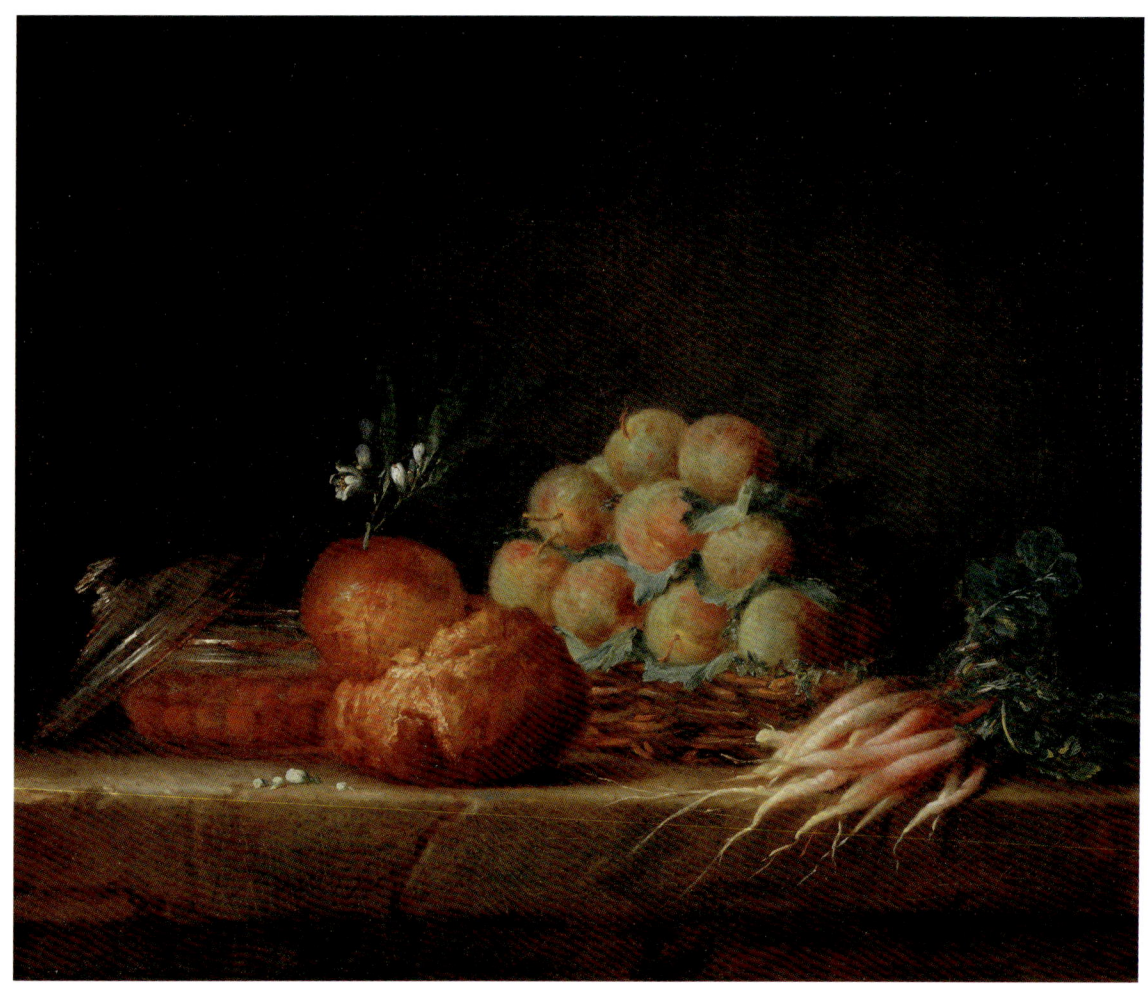

24 Anne Vallayer-Coster, *Still Life with Brioche, Fruit and Vegetables*, 1775, oil on canvas, 45.5 × 55 cm (17 ⅞ × 21 ⅝ in), Nationalmuseum, Stockholm

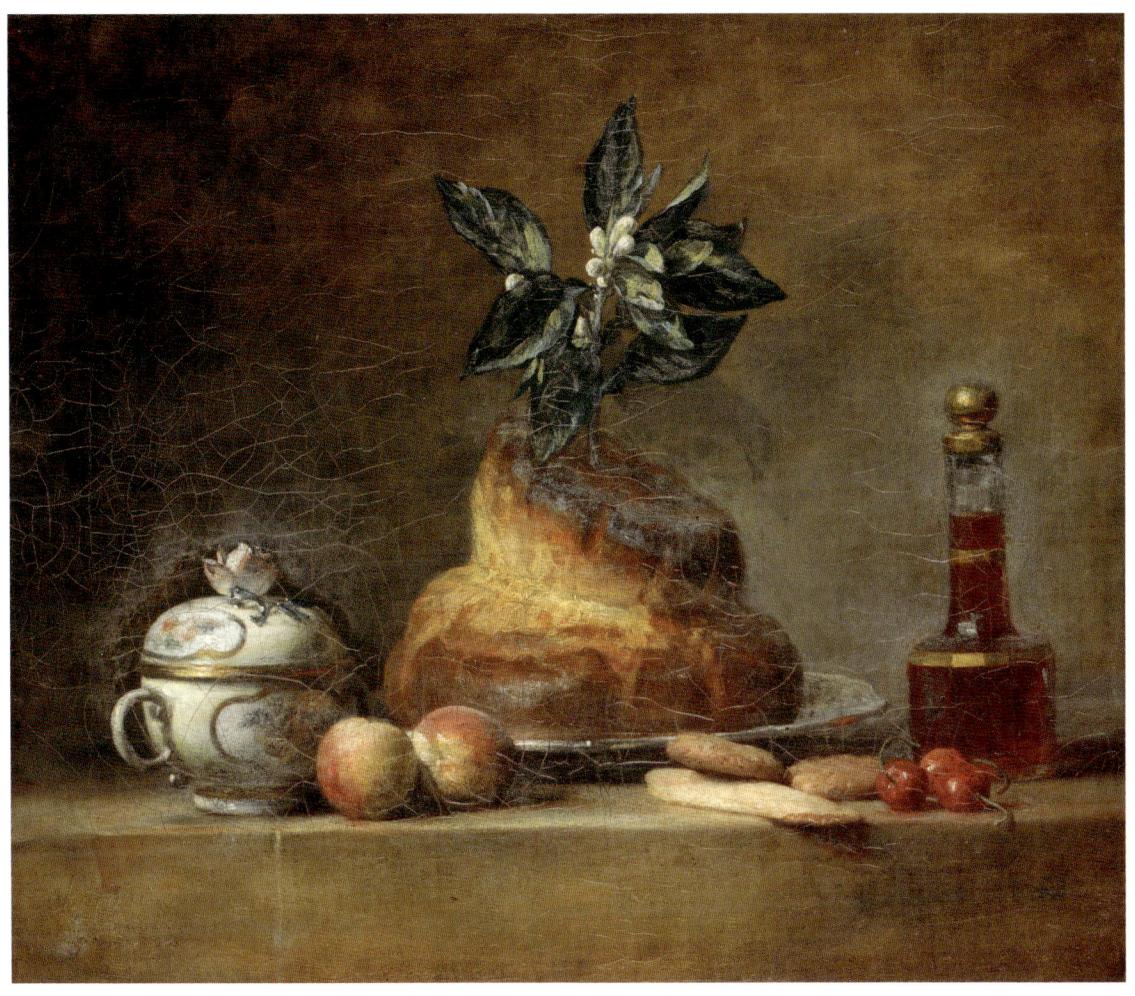

25 Jean Siméon Chardin, *The Brioche*, 1763, oil on canvas, 47 × 56 cm (18 ½ × 22 in), Musée du Louvre, Paris

predecessor, Vallayer-Coster paired her brioche with cherries and peaches. She also similarly topped it with a white floral sprig, a typical adornment for Easter or a wedding.[29] The brioche's ambiguity is further evidenced by the expression '*qu'ils mangeant de la brioche*', frequently misattributed to Queen Marie Antoinette and clumsily translated to 'Let them eat cake!'[30] Whatever the occasion, the sweet-smelling blossom atop a buttery brioche distinguished this particular French baked good from any other, placing it somewhere between quotidian, starchy bread and a sweet sponge cake.

There was also a specific vocabulary to describe various types of pastry makers and bread bakers, whose primary medium was flour – just as there were a variety of terms to denote artists who specialized in different media or genres, as well as their hierarchical rank within the Académie. A *pâtissier* (pastry chef) made sweet pastries, whereas a *boulanger privilégié* (privileged baker) referred only to savory bread bakers who legally owned brick-and-mortar shops in Paris. These bread makers employed apprentices to deliver bread daily to wealthy Parisian households.[31] *Boulangers forains* (stallholder bakers), on the other hand, sold their wares at regularly scheduled markets. According to Diderot's 'Baker' entry in the *Encyclopédie*, 'The city needs 900 stallholders, who come to the markets twice a week . . . Bread markets have grown in size as Paris has increased. There are now fifteen of them.' For Diderot, the centrality of bread to the Parisian diet required no further explanation than this: 'As bread is the most common and necessary food, the bread market is held in Paris on Wednesdays and Saturdays, no matter when these days fall.'[32]

A simple *pain blanc* (white bread) or *pain de campagne* (country bread), sold biweekly by the stallholders of Paris, appears in Vallayer-Coster's *The White Tureen* (fig.26).[33] The painting features a chunky, oblong loaf with a golden crust, comprised of dashes of red, burnt orange and yellow paint. The bread has been halved to expose its starchy interior, punctuated

by yeast-induced air bubbles and loosely wrapped in a plain white cloth. The loaf is paired with a modest white soup bowl, the simplicity of which suggests a midday meal; as Brillat-Savarin noted, 'between one and two P.M., we take soup or *pot au feu* according to our positions'.[34] Though the contents of that vessel are not visible, the thick steam emerging from the unlidded bowl suggests an aromatic stock or stew. Vallayer-Coster offers no other clues as to the specific ingredients contained within the bowl, yet thick wafts of steam invite specific memories: salivation in response to a savory smell and the satisfaction of consuming hot soup and bread.

However humble the materials depicted in this monochromatic composition, the painting appealed to critics and patrons alike. When the work appeared at the Salon of 1771, Diderot praised the veracity of Vallayer-Coster's representation of bread, in particular, as 'true and like nature, but without rawness'.[35] For Diderot, the smooth, well-baked quality of her work formed a contrast to Chardin's 'rough and uneven way of painting'.[36] Abel-François Poisson de Vandières, marquis de Marigny (1727–81) – the brother of King Louis XV's mistress, the marquise de Pompadour – likely acquired this painting sometime before he retired from his post as Director of the King's Buildings in July 1773; the work was subsequently sold at his 1782 estate sale.[37]

WINE AND HAM

In *The White Tureen*, the soup or stew is paired with dark glass bottles, probably containing wine. Similar bottles also appeared in two of Vallayer-Coster's earliest known canvases: *Still Life with Ham, Bottles and Radishes* (fig.27)[38] and *Hare, Partridge and Ham* (fig.28).[39] The frequency with which wine bottles appear in Vallayer-Coster's early paintings is unsurprising; in the words of Mercier, 'In Paris, wine still holds sway'.[40] Indeed, the social and cultural significance of wine would be difficult to

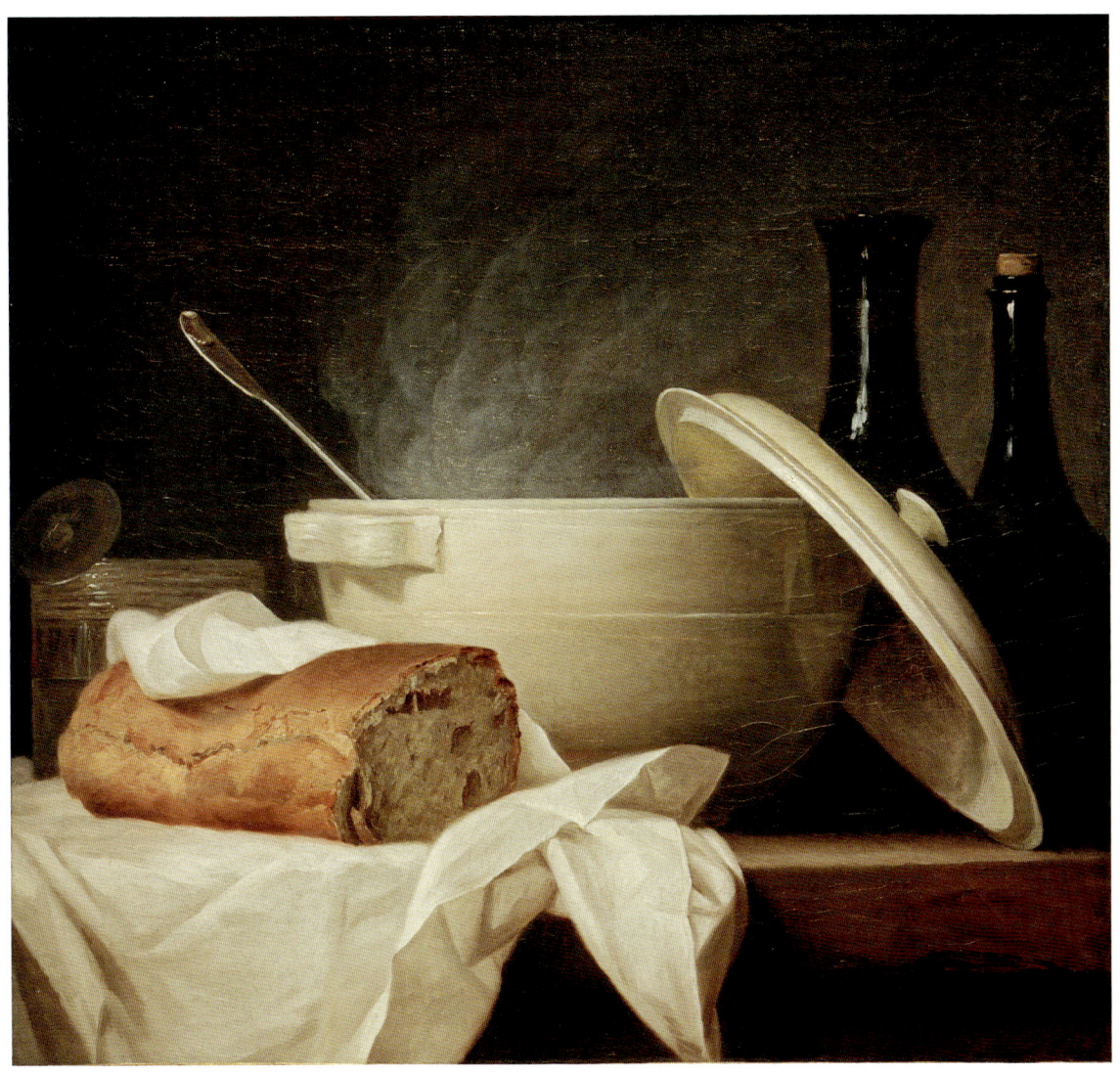

26 Anne Vallayer-Coster, *The White Tureen*, 1771, oil on canvas, 54 × 62 cm (21 ¼ × 24 ⅜ in), Private collection

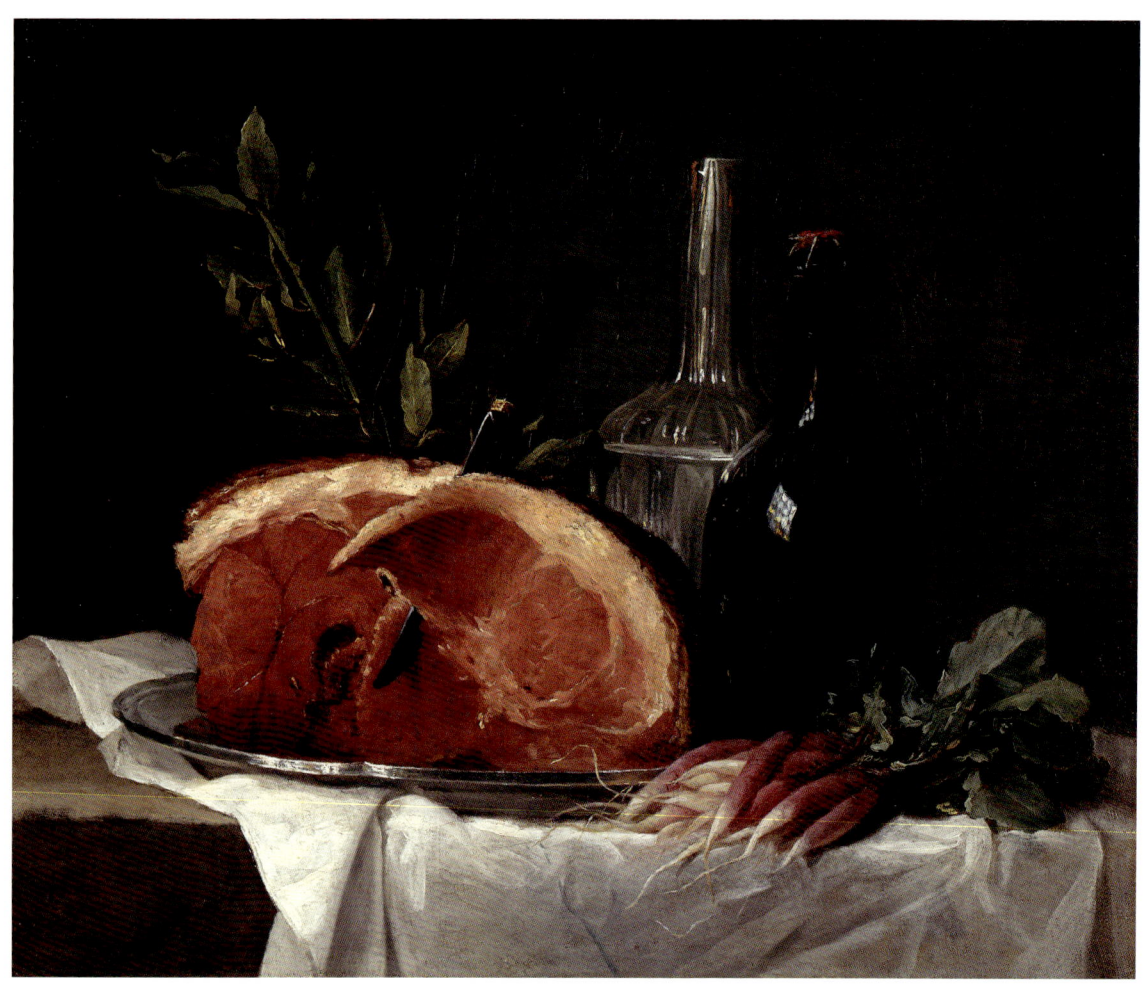

27 Anne Vallayer-Coster, *Still Life with Ham, Bottles and Radishes*, 1767, oil on canvas, 46 × 45.6 cm (18 ⅛ × 18 in), Staatliche Museen zu Berlin, Gemaldegalerie

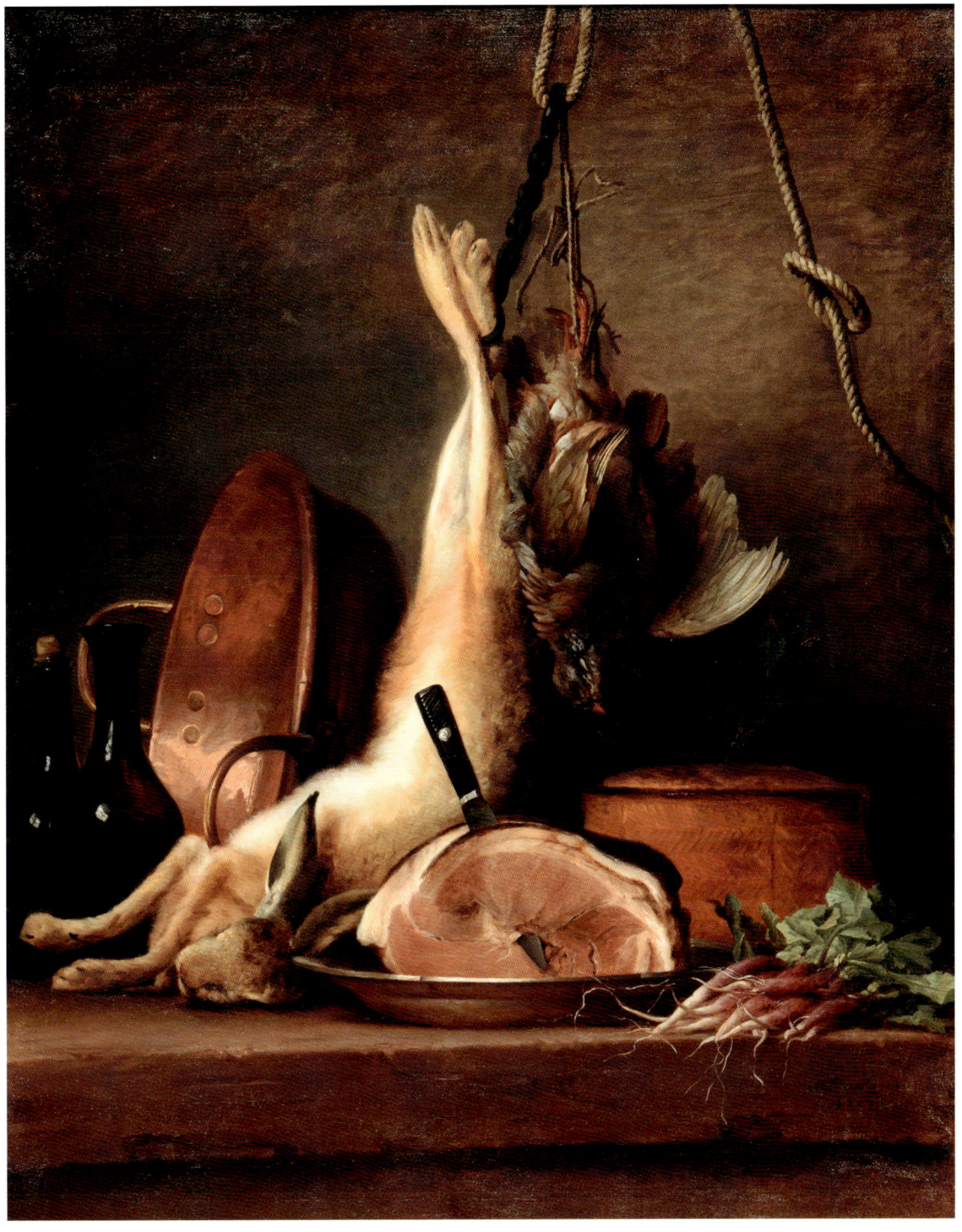

28 Anne Vallayer-Coster, *Hare, Partridge and Ham*, 1769, oil on canvas, 101.6 × 81 cm (40 × 31⅞ in), Musée des
Beaux-Arts, Reims

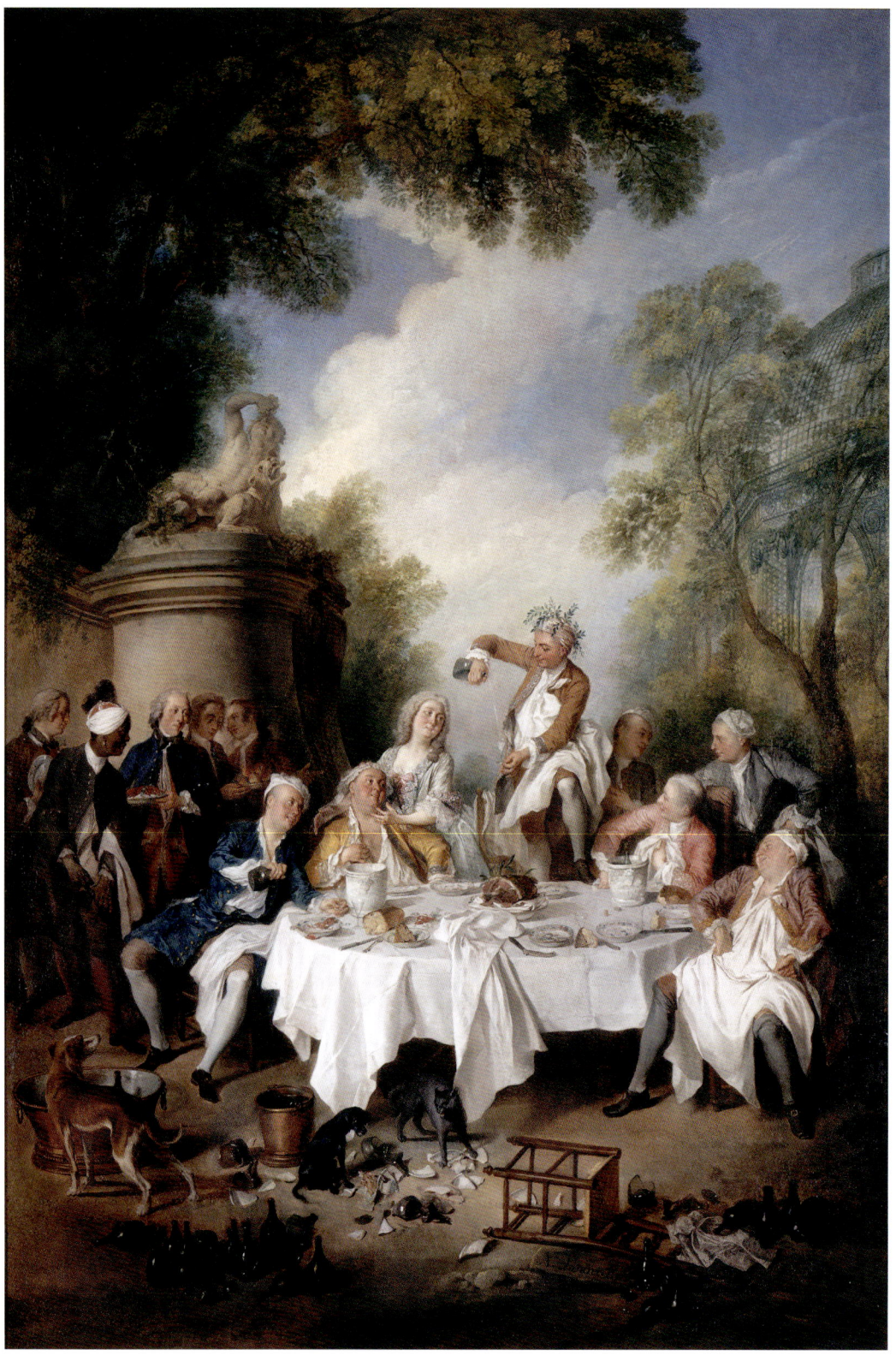

29 Nicolas Lancret, *Ham Luncheon*, 1735, oil on canvas, 188 × 123 cm (74 × 48⅜ in), Musée Condé, Chantilly

overstate. Sometimes diluted with water, wine was a ubiquitous beverage that Parisians drank at nearly every meal. Bourgeois and aristocratic customers alike purchased casks to store in private cellars and periodically refilled their own glass bottles. High rates of wine consumption are evidenced in part by the vast number of barrels imported from Parisian wholesale wine traders during this period. Despite the remarkable quantity of wine drunk in Paris in the eighteenth century, quality was still of great importance – especially to elite connoisseurs, who debated a wine's merits of color, body and taste.[41]

In addition to wine bottles, these two paintings are also linked by their mutual representation of ham, the hind leg of a pig that has been boiled and cured with dry salt or wet brine. The chevalier de Jaucourt explained the process and merits of curing meats in his 'Cuisine' entry in the *Encyclopédie*: 'Meats and fish that are prepared in this fashion keep better than by any other method.'[42] Unlike *traiteurs*, butchers who sold raw meats, *charcutiers* provided preserved hams to urban markets.[43] Ham became more accessible to consumers over the course of the eighteenth century but maintained its associations with celebratory indulgence, due in part to the Catholic restrictions on meat consumption during fast days; the Crown only began to relax laws surrounding the sale of meat during Lent in 1774.[44] As Brillat-Savarin observed in *Physiologie du goût*, 'The prime elements of our pleasures are difficulty, privation, desire and accomplishment. All these came together in the act of breaking abstinence, and I have seen two of my grand-uncles, both strong and level-headed men, half swoon with joy when they saw the first slice cut from a ham … on Easter day.'[45]

Boozy, carnivorous ecstasy took visual form in Nicolas Lancret's (1690–1743) *Ham Luncheon* (fig.29), a painting commissioned to decorate Louis XV's dining room at Versailles in 1735, which was widely reproduced in print thereafter.[46] The image features a boisterous group of aristocratic young men carousing in a garden littered with empty wine bottles, around a table set with a plump ham punctuated with aromatic bay leaves. *Ham Luncheon* celebrates the same tandem delights of alcohol and meat depicted in Vallayer-Coster's work, which clearly had an appeal beyond Versailles.

In both of Vallayer-Coster's ham paintings, the knife is mid-cleave, propped up by the very meat it has just incised. The erect knife emphasizes the immediacy of the act of slicing and eating the ham, as well as the materiality of the (yet to be consumed) meat. But for the orientations of the knives thrust inside them, the two paintings feature nearly identical hams, situated on the same silver platter. In both, Vallayer-Coster oriented the succulent interior cut of the meat toward the viewer. Using a series of slick brushstrokes, she quickly summarized the color and texture of the ham's rough, desiccated brown skin, thick layer of white fat and marbled rosy-brown flesh. Both paintings also feature fistfuls of pink and white radishes, cleaned of their dirt but still attached to their stringy roots. The raw radishes provide yet another visual, textural and savory contrast to the chewy cured meat.

Despite their manifold similarities, Vallayer-Coster's Berlin (1767) and Reims (1769) hams appear in two slightly different settings. The Reims ham has been placed on a dimly lit stone ledge, along with two pieces of wild game: a lean hare and a gray partridge, both suspended by their legs with a coarse rope to relax and tenderize their muscles. The freshness of the game (unskinned, unplucked), in combination with the cooking utensils that surround them (a gleaming copper cauldron and a woven basket), suggests that they are in a dimly lit kitchen nook.

In the Berlin painting, in contrast, the ham has been set on smooth white cloth alongside a fluted crystal bottle and studded with a few sprigs of green bay leaves, valued for its decorative and aromatic qualities. The savory flavor combination of ham and bay leaves, which also appears in Lancret's *Ham Luncheon*, was specifically recommended to cooks in

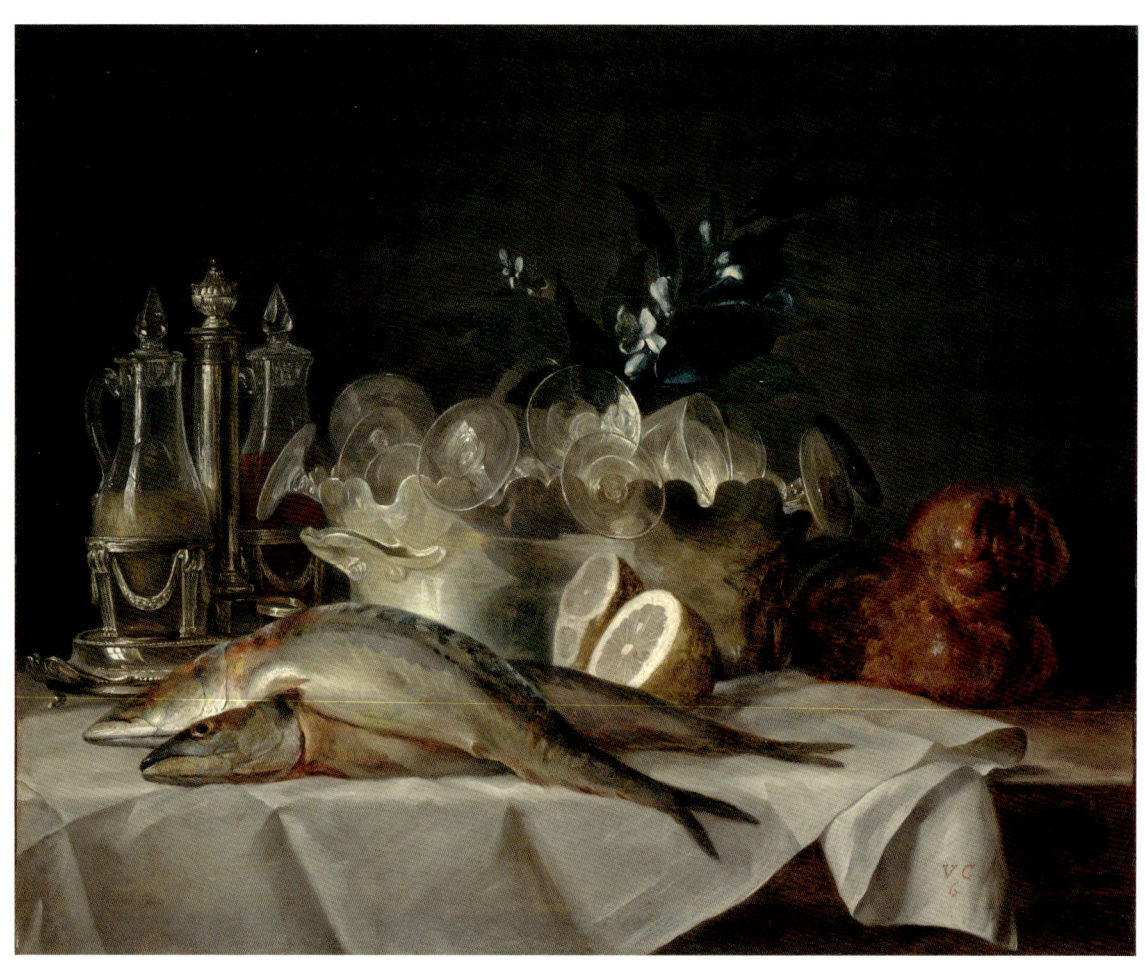

30 Anne Vallayer-Coster, *Still Life with Mackerel*, 1787, oil on canvas, 49.5 × 61 cm (19 ½ × 24 in), Kimbell Art Museum, Fort Worth, TX

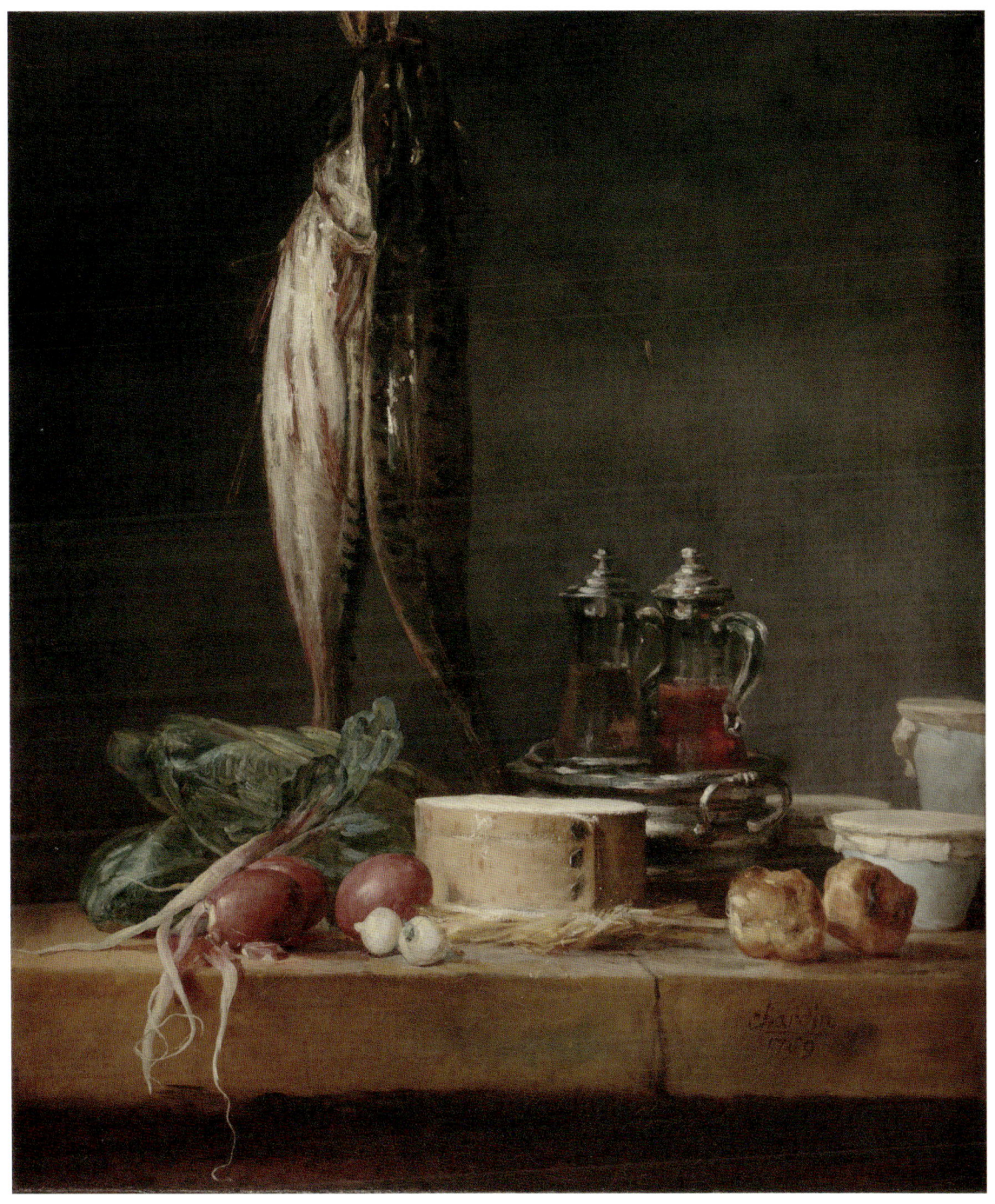

31 Jean Siméon Chardin, *Still Life with Fish, Vegetables, Gougères, Pots and Cruets on a Table*, 1769, oil on canvas, 68.6 × 58.4 cm (27 × 23 in), The J. Paul Getty Museum, Los Angeles, CA

Menon's *Les soupers de la cour* (*Court Suppers*, 1755).[47] These accompaniments suggest a proximity to the ham's consumption at the dining table, rather than its preparation in the kitchen.

SEAFOOD

As her career progressed, Vallayer-Coster distanced herself from the humble foodstuffs and utensils that also characterized Chardin's paintings. Her later food still lifes show a preference for finer, more delicate materials – glass, silver, porcelain – whose gleaming reflective surfaces produce interesting illusory effects. This is true of the three seafood still lifes that Vallayer-Coster produced in the 1780s and beyond. *Still Life with Mackerel* (fig.30), for example, was identified by its depiction of silverware at the 1787 Salon, where it appeared as *Une verrière d'argent avec des verres, des maquereaux, un huilier, etc.* (*A Silver Basin with Glasses, Mackerels, a Cruet, etc.*).[48]

The *verrière* is a vessel characterized by its scalloped rim, designed to accommodate the stems of several wine glasses. In Vallayer-Coster's painting, the bases of the glasses emerge from the mouth of the basin like a crystal bouquet. On the body of the *verrière*, the distorted reflections of surrounding objects are rendered with strokes of yellow, white, gray and brown. These liquid abstractions of color float on the shiny silver surface (recall that her father trained as a goldsmith and, along with her mother, produced military medals in the family workshop). The *verrière* rests on a white tablecloth, 'monogrammed' in red thread with the initials of the artist's maiden and married name ('VC') – a *trompe-l'oeil* signature that suggests this is the artist's own table. This rather personal painting remained in Vallayer-Coster's household for the remainder of her life and was only sold at her husband's estate sale in 1824.[49]

The painting contains other elite dining accessories: *huiliers* and *vinaigriers*, glass cruets containing oil and vinegar. The bottles are set within a neoclassical silver holster, festooned with silver floral garlands and fluted columns. The fatty and acidic duet of oil and vinegar was a popular pairing with fish: similar (if less luxurious) cruets appear alongside fish in another late Chardin painting, *Still Life with Fish, Vegetables, Gougères, Pots and Cruets on a Table*, dated to 1769 (fig.31).[50] Chardin's fish painting is brutally frank: two fish dangle vertically from a hook and one is partially flayed, its interior crudely etched with dry streaks of white, gray and deep red paint. In contrast, Vallayer-Coster's fish flop, one over the other, in a sensual embrace. She employed delicate yellows and silvery grays to evoke the feel of the mackerel's slick belly and jelly eyeball, as well as the waxy rind and citrusy tissue of the halved lemons next to them. The palpable texture of the depicted substances is belied by the 'wet', undisguised touch of Vallayer-Coster's brush. Quick, unblended dabs of vermillion at the mackerel's gills, for example, stand for residual blood – the only reference to the violent means through which the fish were extracted from the sea.

Still Life with Mackerel is Vallayer-Coster's only extant painting to feature scaled fish. This may be attributed to the relative expense and difficulty of importing fresh fish to Paris. Fish were typically acquired on commercial sailing vessels known as *chasse-marées*, and transported by land from the port cities to Paris, occasionally thwarted by storms or excessive heat.[51] Oily fish, like mackerel, were cured with salt prior to shipment in order to deter spoilage, with varying degrees of success. In *Tableau de Paris*, Mercier bemoaned the malodorous proliferation of fish vendors in Paris ('the fish stalls are unspeakable … our modern fishwives will not part with a scale or fin until it begins to stink').[52] Still, Mercier notes that these putrid aromas did little to dampen the French appetite for seafood: 'There is no one in the world like the Parisian for eating what revolts the sense of smell.'[53] The fish stalls of Les Halles, near Vallayer-Coster's family home on rue de Roule, must have offered a salient sensory experience.

Beyond its odor, the fish market was also associated with the *poissarde* ('fishwife' or female fishmonger) – more specifically, the sound of her. The *poissardes* of Les Halles were renowned for the volume and vulgarity of their street cries; in the words of the popular *Fishwife Song* of 1789, 'There are more words in their lungs than in the *Encyclopédie*'.[54] The fishwife also assumed a specific political agency in the final decade of the *ancien régime*. In 1787, the same year that Vallayer-Coster painted and exhibited *Still Life with Mackerel*, the absence of *poissardes* from Queen Marie Antoinette's annual Assumption Day festivities was interpreted as a sign of dissatisfaction with the monarchy in the popular press. This act of defiance foreshadowed the notorious march of the market women on Versailles two years later – one of the events that marked the beginning of the Revolution.[55] Vallayer-Coster was certainly familiar with these local purveyors of seafood. To the Salon of 1783, she submitted a small oval painting titled *Marchande de marée* (*Female Fish Seller*), paired with a flower seller, both now lost.[56] Despite her representation of market women in the mid 1780s, the artist's political sympathies likely lay elsewhere during the Revolution – in part because she relied on the patronage of the monarchy and aristocracy.

In the absence of any explicit evidence of Vallayer-Coster's political inclinations, however, a duo of lobster paintings offers interesting clues. The first lobster, painted in 1781, belonged to a wealthy Parisian banker at the height of the *ancien régime* (fig.32).[57] The second lobster appeared at the Salon of 1817, as part of the collection of a restored Bourbon King Louis XVIII (fig.33).[58] Though separated by several decades and a rapid succession of political regimes, these two paintings are linked by their nearly identical, evocatively textured lobsters. Spongy fields of red form the mottled surface of the body, and looser dabs of maroon and pink color the serrated claws, which are crusted with spherical white barnacles. In both works, Vallayer-Coster evoked the craggy texture of the lobster shells by grinding chunks of lead, stone or shell into her red paints. Some seventeenth-century Dutch still-life artists are thought to have employed this same technique.[59]

Vallayer-Coster's lobster paintings must have appealed to collectors of the seventeenth-century Dutch *pronkstilleven* (display still life), a category renowned for its complexity and opulence. However, her treatments of the lobster are much more modest in contrast. This difference may be attributed to the relative accessibility of lobsters in France and the Netherlands. According to Henri-Louis Duhamel du Monceau's *Traité général des pesches, et histoires des poissons* (*General Treatise on Fishing and the History of Fish*, 1769–77), commercial fisheries operating on the rocky coast of Normandy easily filled the Parisian demand for mollusks and crustaceans (which, unlike scaled fish, could feasibly be transported to the capital city while still alive). However, because lobsters were less plentiful along the sandy Dutch coast, they were significantly more costly in Dutch fish markets – and were thus a stronger symbol of visual and culinary opulence in that context.[60]

Though they were not an especially rare delicacy in French cuisine, shellfish were nonetheless prized for their aphrodisiac qualities. As Nicolas Venette (1633–98) stated in *Tableau de l'amour conjugal* (*The Mysteries of Conjugal Love*), 'those who live almost entirely upon fish and shellfish . . . are more ardent in love than all others'.[61] Brillat-Savarin, writing almost a century later in *Physiologie du goût*, agreed that seafood generally 'acts strongly on the genesic sense and awakens in both sexes the instincts of reproduction'.[62] This connotation may be attributed to the passionate gestures required to strip the oyster, clam or lobster of its outer shell and devour the meat inside – or perhaps to the peculiarities of its salty, alien smell.

The lobster, in particular, exemplifies the erotic tension between revulsion and desire, but also the tension between life and death. Vallayer-Coster's

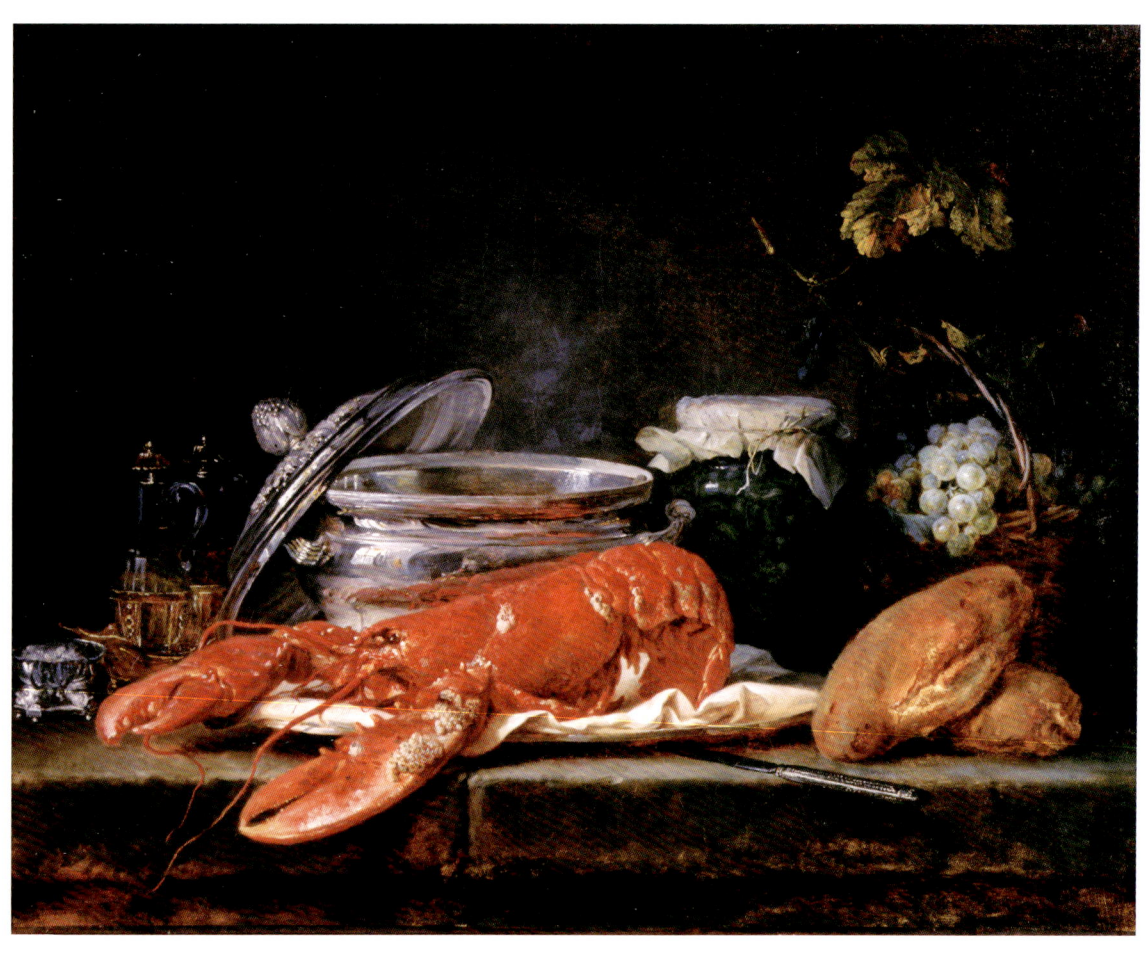

32 Anne Vallayer-Coster, *Still Life with Lobster*, 1781, oil on canvas, 70.5 × 89.5 cm (27 ¾ × 35 ¼ in), Toledo Museum of Art, OH

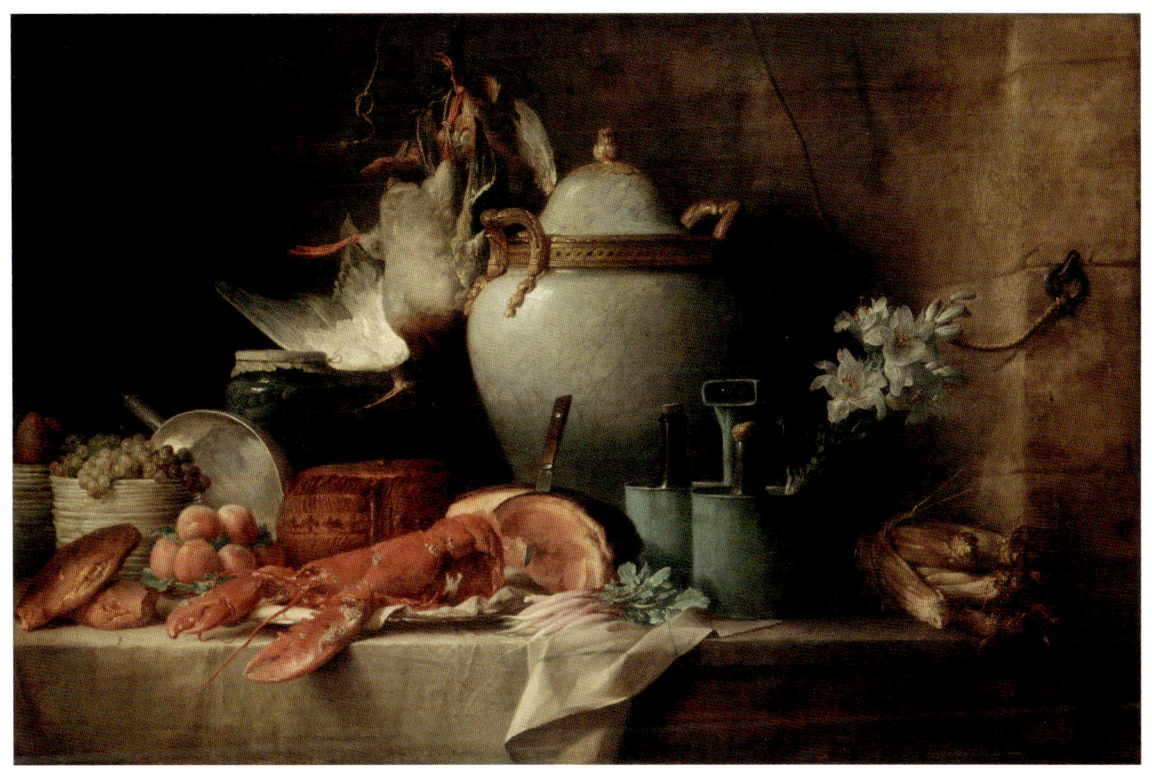

33 Anne Vallayer-Coster, *Still Life with Lobster*, *c.*1775 [previously dated 1817], oil on canvas, 116 × 178 cm (45⅝ × 70 in),
Musée du Louvre, Paris

representations of lobsters are demonstrably dead, the blood red-orange color an indication of having been boiled, but they still possess an uncanny, animate quality. In both works, the lobsters' pleated abdomens are tentatively arched, their stringy antennae and sharp pincers creep beyond the stony ledge toward the viewer, as if fully alive. Real or painted, the insectile lobster could be a rather fearsome sight; the princesse de Lamballe, a favorite of Queen Marie Antoinette, was said to have once fainted at the sight of a particularly lifelike painting of a lobster.[63]

Tentacles and barnacles did not otherwise diminish the Parisian taste for lobster meat or for paintings of them. In Vallayer-Coster's 1781 *Still Life with Lobster*, the lobster is pictured alongside a number of savory accompaniments, an assortment of sweet, tart, sour, fatty and salty: from right to left, two crusty loaves of bread, a basket of pale green grapes, a glass jar of cornichons, cruets of oil and vinegar and a silver dish piled with flaky salt. As with the silver *verrière* in the 1787 *Mackerel* painting, the surface of the silver tureen here produces an almost hallucinatory, distorted reflection of the lobster as well as the surrounding room, perhaps the artist's own studio at the Louvre. The reflection consists of a four-paned window and the hint of a figure, likely that of the artist herself, dressed in orange. This painterly practice of 'signing' ones work with a subtle, reflected self-portrait was typical of early modern still life in Northern Europe.[64]

Vallayer-Coster's 1781 lobster found a buyer in the banker Jean Girardot de Marigny (1733–96), who probably acquired the canvas soon after its completion. The stretcher of this canvas is inscribed '*2e étage sale a Manger*' (second floor dining room), which may refer to Girardot de Marigny's Parisian apartment on 44 rue Vivienne or perhaps a subsequent owner. This inscription indicates that the work, and likely its pendant, *Still Life with Game* (see fig.40), were at some point installed in a private room dedicated to culinary consumption.[65] In 1783, Girardot de Marigny also lent it to the curator and dealer Pahin de la Blancherie

(1752–1811) for a public exhibition on French painting from the sixteenth through the eighteenth centuries.[66]

A second lobster painting, which belonged to King Louis XVIII, appeared at the Salon of 1817 (fig.33). In the nearly 40 years since 1781, the French Revolution had dismantled the monarchy and enabled the rise and fall of Napoleon Bonaparte's empire. In the wake of the Emperor's exile in 1814, King Louis XVIII, younger brother of Louis XVI, restored the Bourbon monarchy and took up residence once again in the Tuileries Palace in Paris, across from the Louvre. In the early years of the so-called Bourbon Restoration, the Crown struggled to articulate a 'new' visual identity, while contending with its own troubled history. However, this provided opportunities for artists of all generations to contribute to the iconography of the restored monarchy.[67]

In Vallayer-Coster's second work, the lobster is once more the protagonist, surrounded by a familiar supporting cast: piles of pears and grapes, a pair of bread loaves, a pyramid of peaches, a jar of cornichons, a ham mid-slice, a fistful of radishes, glass wine bottles and a woven basket are all set on a slightly rumpled white tablecloth. New additions to the composition include a large Chinese celadon porcelain vase mounted with gilt-bronze twisted rope handles (a hallmark of *ancien régime* luxury) and a fresh bouquet of white lilies (a naturalistic nod to the Bourbon heraldic symbol of the *fleur de lis*).

Vallayer-Coster was 73 years old when *Still Life with Lobster* was shown at the Salon of 1817. Art historians Sophie Mouquin and Christophe Huchet de Quénetain have recently suggested that this canvas was not painted that year, but rather much earlier in the artist's career. They argue that the painting was first exhibited at the Salon of 1775, under the title *Urn, Fruits and a Lobster*. According to the 1775 Salon catalogue, that painting measured six by four feet and belonged to a M. Montullé. Colin Bailey identified the owner of that canvas as Jean-Baptiste-François de Montullé (1721–87), a former secretary to the late

Queen Marie Leszczyńska who subsequently become an honorary member of the Académie. Montullé's extensive collection of French art included two floral paintings by Vallayer-Coster (see Chapter 6, figs 57–8), as well as several celadon porcelain vases.[68] The description and dimensions of Montullé's 1775 lobster roughly match those of the 1817 Salon picture.

If we assume that they are the same, more than 40 years had transpired since the first and the second Salon appearances of the painting, during which time the French monarchy acquired the painting. We know that Louis XVI purchased a Jan van Huysum still life from Madame Montullé in 1784, so it is possible that Vallayer-Coster's lobster was absorbed by the Crown from the Montullé collection prior to the Revolution.[69] In any case, by 1817, this lobster belonged to Louis XVI's surviving younger brother, the recently crowned Louis XVIII.[70] Was the 1817 Salon loan initiated by the restored King or the artist herself? Might this signal Vallayer-Coster's desire to align herself with the new King? Or was this simply a regurgitation of the tastes of the resurrected monarchy?

Although the Bourbon kings had returned to power, the food culture of the *ancien régime* was long gone and much had changed about the ways Parisians ate. A new generation of gastronomic literature had further democratized access to modern cuisine, and the proliferation of cafés and taverns had thrust the formerly private acts of eating and drinking into the public sphere.[71] These profound post-Revolution shifts in food culture and politics do not seem to register in *Still Life with Lobster*, which was likely painted just after the coronation of Louis XVI and Marie Antoinette. In any case, at the Salon of 1817 – just one year before her death – the artist's favorite ingredients were reassembled in public for one final, flavorful feast.

4

Guns and Game

Vallayer-Coster painted just a few representations of the hunt throughout her career.[1] At first, these works seem to adhere to a formula established by her academic forefathers, the animal painters François Desportes (1661–1743) and Jean-Baptiste Oudry (1686–1755): thick piles of dead game, guns and gunpowder in a wooded landscape.[2] Unlike her male predecessors, however, Vallayer-Coster was obliged to imagine the hunt's pleasures from a distance. She did so by closely examining its material attributes, emphasizing the textures of the dead animal bodies, as well as the weapons used to kill them.

Several art historians have explored the political and cultural dimensions of the hunt, as well as its visual representation in eighteenth-century French painting. Amy Freund, for example, has described Desportes's and Oudry's hunting portraits as celebrations of patriarchal power and violence, in which the viewer is meant to identify with the male hunter. Freund explains, 'We the viewers take the position of that man, surveying what we have killed, and what still remains to be killed.'[3] Desportes's reception piece, *Self-Portrait in Hunting Dress* (fig.34), illustrates this complicity of the hunter, artist and viewer. In that painting, Desportes presents himself as the protagonist of the hunt; we can imagine that the artist himself hunted and killed the very animals that he depicts lying in a heap beside him. He allows his

viewers (and potential patrons) to imagine themselves in a position of masculine dominance over nature.[4] The Académie installed Desportes's self-portrait in the assembly room of the Académie at the Louvre – where meetings were held and where Vallayer-Coster was admitted in 1770.

Desportes's self-portrait also offers evidence of the hybridity of the genre of the hunt. He was received as an animal painter, yet his subject also required fluency in painting the human body, landscape, animals dead and alive, as well as weapons and other inanimate objects. Desportes went on to paint dozens of hunting trophies, as well as portraits of Louis XIV's beloved hunting dogs. He also regularly attended the *chasse royale* (royal hunt), sketchbook in hand, thereby gaining access to the greatest hunter and patron of all, the King. Desportes thus allied himself with the 'hunter-patron' and produced images that recalled his own trials and successes in the woods.[5] This subject matter must have appealed to members of the court who participated in the *chasse royal*, but also to the hunters of the humbler *petite chasse*: the individual pursuit of small game that was widely and illicitly practiced by non-royals.

What, then, do we make of Vallayer-Coster's paintings of the hunt? As the daughter of a goldsmith, who lived nearly her entire life in Paris, Vallayer-Coster probably never participated in this

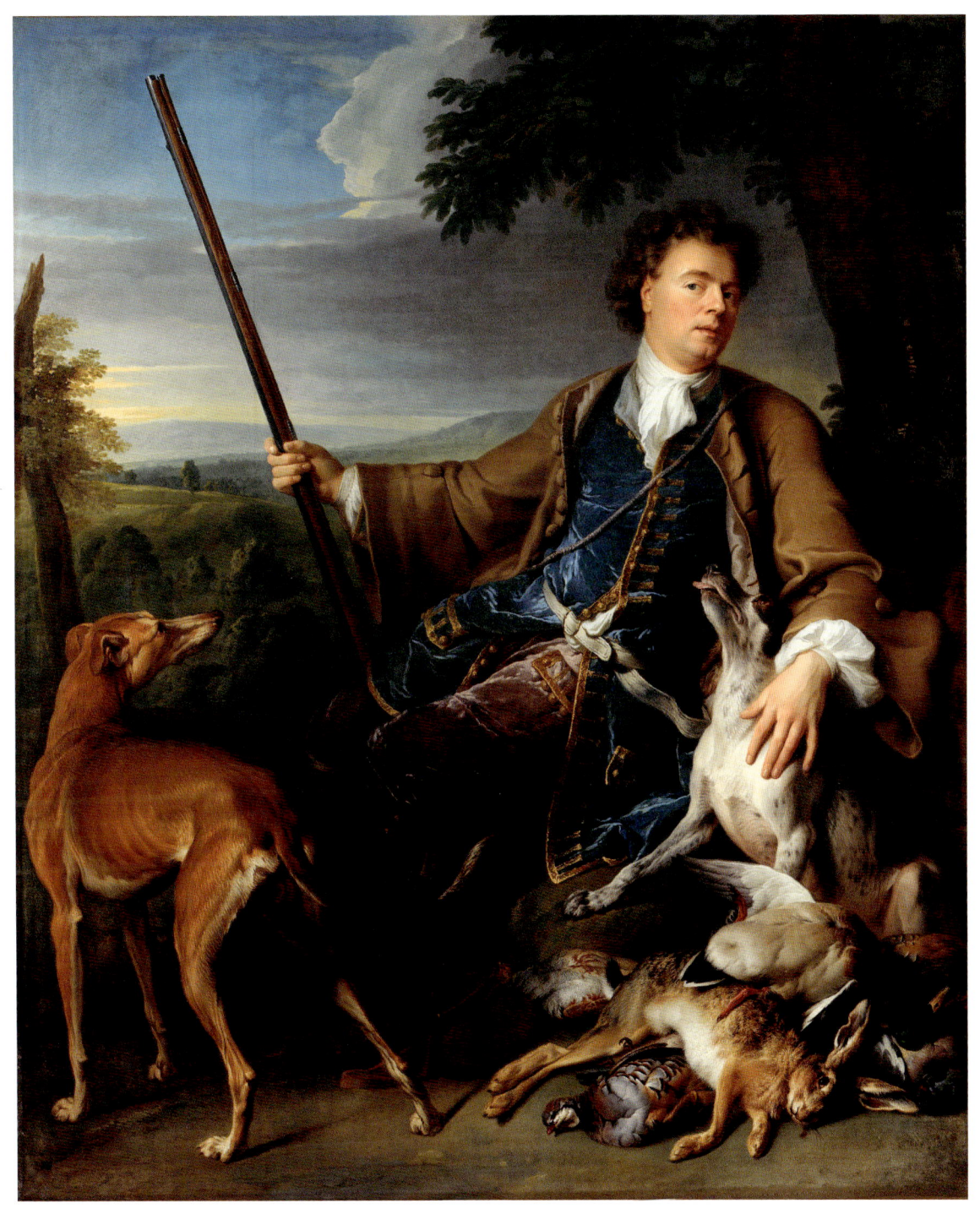

34 François Desportes, *Self-Portrait in Hunting Dress*, *c.*1699, oil on canvas, 197 × 163 cm (77½ × 64 ⅛ in), Musée du Louvre, Paris

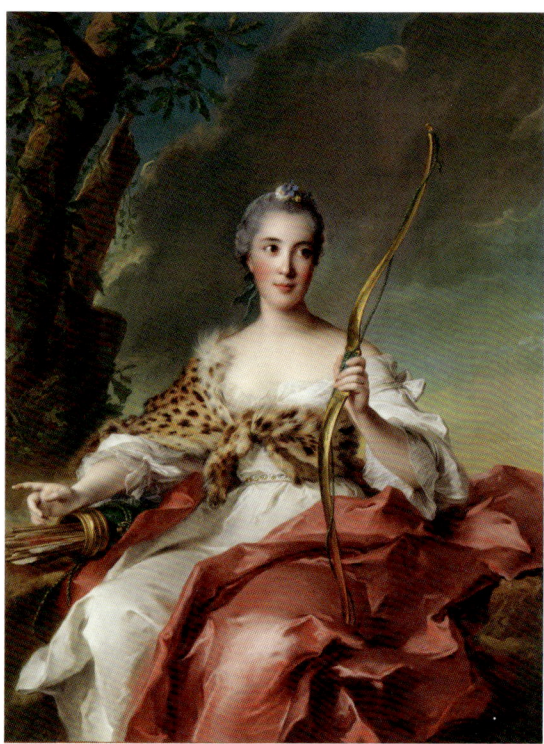

35 Jean-Marc Nattier, *Madame Bergeret de Frouville as Diana*, c.1756, oil on canvas, 136.5 × 105.1 cm (53 ¾ × 41 ⅜ in), The Metropolitan Museum of Art, New York

primarily masculine, elite exercise. What did it mean for a woman to paint a gun in the eighteenth century – much less to wield one? If hunting was primarily a sport for men, what vicarious pleasure did such paintings offer women? Let us begin by exploring contemporary beliefs about women, guns and game, and then use these ideas to analyze Vallayer-Coster's contradictory paintings of them.

WOMEN ON THE HUNT

Even if Vallayer-Coster never attended or participated in a hunt, there is evidence that some

royal women did. The hunt was, after all, a primarily royal pursuit – and a fairly regular one at that. Louis XV hunted three times per week on average. During the reign of his grandson, Louis XVI, the ritual took place almost daily. The *chasse royale* was more than just a monarchical activity; it was also an expression of absolutist power over people, animals and land. French law defined hunting as the exclusive privilege of the nobility, but the royal hunt was the largest and most elaborate performance of all.[6] While it was common for female members of the court to follow the course of the hunt on horseback or in a carriage, only a few seem to have actively participated in it. Two women close to Louis XV, for example, were known to regularly attend the *chasse royale*: his mistress, Jeanne-Antoinette de Pompadour (1721–64) and his grandson's bride, the future Queen Marie Antoinette (1755–93).[7]

Pompadour's meteoric rise from a tax farmer's wife to the King's favorite may be partially attributed to Louis XV's enthusiasm for the hunt. During one hunting expedition, Louis XV took notice of Pompadour riding in a carriage through the forest – a spectacle designed to draw the attention of the King. Later, at a masked ball at Versailles, the King (wearing the costume of a tree) and Pompadour (dressed as a wood nymph) first exchanged words.[8] A portrait of Madame de Pompadour in the guise of Diana, the Greek goddess of the hunt, by Jean-Marc Nattier (1685–1766) was subsequently installed at the Château de Fontainebleau, one of Louis XV's favorite hunting lodges.[9]

Nattier employed the same Diana theme for nearly a dozen *portraits déguisés* (allegorical portraits) of other women (fig.35).[10] His subjects all appear with cheeks rouged and hair tightly curled, wearing sheer white chemises and leopard furs, bearing gold quivers and bows. Their flimsy garb, delicate, symbolic weapons and the absence of dead game seem to preclude these Dianas from participating in anything resembling the contemporary sport; it is difficult to imagine them engaged in the bloody and sweaty enterprise of chasing and shooting an animal. Nattier's Diana *portraits déguisés* are mythological fantasies, rather than mortal hunting portraits.

The fantastical, feminine nature of Nattier's Diana portraits is evident when they are contrasted with Desportes's more rugged, masculine self-portrait. Desportes espouses a cool masculine swagger, with one arm embracing his loyal dog and the other gripping the long barrel of his modern rifle, which projects upward and outward from his thigh. The artist-hunter grips the gun with the same confidence and ease with which he wields his brush; as Freund wrote, 'The gun . . . functions as an extension of his person. Because of its identification with the man who owns it, the gun is naturalized as an integral part of the elite male body.'[11] Given this phallic understanding of the weapon, it is perhaps unsurprising that women are almost never depicted wielding a gun – or that female artists, like Vallayer-Coster, would be considered unlikely to paint them.

There do exist a handful of paintings of royal women dressed in contemporary hunting garb. Even in these exceptional images, the tools of the hunt are almost entirely absent. Marie Antoinette's fondness for attending the hunt has been well documented, and while she was occasionally depicted on horseback, she was never visually represented holding a weapon or dead game. Still, there is evidence that the Queen bought (and perhaps used) guns herself. Marie Antoinette owned at least one luxurious, gilded flintlock gun crafted by Pierre de Saintes, the official gunmaker to the King.[12] In 1784, the Queen and her brother-in-law, the comte d'Artois (1757–1836), co-purchased the duc d'Orléans's hunting equipment, which included several guns.[13] The Queen also gifted a set of hunting rifles, along with a velvet-lined case filled with tools to clean and maintain the weapons, to her mother, Empress Maria Theresa of Austria.[14]

Royal French women had the power to buy expensive, luxurious guns, even if contemporary

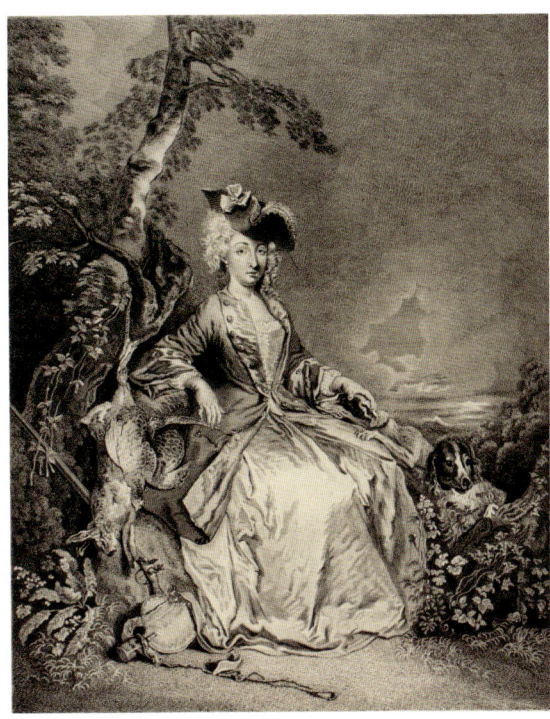

36 Benoît Audran II after Jean-Antoine Watteau, *Return from the Hunt*, 1727, etching and engraving, 44.4 × 33.3 cm (17 ½ × 13 ⅛ in), Philadelphia Museum of Art, PA

paintings depict them as impotent spectators of the hunt. Did non-royal women enjoy the same privilege? The cost of a standard firearm in the eighteenth century was relatively low: a basic firearm cost as little as 7 *livres*.[15] Yet, the vast majority of gun owners and users were probably men. Louis-Sébastien Mercier notes one important caveat in *Le tableau de Paris* (1781): as was true in many family workshops in the *ancien régime*, the wives of gunmakers often interacted with customers. This role required them to become familiar with the making and function of their products, if not to operate them recreationally.[16]

According to one author, the primary deterrent to female gun ownership and operation was the feminine sensitivity to the smell of gunpowder and the gun's explosive sound ricochet – that is, the sensory experience of shooting a gun. In *Mémoires sur l'ancienne chevalerie* (*Memoirs of Ancient Chivalry*, 1781), Jean-Baptiste de La Curne de Sainte-Palaye wrote of women: 'There are only a very small number to be found among them who dare to familiarize themselves with the noise of firearms and the idea of the dangers to which their usage sometimes exposes [the user].'[17] This writer assumes that a woman's gentle nature and aversion to violence made her ill-suited to operate a firearm. After all, boys became men through hunting and warfare. In Jean-Jacques Rousseau's *Emile* (1762), the narrator-tutor argues that hunting purged a young man of 'the dangerous inclinations born of softness' – the feminine influences of childhood. He continues, 'The hunt hardens the heart as well as the body. It accustoms one to blood, to cruelty.'[18] Previously, in *Le Discours sur l'origine et les fondements de l'inégalité* (*Discourse on Inequality*, 1754), Rousseau identified early man's proclivity for hunting, in contrast with his female counterpart's passive, sedentary nature, as the anthropological origin of the differences between the sexes.[19] That sentiment persisted into the Revolutionary era, when one politician declared: '[Nature] has said to man: "Be a man: hunting, farming, political concerns, toils of every kind, that is your appanage."'[20]

If hunting was considered central to the formation or 'hardening' of the male ego, and the gun was a phallic symbol of this emotional and physical transformation, then the armed huntress was truly exceptional, even paradoxical. Consider the utter strangeness of a portrait by Jean-Antoine Watteau (1684–1721), known through an engraving by Benoît Audran II (1698–1772; fig.36).[21] The engraving depicts a woman seated in a landscape, accompanied by two hunting dogs. With one hand, she pats her furry companion; with the other, she fingers the feathered wing of a dead partridge. The still-life arrangement at

her feet, a hunting purse and a single-barreled rifle, offers evidence of her role in the kill and aligns her with the hunter portraits of Desportes and Oudry. The woman's full skirt and corseted waist are the only material markers of her femininity. Different theories persist as to the name of this exceptional huntress,[22] yet the historical identity of the portrait subject becomes less significant given the form in which the huntress's image circulated: as a monochromatic print, bearing the vague title of *Retour de chasse* (*Return from the Hunt*), first published in the *Mercure de France* in 1727.[23] Engraved, colorless and anonymous, the woman's transgressive potential is mitigated. Women were, at best, peripheral to the gun culture of eighteenth-century France.

Like Watteau's portrait of a huntress, Vallayer-Coster's paintings engage less with the pomp of the *chasse royal* than the humble material culture of the *petite chasse*. In *Emile*, Rousseau's narrator recalls his father's love of hunting alone, and specifically names the objects associated with the *petite chasse* that also populate Vallayer-Coster's few paintings of the hunt. He considered the rifle, kit and game bag essential to the formation of the hunter and his recreation in the woods.[24]

While Vallayer-Coster likely never knew the pleasure of pursuing and shooting an animal as Rousseau described it, she painted these accessories several times. How, then, can we describe the artist's relationship to these objects? We find one possible approach in the writing of the cross-dressing British actress, Charlotte Charke (1713–60). In her memoir, Charke described her beloved childhood gun and the adolescent trauma of being disarmed by her mother, who was appalled by her daughter's 'ungentlewoman[ly]' delight in the weapon. In remembering and writing about her gun, however, Charke rediscovers the happiness it once provided her, and is thus able to transcend gendered limitations.[25]

We can use Charke's writing about her gun as a way of understanding Vallayer-Coster's paintings of them. For Vallayer-Coster, a *Parisienne* painter, the hunt remained a distant fantasy: the glory and satisfaction of being alone in the woods, wielding a gun and conquering prey were foreign to her. In painting its material culture, however, Vallayer-Coster gained imaginative access to the hunt. Through her art, she exceeded the culturally determined boundaries of her own body – and simultaneously catered to the violent appetites of her patrons.

GUNS

The guns in Vallayer-Coster's paintings vary slightly, but they are all examples of single- and double-barreled flintlock rifles. The flintlock technology was invented in the early seventeenth century and had become ubiquitous in Europe by the late eighteenth century. Though less volatile than older mechanisms, the flintlock was still complicated and unwieldy to operate. In order to load the gun, the hunter had to place gunpowder into the barrel and secure it with a lubricated wad of paper or fabric, followed by ammunition (small metal bullets) and yet another wad. The hunter loaded each layer of material into the barrel with the aid of a thin ramrod, then dispensed a dash of gunpowder into a small pan directly underneath the flintlock mechanism.[26]

To fire the loaded gun, the hunter gripped the gun with both hands, placed the butt against his shoulder, pressed his cheek against the stock, aimed and pulled the trigger. In response, the hammer or cock gripping a piece of flint would strike a piece of steel, known as a frizzen. The resulting spark ignited the powder in the pan below and propelled the ammunition out of the open-ended barrel of the gun. As the ammunition discharged, the gun would recoil, suddenly and hard, into the shoulder of the user. The igniting powder simultaneously produced a bright flash of light, a small burst of sulfurous smoke and a sharp boom. In order to fire another shot, the hunter had to repeat this entire process.[27]

Flintlocks all functioned in much the same way, but could be differentiated by the length, texture and number of barrels. Pistols have short barrels, ideal for close-range shots. Rifles and muskets have much longer barrels, typically between four and five feet, and were designed to hit long-distance targets. Rifle barrels have grooved interiors, while musket barrels are smooth. The grooves improved the rifle's accuracy, but required frequent cleaning in order to function properly. For these reasons, more accurate grooved rifles were preferred on the hunt and quicker, more efficient smooth-bore muskets were used on the battlefield (see figs 13 and 18). Although we cannot see the entire length or the interior of Vallayer-Coster's barrels, a contemporary viewer would likely have identified them as rifles based on their context. Finally, Vallayer-Coster's paintings depict both single- and double-barreled rifles. Multi-barreled guns enabled users to fire two shots without stopping to reload, but were more expensive and riskier to load and fire.[28]

Vallayer-Coster's representations of guns may be precise enough for us to identify their type, but her treatment of them is as equivocal as her representations of game. In the aforementioned self-portrait by Desportes (see fig.34), the entire length of the *fusil de chasse* is pictured: the barrel projects into the air, ready to shoot. In contrast, Vallayer-Coster's guns lie prone, buried underneath a thick pile of dead game. She provides only a fragmented view by obscuring the triggers and barrels, rendering the weapons impotent. The guns have been arranged in visually frustrating orientations, but the unusual angles from which she paints them suggests that she observed a gun directly, rather than copying a representation of one. Contemporary prints described the gun's profile and dissected its individual parts, but did not provide the skewed perspectives represented in Vallayer-Coster's paintings (fig.37).

Vallayer-Coster offers us glimpses of a few different types of guns, accompanied by a leather

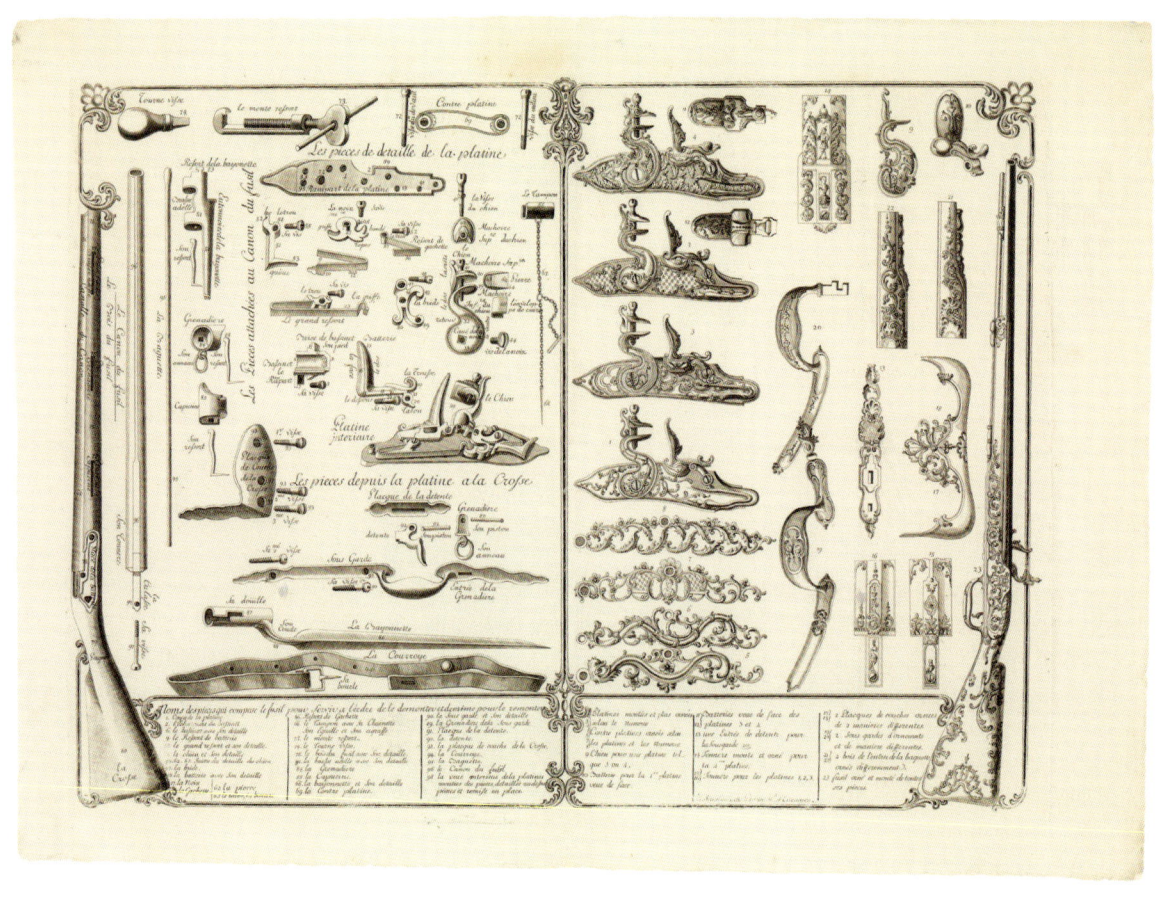

37　Perrier, *Engraving of Firearm Parts*, *c*.1750, engraving, 47.5 × 64 cm (18 ¾ × 25 ¼ in), The Metropolitan Museum of Art, New York

hunting purse designed to carry ammunition and a *pulvérin* (powder horn) made of porcelain with a gilded spout. The gun that appears in *The Attributes of Hunting and Gardening* (fig.38) is a simple weapon; faced with the butt of the gun, we can see its wooden exoskeleton but little else. More elaborate models appear in *Trophies of the Hunt* (fig.39) and *Still Life with Game* (fig.40). In the former, the edge of the silver-plated butt of a single-barreled flintlock, further adorned with a red velvet cheek pad, is visible. The bodies of the dead game obscure most of the gun's mechanisms, though we can discern the serpentine shape of the metal flintlock. In the latter painting, we view a double-barreled gun from above. We cannot see the barrels themselves, but we can see the silver-plated cleavage between the two barrels, and flintlocks on both sides of the gun. The legibility of these mechanisms is compromised by the peculiar angle of the weapon.

The gun in *Still Life with Game* is further adorned with a delicate marquetry design between the lock and the dark turquoise velvet cheek pad. Only a handful of flintlocks with velvet cheek pads survive today, but it was undoubtedly a more expensive modification. Velvet was a densely tufted textile typically associated with luxurious objects that came in close contact with the body, such as a coat or a chair. These guns with velvet cheek pads were likely designed for elite consumers who preferred to press their cheeks against a soft, rich fabric, rather than hard wood or cold metal.

The velvet cheek pad served Vallayer-Coster's artistic purposes, as well – that is, her interest in representing a range of organic and handmade textures: shiny metal, smooth wood, luxe velvet, worn leather, frayed ribbon, ruffled feathers and fur matted with sweat and blood. The artist's interest in these textural elements comes at the expense of the gun itself. By making the gun's shape strange and nearly unrecognizable, and draping it with velvet and fur, the artist compromises its legibility and potency – perhaps betraying her own inexperience with guns,

but also subtly undermining its lethal function and its proud symbolism of masculine violence and power.

GAME

In addition to guns, Vallayer-Coster's hunting pictures include representations of dead game. The artist probably first encountered dead animals in the kitchen, and she painted them in a handful of early works (see figs 28 and 41).[29] Dead animals were often strung upside down in order to drain excess fluids, facilitating the preservation and tenderization of their meat. The furry hare and feathered partridge (perhaps domesticated livestock, reared by a farmer and sold at a Parisian food market)[30] are not ready to cook or eat, but in these paintings they are situated in the context of the edible.

In several later works, however, the artist positioned wild animal bodies not in the kitchen, but closer to their source in nature: vivid blue skies and untamed pastoral landscapes form the backdrop of her compositions (see figs 38–40 and 43). Hunting was considered to be one of the primary means of experiencing the rural landscape; as Rousseau's narrator in *Emile* mused, 'Is one really in the country if one does not hunt?'[31] Here, the animal bodies have not yet entered the cycle of distribution, preparation and consumption that characterize Vallayer-Coster's food still lifes, and are instead embedded in the recreational sphere of the hunt. The potential use value of the animal – the consumption of its meat or application of its fur – was secondary to the glory that its death represented: the hunter's personal triumph over nature.[32]

The hunter's pursuit of game finds a parallel in the painter's visual pursuit of her subjects. Jean Siméon Chardin, for one, approached paintings of small game with a rigorously formal approach, making himself 'forget' the hare – his own personal memories and experiences – in order to produce a truthful representation of it (fig.42).[33] Like Chardin,

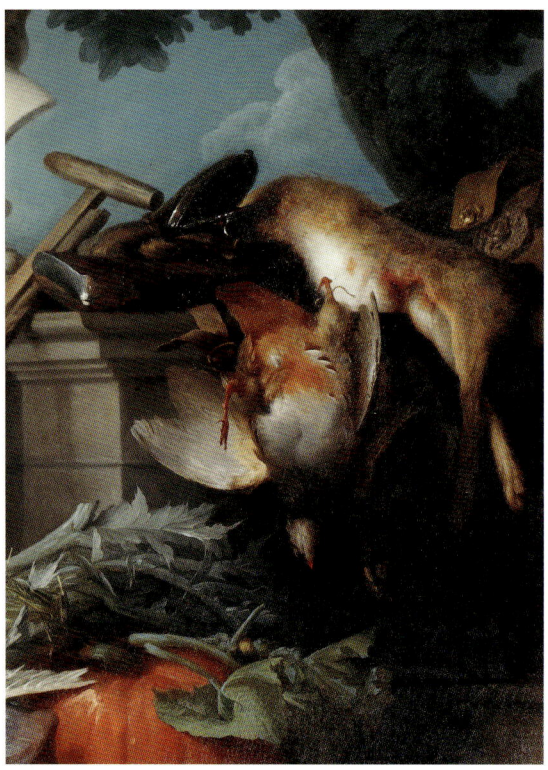

38 Anne Vallayer-Coster, detail of *The Attributes of Hunting and Gardening*, 1774, oil on canvas, 152 × 137 cm (60 × 54 in), Basildon Park, Berkshire

Vallayer-Coster carefully studied the material qualities of the dead animals, and her paintings similar compel us to examine their textures and forms. Her painterly facture invites us to dwell on the tufts of fur along the hares' bellies, as well as the densely plumed breasts of pheasants. However, like a male hunter, Chardin had the privilege of adopting a totally 'disinterested' formal perspective of hunting game and accessories. Vallayer-Coster's relationship to this material was inevitably more complicated because of her limited access to the sport that it represented.

One way that Vallayer-Coster's work conveys this complexity is by emphasizing the sensuality of intertwined animal bodies, belying their deadness.[34] Perhaps the most voluptuous example is the interspecies orgy in *Still Life with Game* (fig.40). The banker and contemporary art collector Jean Girardot de Marigny owned this canvas, along with its pendant, *Still Life with Lobster* (see fig.32); he later lent the painting of game to the Salon of 1783.[35] In *Still Life with Game*, the tawny hare, gray rabbit and pheasants are so entangled in a post-mortem embrace that they are nearly indistinguishable from one another. The freshly killed game thus simultaneously attract and repel, because they seem neither fully dead nor alive. So close to the moment of death, their bodies may still be soft and warm, though we know stiffness and decay are imminent. Moreover, their flesh and fur have yet to be harvested, so while they are no longer wild prey, they are not consumable commodities.

Vallayer-Coster's representations of dead game are not entirely sympathetic to the animals themselves. In addition to her frank portrayal of their wounds, consider the fact that the artist frequently draped their dead bodies over the very tools of their execution – weapons rendered with the same textural detail. Neither was the artist totally squeamish in describing her dead game's wounds, although she refrained from excessive gore. In *The Attributes of Hunting and Gardening* (see fig.38) and *Trophies of the Hunt* (see fig.39), two pieces of game are draped off a ledge: pheasants hanging by the tail feathers, with their spindly limbs unnaturally splayed, and hares, limp and belly-up, with subtle wounds in their lower abdomens. In *The Attributes of Hunting and Gardening*, Vallayer-Coster employed a deep crimson pigment at the center of the cut, alluding to the hare's visceral interior, and a lighter rust color to indicate the dried blood stains on the white belly fur. In *Trophies of the Hunt*, she added an additional liquid detail: several droplets of bright red paint trickling from between the hare's legs.

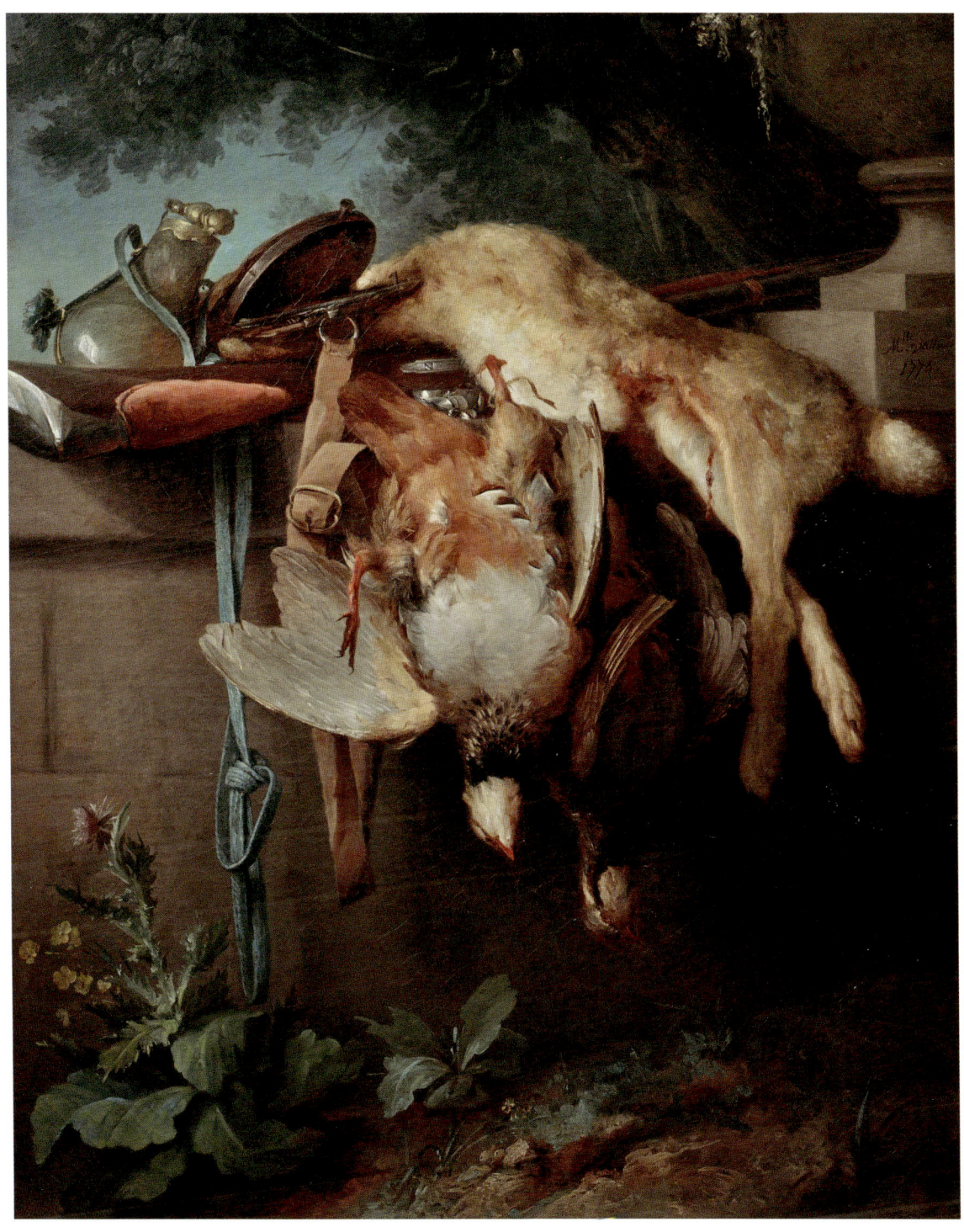

39 Anne Vallayer-Coster, *Trophies of the Hunt*, 1774, oil on canvas, 91 × 73 cm (35 ⅞ × 28 ¾ in), Private collection

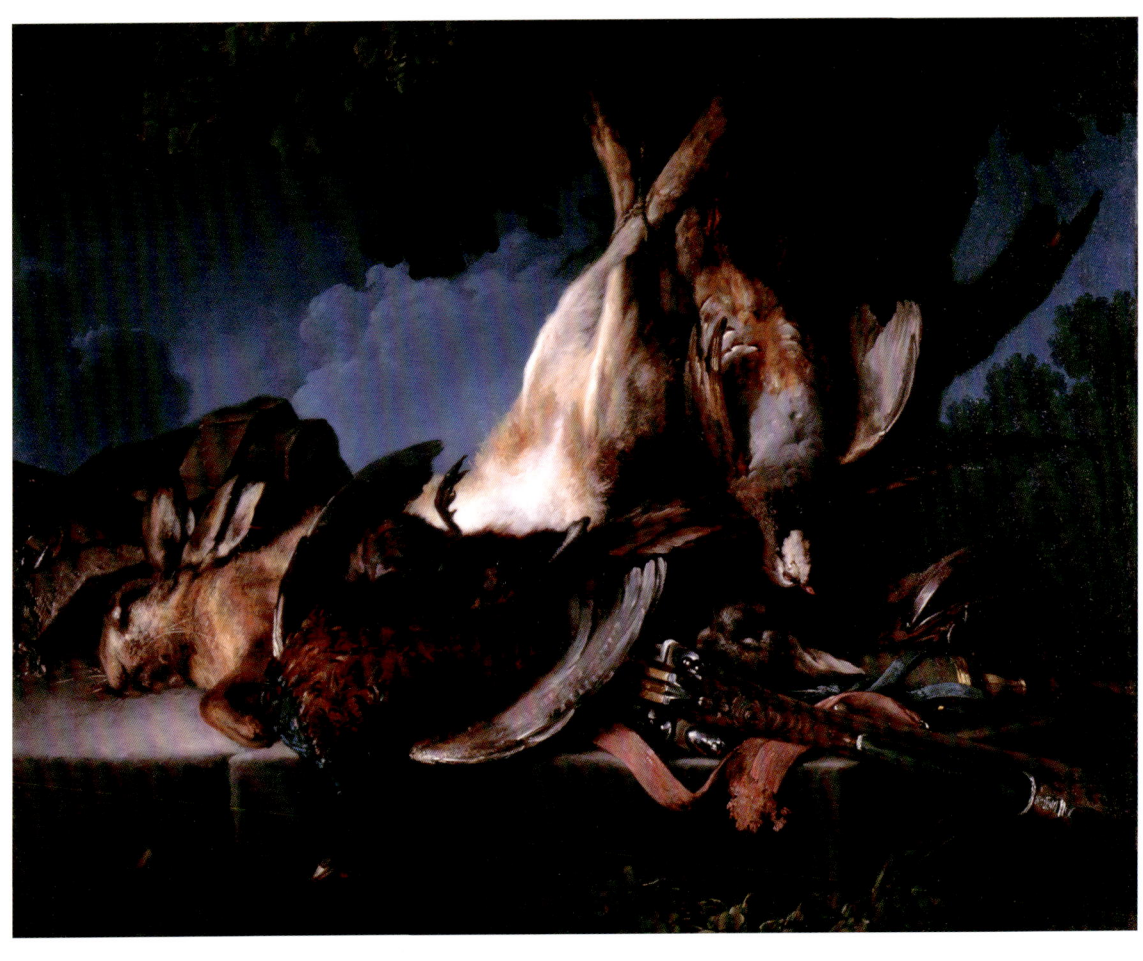

40 Anne Vallayer-Coster, *Still Life with Game*, 1781, oil on canvas, 70.5 × 89.5 cm (27¾ × 35¼ in), Toledo Museum of Art, OH

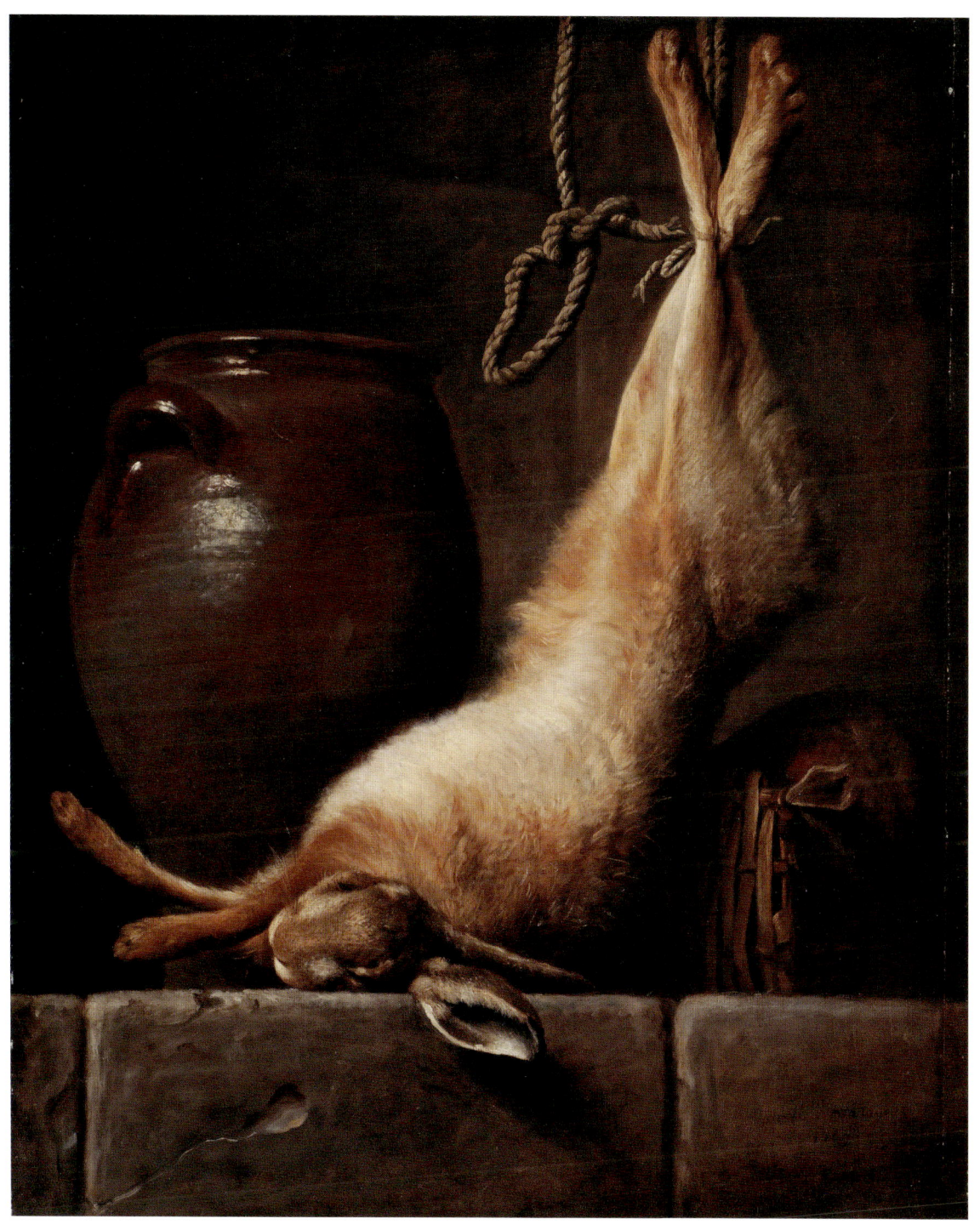

41 Anne Vallayer-Coster, *Still Life with Dead Hare*, 1769, oil on canvas, 74.5 × 60.5 cm (29 ⅜ × 23 ⅞ in), The Horvitz Collection, Wilmington

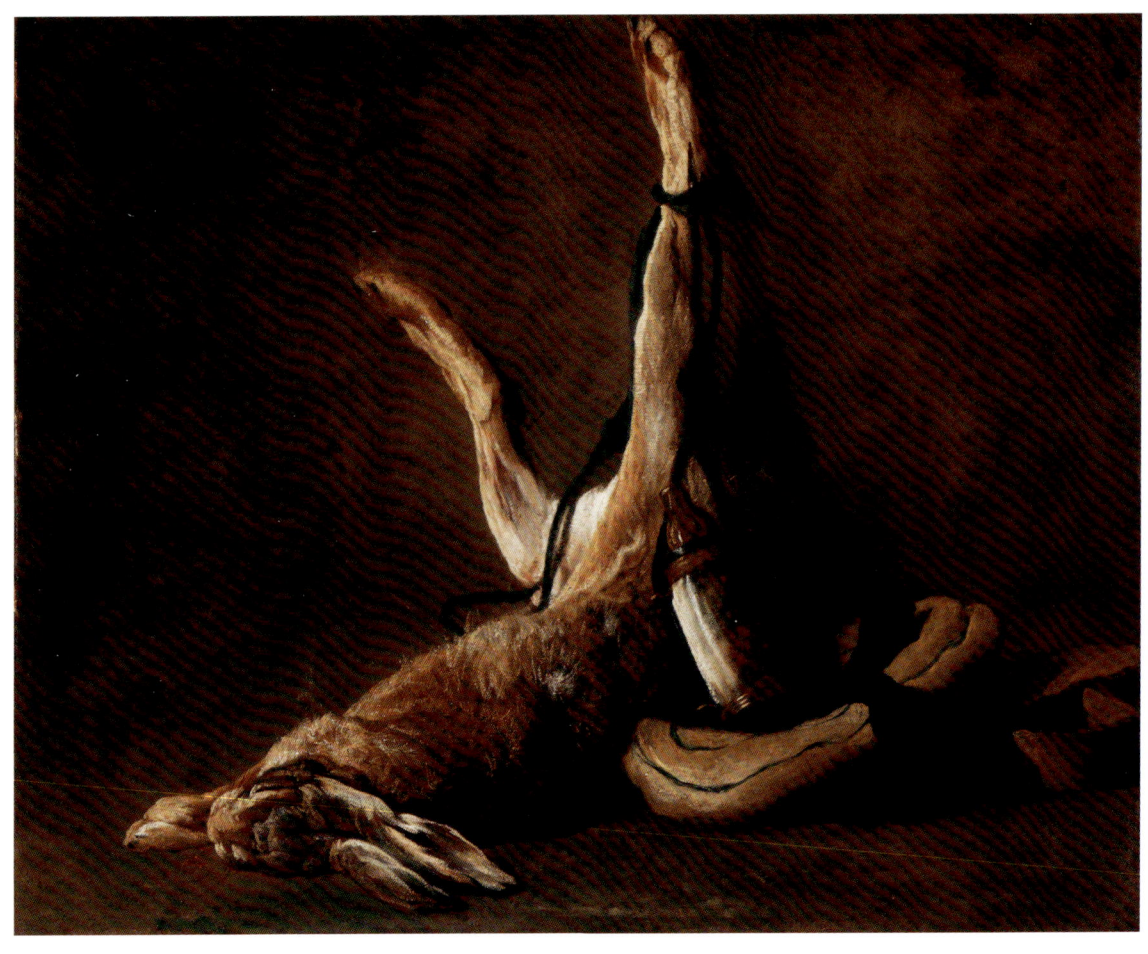

42 Jean Siméon Chardin, *Still Life with a Hare*, c.1730, oil on canvas, 65.1 × 81.3 cm (25 ⅝ × 32 in), Philadelphia Museum of Art, PA

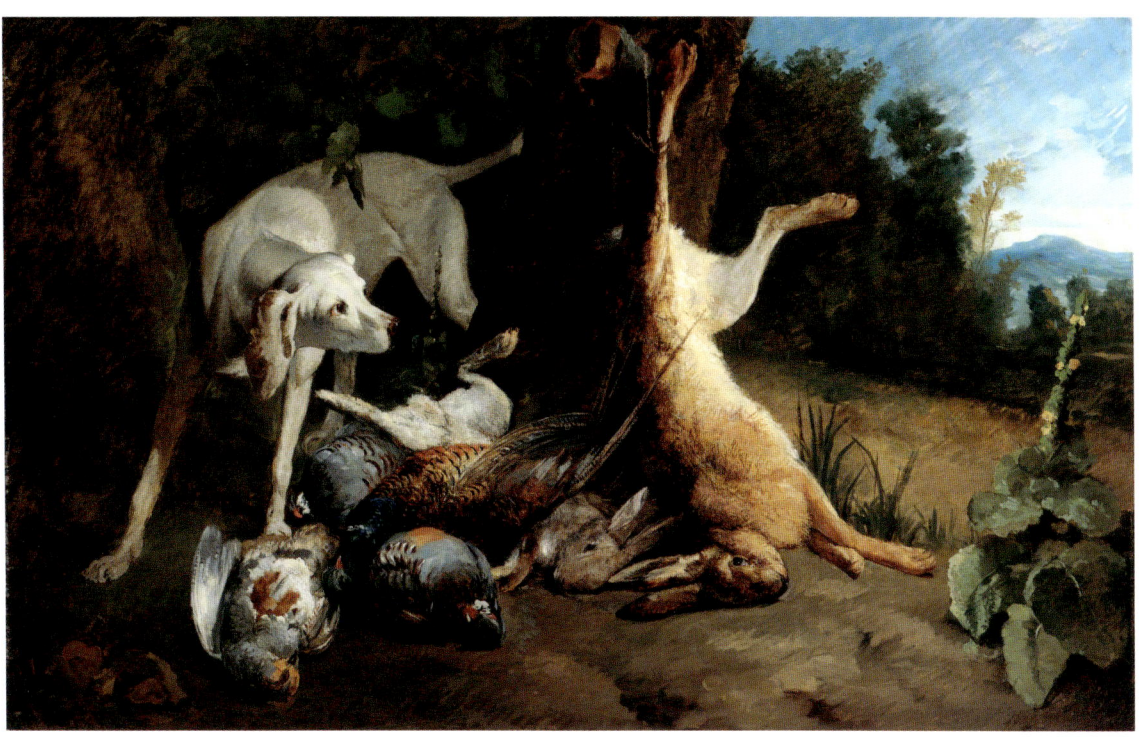

43 Anne Vallayer-Coster, *A Hound with Dead Game in a Landscape*, 1785, oil on canvas, 87 × 141 cm (34 ¼ × 55 ½ in),
Private collection

These incisions are most likely not the result of the fatal gunshot, but rather refer to the traditional method of field dressing: slicing the dead animal from ribcage to groin and removing the internal organs by hand. Field dressing was performed as soon as possible after the kill in order to preserve the quality of the meat and to lighten the triumphant hunter's load.[36] (Chardin similarly painted a disemboweled, castrated hare in a 1728–30 painting.[37]) Just as the hunter was required to manually probe the interior of his dead game soon after its execution, so too did the artist investigate and reimagine her subjects' blood in paint – in pursuit of her own painterly 'glory'.

Vallayer-Coster only painted the subject of the hunt three more times: one painting dated to 1785, which sold on the Parisian art market in 2014 (fig.43),[38] and two other examples that were exhibited at the Salons of 1785 and 1787, now lost.[39] These three later paintings all represent a hunting dog, who acts as a mammalian surrogate for his human master, guarding the feathered and furry profits of the hunt.[40] Vallayer-Coster's juxtaposition of live and dead animals is typical of the work of both Desportes and Oudry. Like them, her work was designed to celebrate man's violent command over nature – and to flatter her male clients, whose own political and cultural authority was predicated upon this idea.

Still, Vallayer-Coster's exploration of the hunting fantasy is rife with contradictions. Her paintings of guns and dead game certainly celebrate the hunt, but she also must have executed them with some degree of alienation. Vallayer-Coster's hunting scenes emphasize sensual textures of the dead game and effectively neuter the gun, betraying a sense of ambivalence about the material she paints. Perhaps because she was personally detached from the experience, her paintings perform the fantasies and frustrations of the hunt from a distance. In this sense, Vallayer-Coster's work differs significantly from that of nineteenth-century French animal painter Rosa Bonheur (1822–99), who donned a man's trousers in order to pursue her subject matter at farms, horse fairs and slaughterhouses – physically transgressing the boundaries that Vallayer-Coster could only imaginatively transcend.[41]

5

Shells

At the Salon of 1771, her first as an *académicienne*, Vallayer-Coster exhibited two large paintings: *Still Life with Seashells and Coral* (fig.44) and its now lost pendant, *Still Life with a Porcelain Vase, Minerals and Crystals.* These paintings, characterized by bold compositions and brilliant color, were a critical success and clearly distinguished Vallayer-Coster from her predecessor Jean Siméon Chardin, who never took natural history as a subject.[1] Vallayer-Coster would go on to paint shells a few more times throughout her career, including *Still Life with Porcelain Vase, Marine Plants, Shells and Various Mineralogical Specimens* of 1776;[2] *Vase of Flowers with Shell* of 1780 (fig.45);[3] and *Still Life with Minerals* of 1789.[4]

In the eighteenth century, shells and minerals conveyed a wide range of cultural meanings. During this period, elite French collectors began to acquire panoplies of shells and to display their collections in curiosity cabinets. There, they came to be viewed as objects of material and aesthetic value, as well as scientific inquiry. Long prized for their natural beauty and exotic origins, shells were now also subject to the Enlightenment impulse to label and classify things. French *curieux* (collectors of curiosities) came to rely on auction catalogues, illustrated guidebooks and taxonomic texts to identify the shells in their collections.

Here, Vallayer-Coster's shell paintings are placed in dialogue with contemporary ideas about shells. Her work exemplifies the twin systems of meaning that structured both curiosity cabinets and conchological texts: the aesthetic and the scientific; the visual and the haptic; the masculine and the feminine. Though seemingly contradictory, these dual concepts were intricately connected in practice – in Vallayer-Coster's painting practice and in the collecting practices of her patrons.

VALLAYER-COSTER AND THE PRINCE DE CONTI

The catalogue of the Salon of 1771 listed Vallayer-Coster's *Still Life with Seashells and Coral* with its now lost pendant under the joint title, *Deux tableaux représentans divers morceaux d'histoire naturelle* (*Two Paintings Representing Diverse Pieces of Natural History*).[5] The surviving work, measuring 4¼ by 3 feet, depicts 24 distinct plant and animal species imported to France from all over the globe. The painting is dominated by the plumes of a stony white Venus sea fan, as well as red and purple coral extracted from the Caribbean Sea. To the right, Vallayer-Coster positioned a large bivalve mollusk shell with a blood-orange belly, likely from the Mediterranean Sea, buttressed by a pleated, buttercup-yellow sponge.

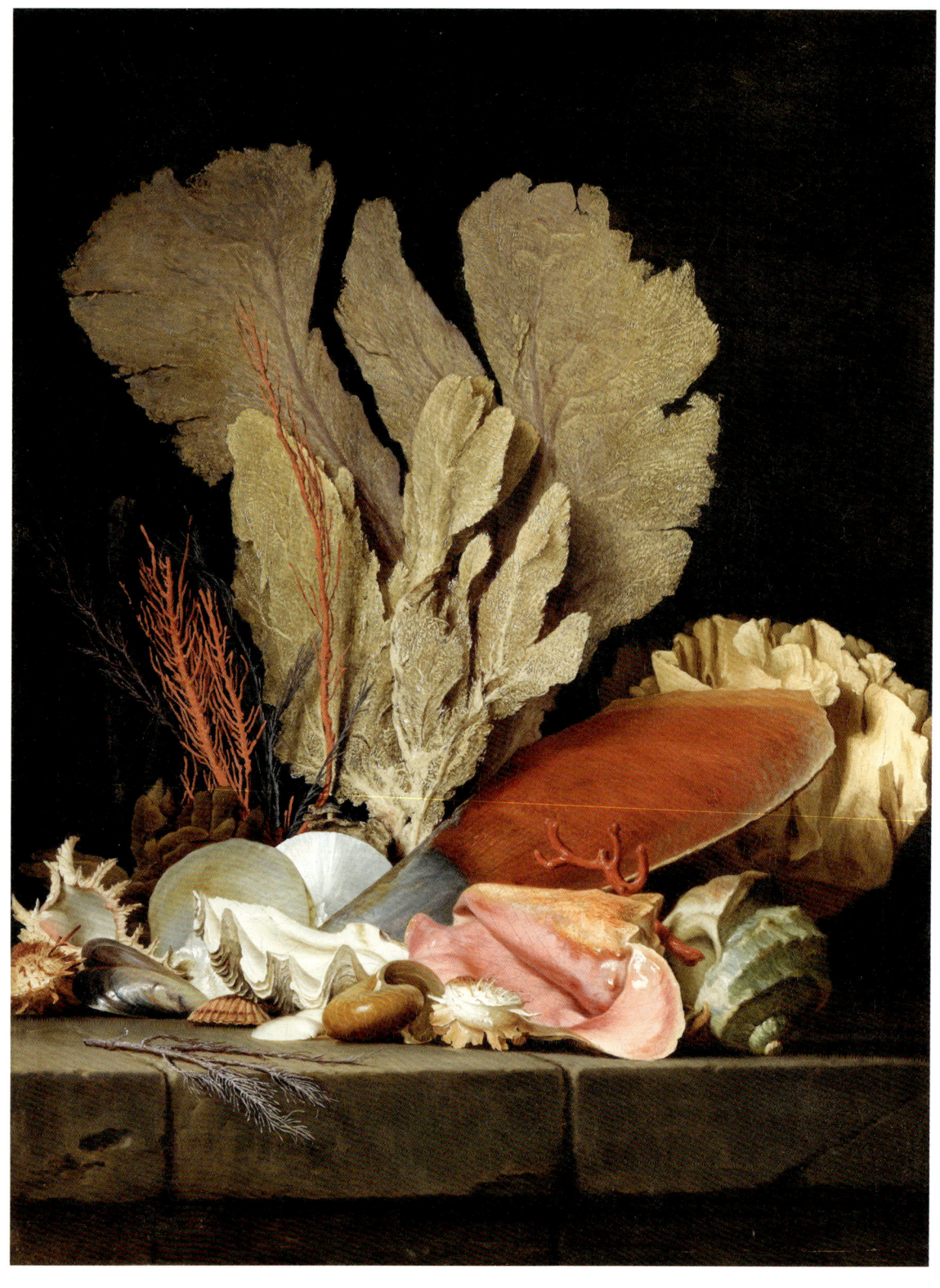

44 Anne Vallayer-Coster, *Still Life with Seashells and Coral*, 1769, oil on canvas, 130 × 97 cm (51 ⅛ × 38 ¼ in), Musée du Louvre, Paris

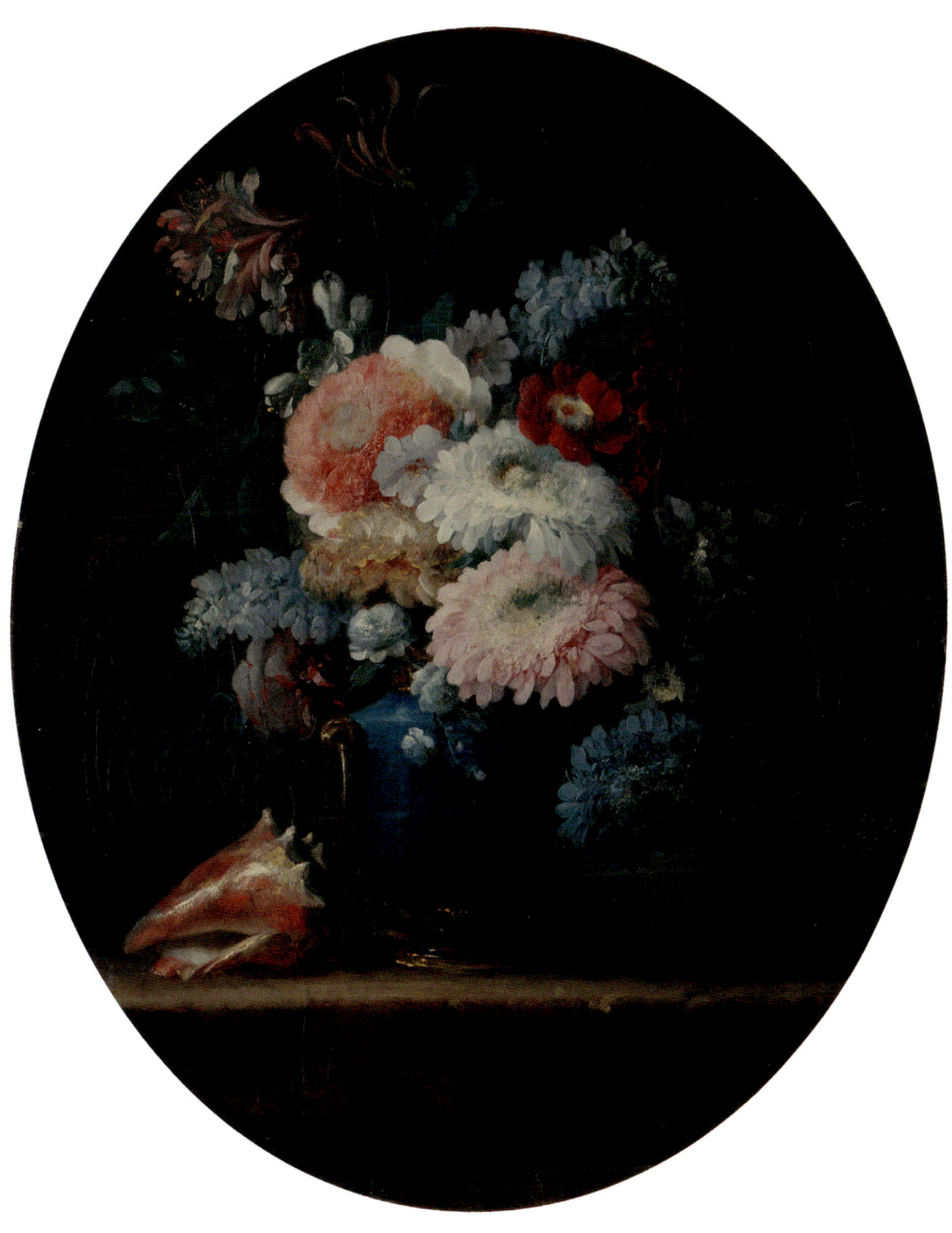

45 Anne Vallayer-Coster, *Vase of Flowers with Shell*, 1780, oil on canvas, 50.2 × 38.1 cm (19 ¾ × 15 in), The Metropolitan
Museum of Art, New York

The artist arranged smaller specimens in the foreground: a mohawked, peach-colored sea snail shell, a fluted white clam and a reptilian green turban shell from the Indo-Pacific Oceans, and a fleshy-pink queen conch shell from the Atlantic.[6]

This triumphant composition is a complex formal exercise, juxtaposing colors (lacquered reds, chalky whites, delicate pinks, iridescent purples and blues, vivid greens), shapes (from tall marine plants to small, tightly wound shells) and textures (spiky, mossy, smooth, slick). At the Salon, these striking formal qualities of Vallayer-Coster's pendants earned significant praise. A *Mercure de France* critic wrote, 'The happy arrangement of these objects, their transparent color, the solidity and the precision of the touch, the artistically placed strokes of light, the well-felt reflections, all contribute to magical canvases that deceive even the most practiced and delicate eye.'[7] Denis Diderot declared the natural history pendants to be masterpieces of the genre, specifically praising the arrangement of what he called the 'polished shell bodies'.[8]

Despite their critical success, Vallayer-Coster's natural history pendants failed to attract an immediate buyer. In December 1775, they appeared in the sale catalogue of Madame du Barry, the last titled mistress of Louis XV of France.[9] Madame du Barry had been exiled to the Abbey du Pont-aux-Dames after the King's death in 1774. When she left the convent in May 1775, she planned to sell her collection in order to reconcile her debts. Vallayer-Coster likely consigned her paintings to the sale through the prominent art dealer Pierre Rémy, who published the sale catalogue. This was a clever act of self-promotion, as the sale promised to be a high-profile event, given du Barry's notoriety.[10] For reasons unknown, the 1775 sale of du Barry's collection never came to fruition, but it may have been through Rémy that Vallayer-Coster's paintings were acquired by Louis-François de Bourbon, the sixth prince de Conti. This cousin of Louis XV purchased the two works for 960 *livres*, just a month after du Barry's cancelled sale.[11]

A habitual and omnivorous collector of beautiful things, both natural and artificial, the prince de Conti was Vallayer-Coster's ideal patron.[12] The prince de Conti's display of Vallayer-Coster's paintings in his Palais du Temple in Paris endowed her paintings with further meaning. There, in the final 20 years of his life, the prince built an enormous collection of natural curiosities, as well as French, Italian and Northern European paintings.[13] Conti typically organized his paintings by school and chronologically therein. For example, he displayed his collection of approximately 100 eighteenth-century French canvases in *les pièces français* (the French Rooms), three connected galleries in the Palais de Temple. Yet, Conti did not hang Vallayer-Coster's paintings in those galleries. Instead, he chose to install her natural history pendants in his *appartement dit le Coquiller* (shell room), one of seven smaller galleries dedicated to his botanical, mammalian and maritime specimens.[14]

Conti's decision to display Vallayer-Coster's still lifes in his shell room, juxtaposing natural artifacts with their painted representation, was a significant departure from his own rigorous system of display.[15] This might be interpreted as a sexist maneuver, isolating a female artist from her male compatriots in the French galleries and thereby undermining the quality of her work.[16] It is also possible that, in the mind of this collector, Vallayer-Coster's paintings were intimately linked with the practice of collecting natural history objects – so much so, that the pendants were displayed to their best advantage in dialogue with the very specimens that they represented. Indeed, Vallayer-Coster's paintings were designed to appeal to this sort of interdisciplinary collecting interest. Conti was precisely the sort of elite connoisseur that she sought to attract with *Still Life with Seashells and Coral*.

The prince de Conti died in August 1776, only six months after he purchased Vallayer-Coster's pendants. In April 1777, the art dealer Rémy organized a sale of the prince de Conti's gargantuan collection: 2117 lots, including paintings, sculptures and curiosities.[17] Despite the wealth of objects represented, the 1777 auction failed to achieve a profit, bringing in 1.1 million *livres* – about a third of the estimated value of the collection. The overwhelming number of objects for sale seems to have diluted the prices. Vallayer-Coster's pendants were no exception: her shell paintings were both acquired by the art dealer Jean-Baptiste Le Brun (husband of the future *académicienne*, Élisabeth Vigée) for a mere 240 *livres*. Sometime after the sale, the pendants were separated. The only remaining visual evidence of the lost painting is a loose sketch by the draftsman Gabriel Saint-Aubin, who drew both paintings on the blank page of the 1777 auction catalogue.[18]

As Conti's display suggests, Vallayer-Coster's *Still Life with Seashells and Coral* is best understood in the context of the Parisian vogue for collecting shells and minerals. Vallayer-Coster married anatomical precision with painterly flourish, suggesting that she herself had gained access to a shell collection – perhaps through the artist Madeleine Françoise Basseporte, a friend of the Vallayer family and the draftswoman of the Jardin du Roi in Paris.[19] Vallayer-Coster may have learned to draw and paint from Basseporte, who produced several representations of shells and coral (fig.46). As noted in Chapter 1, Vallayer-Coster was also said to have enrolled in the drawing school run by *académicienne* Marie-Thérèse Reboul Vien, who herself drew and engraved the illustrations for Michel Adanson's 1757 natural history text, *Histoire naturelle du Sénégal: coquillages, avec la relation abrégée d'un voyage fait en ce pays* (*Natural History of Senegal: Shells, with the Brief Account of the Journey Made to this Country*).[20] Vallayer-Coster almost certainly had access to the shell drawings or prints produced by her teacher and colleague, Reboul Vien.

It may also have been through Basseporte or Reboul Vien that Vallayer-Coster became aware of three important texts that linked collectors, artists

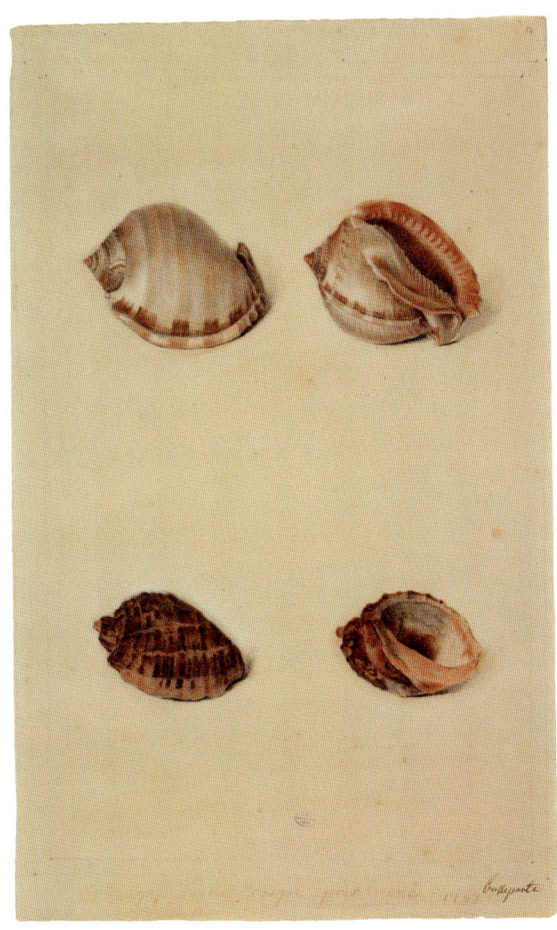

46 Madeleine Françoise Basseporte, *Mollusks*, 1747, red and black crayons on paper, 39 × 24 cm (15 ¼ × 9 ½ in), Bibliothèque centrale du Muséum national d'histoire naturelle, Paris

and natural philosophers across the century: a sale catalogue by Edmé-François Gersaint, a collector's guide by Antoine-Joseph Dezallier d'Argenville and a natural history book by Carl Linnaeus. All of these sources were pivotal in cultivating the luxury market for shells, as well as the aesthetic and scientific discourses surrounding those collecting practices. The

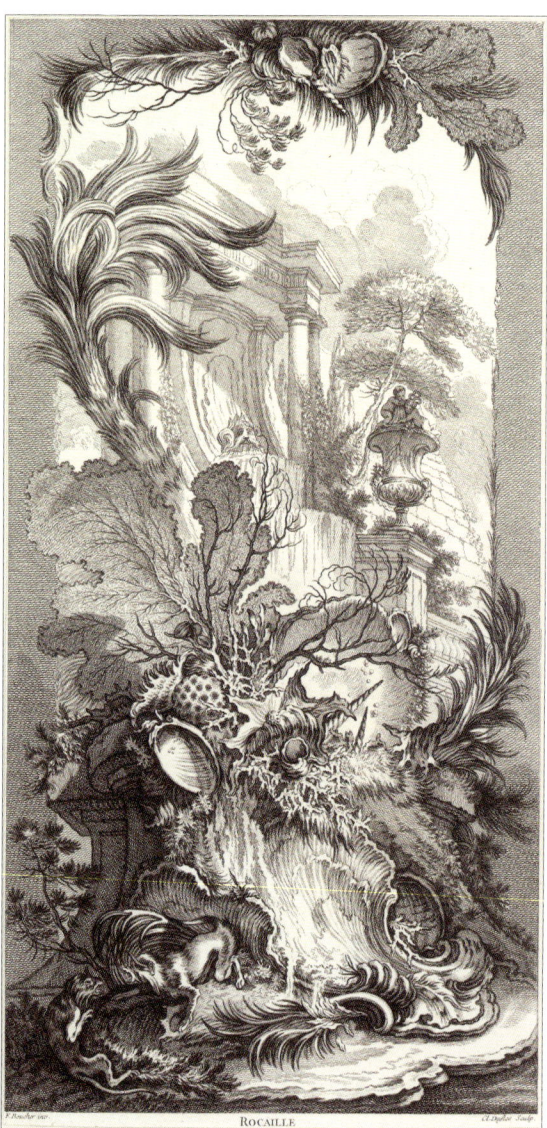

47 Claude Duflos after François Boucher, *Rocaille*, 1737, etching with engraving, 49.8 × 25 cm (19 ⅝ × 9 ⅞ in), The Metropolitan Museum of Art, New York

innovative texts also featured printed illustrations, which probably served as important visual references for the artist.

GERSAINT'S *CATALOGUE RAISONNÉ DES COQUILLES ET AUTRES CURIOSITÉS NATURELLES*

Vallayer-Coster and her patron, the prince de Conti, were probably familiar with the most famous French sale catalogue dedicated to shells: *Catalogue raisonné des coquilles et autres curiosités naturelles* (*Catalogue raisonné of Shells and Other Natural Curiosities*) by the luxury merchant Edmé-François Gersaint (1694–1750). This 234-page catalogue accompanied Gersaint's first major auction of marine specimens on 30 January 1736, which is considered to be the first sale of its kind in Paris. The catalogue listed the shells to be sold and concluded with an extensive, descriptive glossary – an early, if imprecise, attempt to taxonomize shells. Despite its inaccuracies, this glossary continued to serve as an important resource for collectors for several decades after the sale.[21] Serious shell collectors, like the prince de Conti, almost certainly owned a copy.

Gersaint's catalogue was also accompanied by a frontispiece designed by the academic painter François Boucher (fig.47). The vertical, closely cropped image of marine specimens undoubtedly served as a compositional model for Vallayer-Coster's *Still Life with Seashells and Coral*. Boucher and Vallayer-Coster's images both represent shells, minerals and coral in an almost identical arrangement, highlighting the organic irregularity of the diversity of textures, sizes and shapes – though Vallayer-Coster's canvas benefits from the dazzling color and thick facture of oil paint.

Vallayer-Coster's vivid interpretation of Boucher's design would have been instantly recognizable to erudite shell collectors. In the intervening decades since Gersaint's sale of 1736, Boucher's engraved image had become linked to the global market for rare and expensive shells. Gersaint reused Boucher's frontispiece for at least two subsequent auctions.[22] Other dealers, including Rémy, appropriated the same image for their own catalogues, even after Gersaint's death.[23] Boucher's design thus conferred commercial legitimacy to auction catalogues long after its initial engraving in 1736. Vallayer-Coster must have deliberately evoked Boucher's frontispiece, and the flourishing shell economy heralded by his design, in order to engage with the elite circle of connoisseurs who collected both art and shells.

Vallayer-Coster may even have come into contact with Boucher's own extensive collection of over 2500 shells, which he displayed in a cabinet next to his apartments at the Louvre. As Jessica Priebe has demonstrated, Boucher often experimented with displaying his shells in sculptural *mélanges* – three-dimensional arrangements of actual specimens, mounted on a flat base, in compositions that recalled his frontispiece for Gersaint. After Boucher's death, the shells were sold with great fanfare in February 1771[24] – soon after Vallayer-Coster's acceptance into the Académie in July 1770 and just before the debut of her *Still Life with Seashells and Coral* at the Salon of 1771.

DEZALLIER D'ARGENVILLE'S LA CONCHYLIOLOGIE

Vallayer-Coster's shell paintings were informed by another popular conchological text. Antoine-Joseph Dezallier d'Argenville (1680–1765), a connoisseur of art and natural history, published a collecting guide popularly known as *La conchyliologie* (*Conchology*) in 1742, with subsequent editions appearing in 1757 and 1780. Like Gersaint's catalogue, Dezallier d'Argenville's book also featured a frontispiece designed by Boucher (fig.48).[25] This whimsical frontispiece abandons commercial sobriety and scientific exactitude in favor of visual pleasure: a semi-nude merman and mermaid

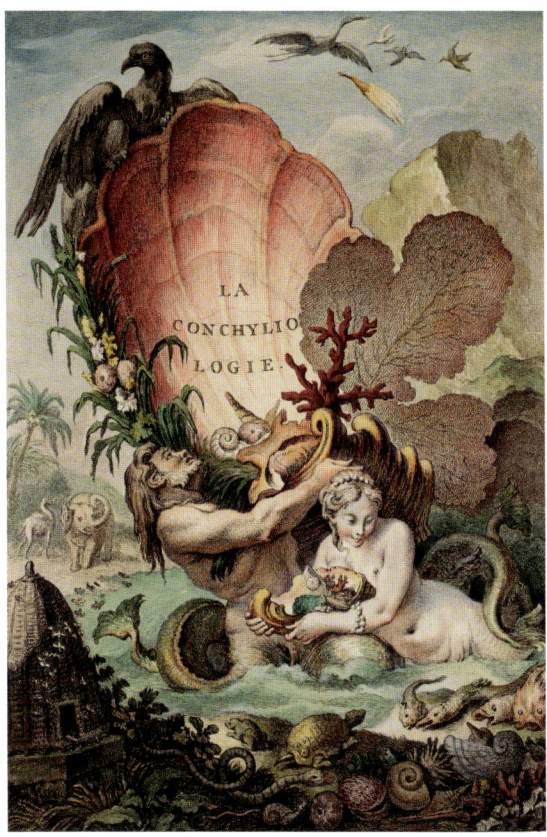

48 François Boucher, frontispiece for Antoine-Joseph Dezallier d'Argenville, *La conchyliologie*, 2nd edn, 1757, hand-colored engraving, 28.6 × 21 cm (11¼ × 8¼ in), American Museum of Natural History, New York

emerge from the sea with armfuls of shells and coral. These specimens were mined from distant waters, as suggested by the palm trees, elephant and camel on shore. Boucher's frontispiece lent artistic value to Dezallier d'Argenville's text, while emphasizing the erotic and exotic qualities of the shells described and illustrated therein.

As Boucher's image suggests, 'exotic' (that is, non-European) shells came from foreign underwater worlds that were sexy and unknowable to French collectors. Throughout the eighteenth century, Parisian dealers like Gersaint acquired shells at auctions in the Netherlands. They were primarily imported via Dutch global trade networks, whose ships combed the Indo-Pacific and Atlantic Oceans for rare marine specimens. By the time these shells appeared on the luxury market in Paris – stripped of sea creatures, slime and grit – their original provenance was often murky. Yet this ambiguity only enhanced their other-worldly appeal for the French collectors, who sought to understand these naked alien specimens by analyzing their color and shape.[26]

In several ways, Vallayer-Coster's painting seems to be a visual articulation of Dezallier d'Argenville's approach toward collecting exotic natural curiosities. In addition to identifying hundreds of different types of shells, *La conchyliologie* drew several explicit comparisons between techniques of painting and displaying shells, blurring the lines between artist and collector. First, Dezallier d'Argenville advocated for the artistic reproduction of the shells as a means of understanding them, writing, 'What better way is there to understand the differences between shells than by drawing them from nature? The slightest fold, the fine details of the shape, the contour, the mouth: nothing escapes the draftsman, and nothing can better reveal their true nature.'[27] Vallayer-Coster answers Dezallier d'Argenville's call to '*dessiner d'après nature*' – to draw after nature, rendering marine specimens with anatomical and textural precision. The author dedicated another chapter to the preparation of shells for display through a series of material interventions – for example, cleaning them with alcohol and applying a coat of egg-white wash in order to enhance the natural shine and hue of the shell.[28] This procedure mimics the early modern practice of varnishing oil paintings, in order to saturate and preserve oil paint, as Vallayer-Coster did with all of her canvases.

Vallayer-Coster's *Still Life with Seashells and Coral* also seems to embrace Dezallier d'Argenville's hybrid strategy for displaying natural specimens in private collections. He distinguishes between two different groups of collectors, first identified by Gersaint in 1736: the Naturalists and the Curious. In Dezallier d'Argenville's words, 'Naturalists arrange shells according to classes and families . . . the Curious, by contrast, who value pleasing the eye above all else, sacrifice methodological order for the sake of varied arrangements, in respect of the form of shells as well as their colors.'[29] Dezallier D'Argenville advised his readers, however, to combine these seemingly contradictory strategies: to group shells by family, but to organize them within that group according to one's own personal taste, in order to achieve a pleasing juxtaposition of color, pattern and texture.

Much like a still-life artist arranging the composition of a painting, Dezallier d'Argenville's ideal collector employed several formal strategies in arranging his or her collection, pursuing symmetry, balance and order, as well as diversity in color and texture.[30] While seeking to better understand the origin and classification of individual specimens, ultimately this ideal collector sought to integrate diverse curiosities into harmonious displays – deriving sensual pleasure from the contrasts between them.[31] Vallayer-Coster's painting appeals directly to this modern sensibility, combining the aesthetic and scientific impulses of a shell collector in arranging her own composition.

LINNAEUS'S SYSTEMA NATURAE

The exuberant composition and the rich colors and textures of Vallayer-Coster's painting were generally informed by the texts and images published by Gersaint and Dezallier d'Argenville. However, the fleshy-pink conch shell in the foreground of her painting finds resonance in another important source: Carl Linnaeus's (1707–78) *Systema Naturae*, the first text to employ a systematic, binomial nomenclature for the natural world. Vallayer-Coster may have encountered Linnaeus's work through Basseporte, who first met Linnaeus during his visit to the Jardin du Roi in Paris in 1737 and thereafter maintained a regular correspondence with him. Basseporte made a strong personal impression on the Swedish naturalist, who declared that he dreamed of her and would like to marry her. Basseporte politely indulged Linnaeus in his flirtation, whether she reciprocated his affections or not.[32]

The tenth edition of Linnaeus's *Systema Naturae*, published in 1758, was the first version of his text to include shelled creatures – possibly a response to the enormous interest in collecting shells and the influx of specimens on the European market.[33] Much like Dezallier d'Argenville's *La conchyliologie*, Linnaeus's system for identifying shells was a superficial one, based primarily on the shape, color, pattern and texture of the shell. This formal methodology parallels the close observation required of a still-life artist. However, because *Systema Naturae* lacked images, Linnaeus cited *La conchyliologie* throughout his text, applying his own Latin terminology to the specimens represented in Dezallier d'Argenville's illustrations. It must have been common for shell collectors to own copies, and to make comparative use, of both authors' texts.

Linnaeus's binomial terminology gained acceptance among European collectors only gradually, due in part to the controversy surrounding his use of sexual metaphor. For example, Linnaeus described one bivalve shell, the *Venus diones*, as reminiscent of female genitalia. He proceeded to label various parts of this shell with the Latin terms for the pubic mound, vulva, labia, hymen and anus – despite the fact that those terms bear no connection to the true biological functions of the animal within the shell. This sexual lexicon was considered controversial by many conchologists. Emanuel Da Costa, the author of *Elements of Conchology* (1776), objected to what he called 'unjustifiable and very indecent terms' because he believed they were inappropriate for women to know and use. Da Costa advocated for more 'chaste'

alternatives, in order to 'render descriptions proper, intelligible, and decent; by which the science may become useful, easy, and adapted to all capacities, and to both sexes'.[34] Da Costa here acknowledged the increasing numbers of female shell collectors, while also revealing contemporary concerns about women gaining scientific knowledge, particularly about their own bodies.

Despite Da Costa's aversion to using the scientific terms for female genitalia to describe parts of shells, Vallayer-Coster's fleshy-pink conch shell in *Still Life with Seashells and Coral* evokes this part of the female body. Fuzzy yellow and peach-colored brushstrokes form the outer edges of the shell. Thick, coagulated touches of white impasto highlight the slick outer lip and a delicate seam of a darker pink stands for the conch's interior fold. We know shells to be as brittle and hard as porcelain, yet the interior of the conch appears as soft and slippery as the body of the sea creature that was once housed within it. In this way, Vallayer-Coster seems to interpret Linnaeus's lexicon of conchology with paint.

BIHERON'S WAX ANATOMICAL MODELS

This visual double-entendre is underscored by Vallayer-Coster's affiliation with anatomist Marie-Marguerite Biheron (1719–95), who specialized in gynecological representations. Biheron took drawing lessons from Basseporte sometime after the latter assumed her post as the official draftswoman at the Jardin du Roi – just as Vallayer-Coster is thought to have trained under the auspices of her family friend.[35] Unlike Vallayer-Coster, who was admitted to the Académie royale de peinture et de sculpture, Biheron was ineligible for membership to the Académie des sciences because she was a woman. Nevertheless, Biheron achieved considerable professional success and developed relationships with several prominent scientists and philosophers, including Diderot. Like Basseporte, Biheron never married; she supported herself by sculpting wax anatomical models and making her cabinet on rue Saint Paul, not far from the Louvre, accessible to the public for a small fee. She also offered private anatomical lessons to young women to prepare them for the biological demands of marriage and motherhood and to familiarize them with the relevant parts of their own bodies.[36]

In 1770, the same year that Vallayer-Coster was admitted to the Académie and a year before she exhibited her *Still Life with Seashells and Coral* at the Salon, Biheron was invited to the Académie des sciences to give a demonstration of her most innovative model: a life-size gynecological and obstetrical wax sculpture. The dynamic imitation of the female reproductive system featured a dilating and contracting uterus, a shifting coccyx and a removable fetus – all rendered in wax tinted to approximate the color of human flesh.[37]

Much like Vallayer-Coster's paintings, Biheron's models were resoundingly praised for their verism. One critic wrote of her anatomy cabinet, 'Mlle Biheron offers a most curious and interesting spectacle . . . she employs all sorts of materials, in order to render the diverse parts most truthful'.[38] Another acknowledged Biheron for having 'imitated nature . . . with a precision and truth which no person has yet achieved'.[39] Sir John Pringle, the Physician General of Britain, crudely exclaimed that Biheron's models 'want nothing but the smell'; they were lifelike in every other sensual capacity.[40]

It is tempting to speculate that Vallayer-Coster's paintings of pink conch shells were inspired by Biheron's anatomical models. While Mary Sheriff has shown that *académicienne* Vigée Le Brun viewed the wax anatomical models sculpted by the Italian scientist Felice Fontana in Florence, we do not know if Vallayer-Coster ever visited Biheron's anatomy cabinet in Paris.[41] Even if she knew Biheron's work, Vallayer-Coster would have been more concerned with the formal resonance between the conch and the vulva, rather than the internal function of the entire

female reproductive system. Still, the fact that the still-life artist and the anatomist shared a personal connection to Basseporte and a major patron in Queen Marie Antoinette suggests that they might have been aware of one another: in 1786, five years after she served as a witness to Vallayer-Coster's marriage, the Queen purchased a set of Biheron's anatomical models for 6,000 *livres*.[42]

THE SENSUAL APPEAL OF SHELLS

Whether or not Vallayer-Coster had access to Biheron's wax anatomical models, the pink conch shell in the foreground of her *Still Life with Seashells and Coral* makes manifest the morphological similarities between the conch and the female sex, which would have been legible and meaningful to a late eighteenth-century audience. This symbolic parallel has ancient roots: the Ancient Greek word *kteis* connoted both the shell and the vagina. The Greco-Roman Goddess Aphrodite/Venus was thought to have emerged from a shell at birth. Although most ancient textual sources fail to mention a shell in their description of Venus's birth, it has long been a part of the visual iconography of the scene: the Imperial Roman fresco in the House of Venus at Pompeii (*c.* first century CE); Sandro Botticelli's Renaissance icon, *Birth of Venus* (1486); and Boucher's rococo masterpiece, *The Triumph of Venus* (1740), are among the most famous examples.[43]

In each of these images, the shell is symbolically genital, a kind of disembodied womb that cradles the ancient goddess of love, beauty and fertility (and the unofficial patron saint of the Rococo). These broad cultural associations of the shell with the feminine cult of Aphrodite/Venus persisted well into the eighteenth century, when the shell became a fetishized symbol of sensual delight. Vallayer-Coster's own painting exemplified the era's fascination with the curvaceous beauty of the shell, the unique allure of its vulval volumes and voids.[44]

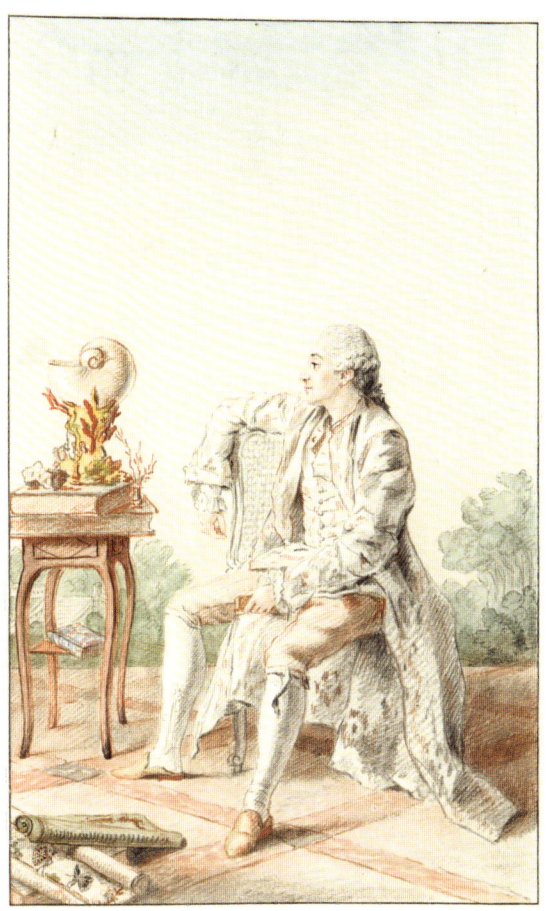

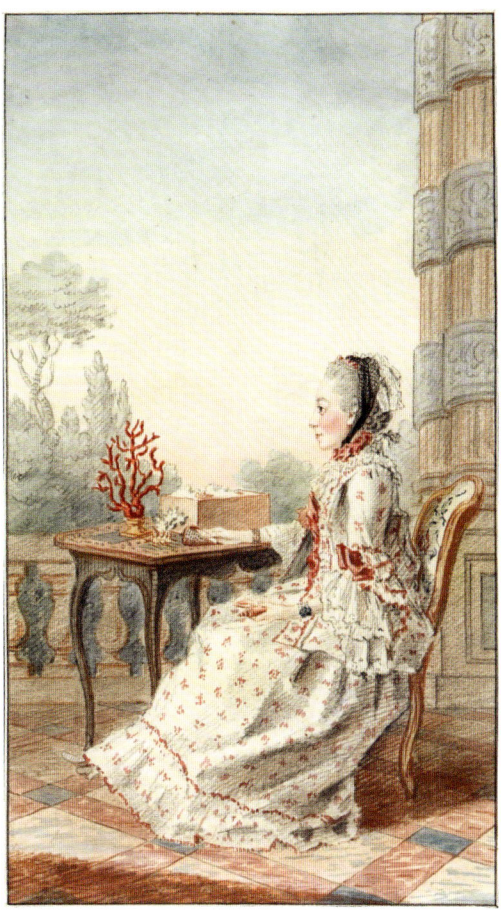

49 Louis Carrogis Carmontelle, *Monsieur de Buchelay*, 1758, watercolor, gouache, sanguine and pencil on paper, 28 × 17 cm (11 × 6¾ in), Musée Condé, Chantilly

50 Louis Carrogis Carmontelle, *Madame Blondel d'Azincourt*, 1760, watercolor, gouache, sanguine and pencil on paper, 29 × 16.5 cm (11⅜ × 6½ in), Musée Condé, Chantilly

Even within the masculine spaces of the natural history text and the curiosity cabinet, the shell never fully shed its association with the erotic and the exotic. There, however, the shell also became the subject of intellectual inquiry – a means of evaluating, understanding and asserting dominance over nature – in addition to being a luxurious object of a collector's lust.[45] These spaces also advocated, and satiated the desire for, a specific kind of look and touch: a way of manipulating shells in order to clean, enhance, arrange and delight in them. Chevalier Louis de Jaucourt articulated this dual compulsion in his entry on 'Painting' in the 1765 edition of *Encyclopédie*, in which he describes the sensual pleasures of both shells and paintings of them: 'It is easy to see how the imitations of painting can move us when one stops to think how a shell . . . excites restless passions and arouses the desire to see them and to possess them. A grand passion ignited by a small object is an ordinary event.'[46]

Still Life with Seashells and Coral appeals to both the visual and the haptic desires described by Jaucourt. Vallayer-Coster achieved this vivid textural illusionism in part through the use of a textured ground: a warm gray layer of primer, mixed with some sort of gritty, ground pebble – perhaps ground shells – applied to the canvas.[47] Vallayer-Coster also employed a unique combination of painting techniques: wet-on-wet paint for the soft, smooth, pink interior of the conch, and a thick dry impasto to articulate the veined, craggy surface of the Venus sea fan coral. This textural specificity reinforces the theory Vallayer-Coster had direct access to a shell collection and that the subjects were seen and felt by the artist herself.

Vallayer-Coster's critics responded directly to the tangible quality of her work. As one author wrote of the artist in 1771: 'You honor the Salon with the perfection with which you have rendered the different subjects that you paint . . . one can imagine touching the objects with a finger and with the eye, as if they were real and protruding [from the canvas].'[48] This

critic imagined touching the varied surfaces of her painted specimens and deriving pleasure from those haptic sensations.

Vallayer-Coster's emphasis on tactility parallels a shift in the eighteenth-century discourse on the very nature of sensory experience. Étienne Bonnot de Condillac's *Treatise of Sensations* of 1754, for example, maintained that a subject understood the boundaries of his or her own body only by touching other objects.[49] Diderot, meanwhile, articulated his belief that touch was the superior sense – 'the most profound and the most philosophical' – in his 1751 essay, *Lettre sur les sourds et muets* (*Letter on the Deaf and Dumb*).[50] Diderot expanded on this idea in *D'Alembert's Dream* (1769), suggesting that knowledge was obtained primarily through bodily interactions with the material world, describing the 'infinite diversity of tactile sensations' that comprise human experience.[51] For Diderot, the subtleties of experience are primarily available through touch, in collaboration with vision and the other senses.

The privileging of touch over vision, however, was a reversal of the traditional hierarchies of the senses that had reigned in centuries past. The sense of sight had long presided because it was associated with objective scientific observation – an intellectual pursuit typically associated with men. Touch, meanwhile, was associated with subjective experiences of pleasure and pain, irrelevant to the pursuit of knowledge – and, therefore, implicitly feminine.[52]

These gendered connotations also existed within the realm of conchology, as illustrated by two drawings by the celebrity portraitist Louis Carrogis, called Carmontelle (1717–1806). In 1758, Carmontelle drew the shell collector Monsieur de Buchelay seated next to a small table, looking pointedly at a group of mounted shells (fig.49). The pile of books (perhaps copies of Gersaint, Dezallier d'Argenville and Linnaeus's texts) at his feet refers to the intellectual discourse surrounding his collecting practice. In 1760, Carmontelle pictured the prominent shell collector

Madame Blondel d'Azincourt using both hands to touch objects from her collection (fig.50).[53] She holds a conch shell in her left hand and fingers a turban shell with her right. Her gaze does not seem to be directed at anything in particular, and she is surrounded by none of the texts that complement Buchelay's portrait. Madame d'Azincourt's touch is a sensual, decidedly feminine one, at least according to the gendered hierarchy in the eighteenth century. Yet we could also describe her gesture as one of ownership, and conclude that the pleasures of owning, looking at, touching and painting shells were not limited to men. Vallayer-Coster's paintings of shells appealed to all of these sensations.

RETURNING TO THE SHELL

Vallayer-Coster would go on to depict shells in at least two other paintings. She submitted *Still Life with Porcelain Vase, Marine Plants, Shells and Various Mineralogical Specimens* to the Salon of 1777,[54] *Vase of Flowers with Shell* to the Salon of 1781 (see fig.45)[55] and, finally, the now lost *Still Life with Minerals* to the Salon of 1789.[56] Her repetition of this subject attests to its enduring appeal to both the artist and her patrons. Vallayer-Coster's shells evoked the collecting practices of the prince de Conti, the economy stimulated by dealers like Gersaint, and the conchological discourses advanced by Dezallier d'Argenville and Linnaeus. Her patrons associated shells with both the masculine curiosity cabinet and the female body; for them, shells ignited visual and haptic desires, connoting both the erotic and the exotic. Vallayer-Coster's shell paintings simultaneously inhabited these overlapping cultural and scientific spheres.

6

Flowers

At the Salon of 1777, Vallayer-Coster submitted 13 paintings, including five still lifes with flowers. Those floral paintings attracted the attention of several critics, including one who wrote: 'Her flowers are so fresh, so vibrant, so brilliant that one is tempted to pick them and make a crown for her. She has, so to speak, treated them like history painting.'[1] The author suggests that Vallayer-Coster has rendered flowers with the complexity more typical of the history painting (biblical, mythological or historical subjects).

This was profound praise for a still-life artist, yet we should also acknowledge the patronizing subtext of the statement. Female artists were largely precluded from the elite title of history painter at the Académie, in part because they were (officially) unable to study the human body.[2] Vallayer-Coster is praised instead for excelling in the representation of a 'simpler' and less prestigious subject. This critic further suggests that the lifelikeness of her flowers is not simply a compliment to her artistic talent, but might form a 'crown' to further ornament her own physical beauty – conflating the attractive qualities of the artist and her subject matter.

Vallayer-Coster's artistic production was by no means limited to flowers, though she was certainly productive in this genre. Of the approximately 140 paintings that are currently attributed to the artist, at least a third are floral. Yet her flower paintings have come to be representative of her entire oeuvre,

perhaps because so many of them were produced in the latter half of her career, when she painted other subjects less frequently. As the dealer Charles Paillet wrote in the 1824 catalogue to the Coster estate sale: '[Vallayer-Coster] constantly maintained, with her adopted genre of flowers, a great reputation she had acquired and defended against the most renowned teachers.'[3] Vallayer-Coster was also remembered as a flower painter in the 1835 memoir of her fellow *académicienne*, portraitist Élisabeth Vigée Le Brun.[4]

Vallayer-Coster's reputation as a flower painter consolidated over the course of the nineteenth and twentieth centuries, in part because she was so prolific in the subject, but also because she was a woman. Flowers have long served as visual metaphors for femininity, symbolizing the colorful but ephemeral beauty of women. Like the shells discussed in the previous chapter, flowers could also serve as symbols for intimate parts of the female body. Consequently, many female artists (especially amateurs) became associated with flower paintings, which are considered simple, pretty and 'easy' to paint.[5] Of course, in the eighteenth century, many professional male artists specialized in painting flowers, including Gerard van Spaendonck (1746–1822) and Pierre-Joseph Redouté (1759–1840). However, their work was more often praised for botanical precision, rather than its decorative qualities. (Jean Siméon Chardin, meanwhile, treated flowers very infrequently and these are his least well-known works.[6])

How then were flowers gendered in eighteenth-century France? How were women associated with the cultivation, arrangement and representation of flowers in various media – but also with their smell? This chapter describes the perceived 'femininity' of Vallayer-Coster's subject matter and painting technique, and situates her flower paintings within the visual, material and olfactory flower culture of late eighteenth-century France. By developing a historically specific understanding of flowers and their fragrances, we can better appreciate the sensual complexity of Vallayer-Coster's work and her distinctive way of approaching this subject. We begin and end with two of the most prominent flower lovers and art collectors of this period: Queen Marie Antoinette and Empress Josephine. These women, whose patronage of Vallayer-Coster marked the beginning and the end of her career, exemplify the conceptual and material links between femininity, flowers and scents in the long eighteenth century.

SMELLING FLOWERS

Vigée Le Brun's famed portrait of Marie Antoinette, exhibited at the Salon of 1783, depicts the Queen holding a rose in front of a flowering bush, representing her own gardens at the Petit Trianon at Versailles (fig.51). Louis XVI had gifted the property to his wife after their coronation in 1774, reportedly saying, 'You are fond of flowers, Madame, so I give you this whole bouquet.'[7] Marie Antoinette transformed the Petit Trianon landscape, in collaboration with the botanists Claude (1705–84) and Antoine Richard (1735–1807), who planted roses and violets in organic patterns that mimicked the informal sprawl of wildflowers.[8]

Contemporary accounts of the Petit Trianon gardens are united in praise of their visual beauty as well their smell, which one visiting nobleman

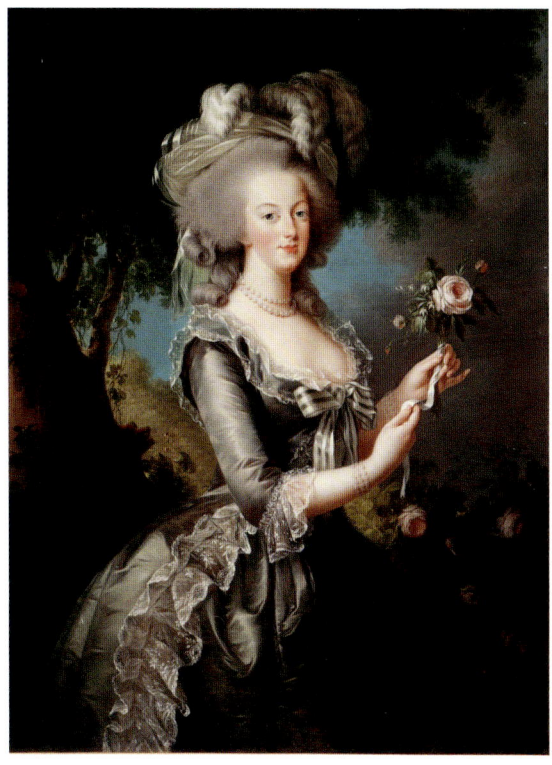

51 Élisabeth Vigée Le Brun, *Marie Antoinette with a Rose*, 1783, oil on canvas, 116.8 × 88.9 cm (46 × 35 in), Collection of Lynda and Stewart Resnick

described as a 'sweet confusion' of iris, jasmine, lavender and lily-of-the-valley. The baronne d'Oberkirch recalled her own visit in her memoir, writing: 'What a charming stroll: the copses of fragrant lilac . . . were utterly delightful. The weather was magnificent; the air was full of the balmy fragrance of spring flowers.'[9] The intertwined visual and olfactory experience of the Petit Trianon gardens was a carefully curated one. As Christian Hirschfeld asserted in *Théorie de l'art des jardins* (*Theory of the Art of Gardening*, translated into French in 1779), the '*artiste jardinière*' (artist-gardener) had the unique power to flatter both the eye and the nose. Flowers offered visual satisfaction, but one also had to account for their variable scents when planting them.[10]

The Queen also plucked flowers from her gardens and displayed them in vases. These fragrant bouquets worked to counteract the fetid funk of the royal château. As Marie Antoinette's perfumer Jean-Louis Fargeon (1748–1806) wrote, 'Versailles could turn the stomach with its dreadful odors. The hallways, the courtyards, the buildings and corridors are filled with urine and fecal matter.'[11] In the early 1780s, Vallayer-Coster expanded her repertoire to include figurative representations of aristocratic women culling and arranging flowers, including members of the Queen's intimate circle. Vallayer-Coster painted at least one portrait of Madame Adélaide Auguié, sister to Jeanne Louise Henriette Campan (whose memoirs contain reference to Vallayer-Coster; see Chapter 1). In this 1781 portrait, Auguié appears draped in silk and pearls, arranging a few stems of roses in a gilded porcelain vase (fig.52)[12] – prefiguring Vigée Le Brun's 1783 portrait of the Queen performing the same task. To the Salon of 1785, Vallayer-Coster also submitted a portrait of famed beauty Mademoiselle de Coigny 'gathering flowers in her garden' – similar to another portrait that she painted of a woman in a diaphanous gown holding a basket of flowers on her lap, which recently reappeared in the Parisian art market (fig.53).[13]

The decorative and deodorant display of flowers was by no means limited to Versailles. In his *Tableau de Paris*, Louis-Sébastien Mercier acknowledged the popularity of private flower gardens, installed in courtyard flowerbeds and windowsill boxes, amongst Parisian housewives. He also described the daily influx of flower vendors to the markets of Les Halles, a familiar sight to Vallayer-Coster.[14] Recall that to the Salon of 1783, she submitted a (now lost) painting of a female flower seller, paired with another of female fish seller.[15] Mercier complained, however, that fresh flowers did little to counteract the stench that plagued the city: a potent combination of sweat, waste and rot

emanating from human and animal bodies, as well as the polluted Seine.[16]

In addition to assembling bouquets in vases, *Parisiennes* and women at the court of Versailles also used flowers to thwart their own personal stink – adorning their hair and necklines with blooms and slathering themselves with their essences.[17] In 1771, the physician and naturalist Pierre-Joseph Buc'hoz published *Toilette de flore, ou Essai sur les plantes et les fleurs qui peuvent servir d'ornement aux dames* (*Toilet of Flora, or Essay on the Plants and Flowers that Serve to Ornament Women*), which contained several homemade recipes to scent and thereby 'ornament' the female body.[18] Similarly, in his *L'art du parfumeur* (*Art of the Perfumer*), Fargeon described the professional techniques of drying, boiling, crushing and concentrating flower petals to extract their oils, and combining them to produce the desired effect – a process he likened to mixing pigments to yield a specific color and texture of paint.[19]

Professional perfumers sold a variety of ready-made fragrances, including oils, perfumes, pomades and powders, in shops. Fargeon operated his own boutique at 11 rue de Roule in Paris – the same street where Vallayer-Coster lived and worked before moving to the Louvre in 1781.[20] The artist must have smelled the profusion of floral, citrus and herbaceous scents wafting from Fargeon's shop on a daily basis. She may even have been a customer, adorning her own body with his concoctions.

Scent professionals like Buc'hoz, Fargeon and others refer to another scented product marketed to women: *portefeuilles*, drawstring bags containing potpourri of dried flowers and spices, or wads of fabric soaked in perfume. Concealed in one's pocket, sleeve or bodice, these satchels emitted a more enduring fragrance than the ephemeral mixtures applied to the skin.[21] Larger pouches embroidered with floral motifs doubled as fashionable accessories, combining the woven representation of flowers with their concentrated scents (fig.54). These bags were also

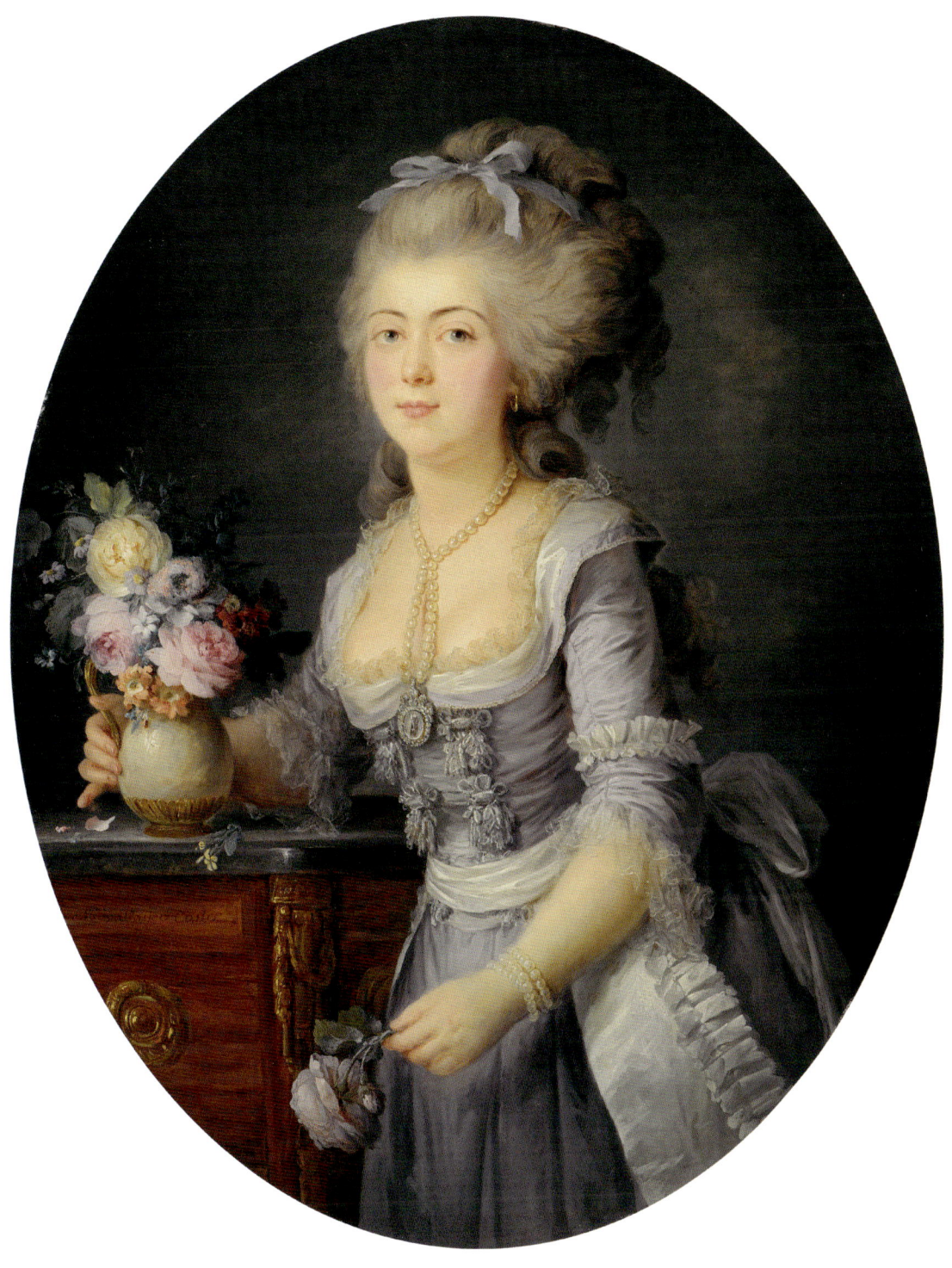

52 Anne Vallayer-Coster, *Portrait of Madame Adélaïde Auguié*, *c*.1781, oil on canvas, 97 × 76 cm (38 ⅛ × 29 ⅞ in),
Private collection

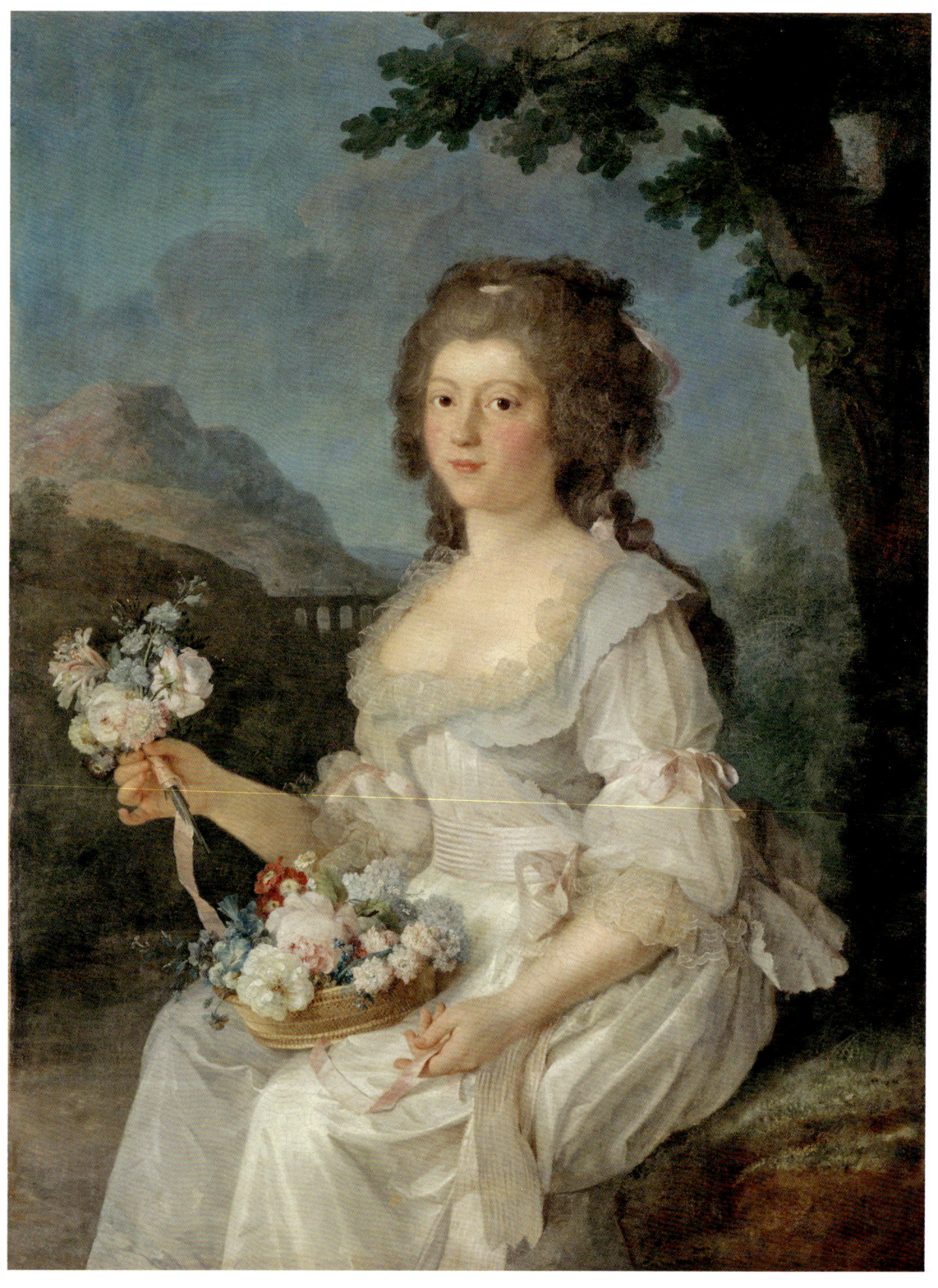

53 Anne Vallayer-Coster, *Portrait of a Woman Holding a Basket of Flowers*, c.1785, oil on canvas, 116 × 89 cm (45 ⅝ × 35 in),
Private collection

depicted alongside fresh flowers in Vallayer-Coster's *Bouquet of Flowers with a Purse* (fig.55) and *Vase of Flowers, Bird's Nest and Purse* (see fig.60).

Floral perfumes were thus closely associated with the female body. Their erotic potential emerges in the work of eighteenth-century *philosophes*. Denis Diderot described smell as the most 'voluptuous' of the senses.[22] Jean-François de Saint-Lambert concurred, writing: 'Odor gives us the most intimate sensation, a more immediate pleasure . . . than the sense of sight.'[23] Jean-Jacques Rousseau's tutor in *Emile, or, On Education* made the same connection, writing,

> Smell is the sense of imagination . . . Its effects are known well enough in love. The sweet fragrance of a dressing room is not so weak a trap as is often thought; and I don't know whether to congratulate or pity that prudent and insensitive man who has never been made to quiver by the smell of flowers on his beloved's bosom.[24]

These fragrant pleasures were not reserved for men alone. In fact, as Hirschfeld wrote in *Théorie de l'art des jardins*, women were considered to be even more sensitive to the 'sweet, delicate, pleasing, and refreshing perfumes' that emerged from flowers. According to him, women experienced their smell differently, more profoundly.[25] The chevalier Louis de Jaucourt observed in Diderot's *Encyclopédie* that 'delicate ladies can scarcely withstand the fine scent which flowers exude'.[26] This notion manifests visually in Jean Honoré Fragonard's (1732–1806) *Progress of Love*, a series of paintings commissioned for Madame du Barry's garden pavilion at Louveciennes, in which episodes of love and seduction are staged in fragrant gardenscapes. In each scene, Fragonard imagines a woman overwhelmed by the possibility or the memory of an amorous encounter, swayed by the smell of flowers all around her.[27]

PAINTING FLOWERS

Now, let us return to the idea of the role of smell and seduction in Vallayer-Coster's still-life paintings of flowers. In the presence of her floral subjects, the artist certainly smelled them. But how did their smell inform the way in which she painted them, or the way that contemporaries reacted to her work? In what ways did her paintings of flowers evoke scent for viewers? Until recently, the relationship between smell and early modern painting has not been well articulated.[28] Of course, oil paint and varnish have their own distinctive odors, derived from the organic materials that produce a specific viscosity and hue. Yet that smell tends to dissipate as paint dries and is not generally thought to contribute to the viewer's experience of the painting.

While one might be able to summon memories of smell in response to *any* representation of a flower, Vallayer-Coster's paintings are distinguished by an 'olfactory texture' – a term borrowed from the historian Alain Corbin, who used it to describe the urban topography of smells of eighteenth- and nineteenth-century Paris.[29] 'Olfactory texture' might also be used to describe the synesthetic effect of Vallayer-Coster's facture – a painting technique that provokes a visual and odorific response.

Her fluid touches of color specifically imitate the liquid sources of a flower's natural, ephemeral scent, as well as the artificial, concentrated perfumes derived from them. The natural oils that effuse from the 'pores' of petals, or the powdery pollens that discharge from central glands, were known to be the primary source of a flower's distinctive perfume – just as sweat and other bodily fluids were understood to be the source of individual human smells. Madeleine Françoise Basseporte's mentor, the botanist Bernard de Jussieu, pointed to the floral organs that 'serve to secrete, in the interior of the flowers, a juice of honeyed liquid modern botanists call nectarium'.[30] Basseporte may have encouraged her own students, perhaps

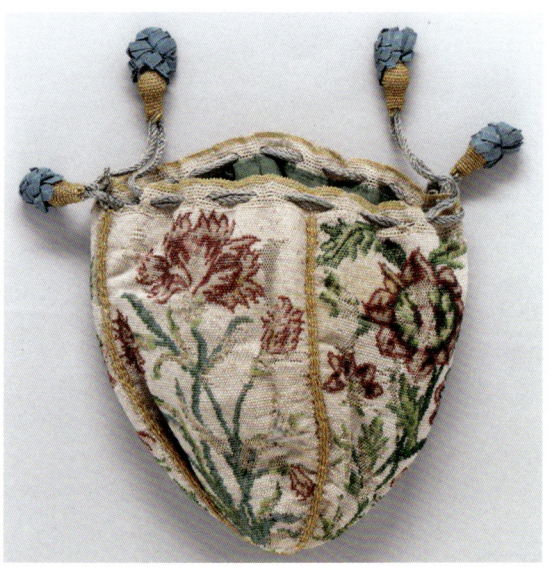

54 French purse, eighteenth century, silk and glass beads, 12.7 × 14 cm (5 × 5 ½ in), The Metropolitan Museum of Art, New York

55 Anne Vallayer-Coster, *Bouquet of Flowers with a Purse*, 1774, oil on canvas, 48 × 58 cm (18 ⅞ × 22 ⅞ in), long-term loan from the Fondation Ephrussi de Rothschild, 2018. Inv. D.2018.1.11, to the Musée Marmottan Monet, Paris

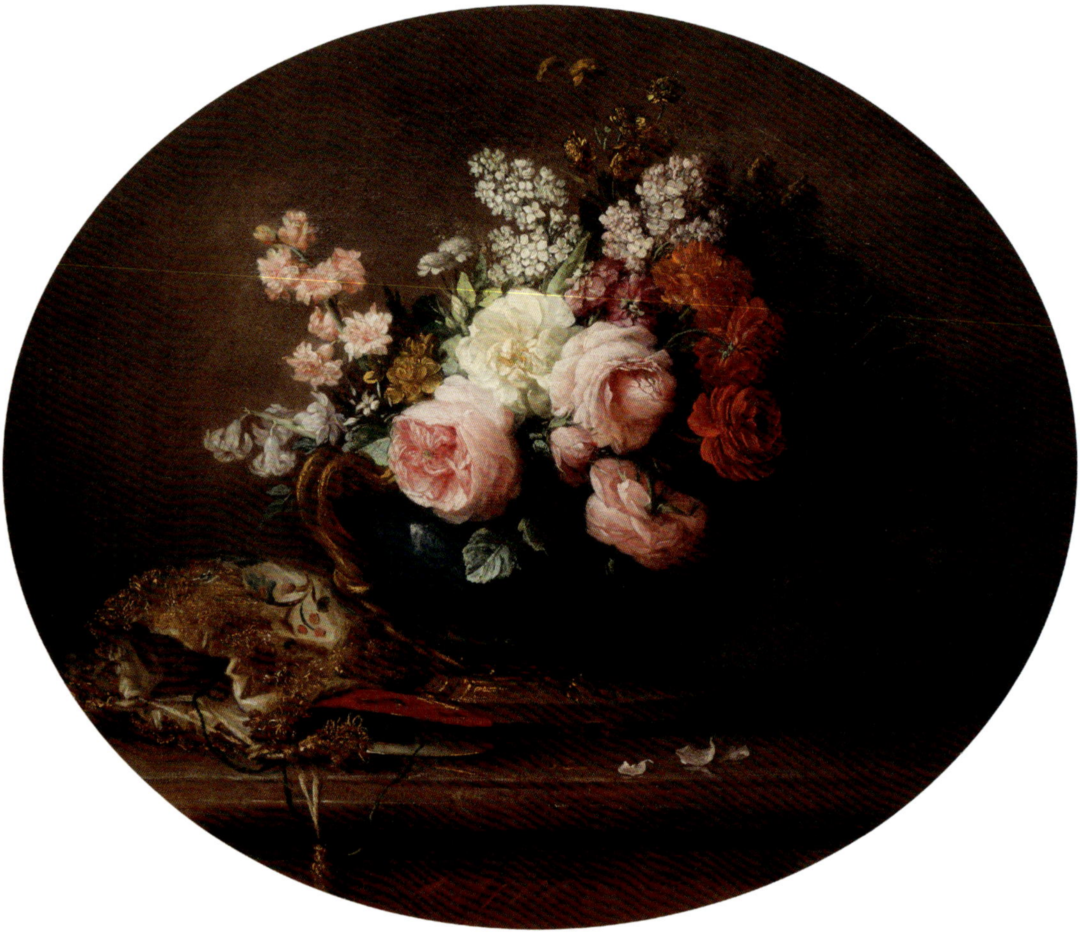

Vallayer-Coster among them, to observe these very parts of the plant. However, Vallayer-Coster seems to have been less concerned with scientific precision than in the sensorial experience of flowers, exploiting the material properties of paint to mimic their look and smell.

VALLAYER-COSTER'S FLOWERS AT THE SALON

Vallayer-Coster first exhibited flower paintings at the Salon of 1775 – one year after Marie Antoinette began gardening at the Petit Trianon and her perfumer Fargeon opened his shop on rue de Roule. At that Salon, the artist submitted two large-scale pendant paintings: *Vase of Flowers with a Bust of Flora* (fig.56)[31] and *The Attributes of Hunting and Gardening* (see fig.11). The pendants measure five feet in height, which are significantly larger than most flower paintings produced in the late eighteenth century and closer in scale to a life-size portrait or figurative genre painting.

Both works, which belonged to the former Director of the King's Buildings, the abbé Joseph-Marie Terray, also feature parallel sculptural busts: Flora, Roman goddess of flowers, and Ceres, the Roman goddess of agriculture. Flora is situated in a contemporary interior, on a Louis XVI wooden desk; she 'peeks' out coquettishly from behind a blue Chinese porcelain vase, mounted with gilded rope handles and overflowing with flowers: white hollyhocks, pale pink roses, bright blue morning glories and hydrangeas, orange day lilies, red poppies and deep purple daisies among them.[32] Vallayer-Coster likely based this composition on individual studies of flowers, which could subsequently be 'assembled' in a bouquet within a larger painting. This procedure enabled the artist to paint impossibly fresh arrangements of flowers that bloomed at slightly different times, an artistic elision of nature that was also typical of seventeenth-century Dutch and Flemish artists.[33] Vallayer-Coster probably trained in this method under Joseph Vernet

or Marie-Thérèse Reboul Vien, both of whom executed floral still-life paintings (see Chapter 1).

Also at the Salon of 1775, Vallayer-Coster showed two smaller oval pendants, *Bouquet of Flowers with Grapes* and *Bouquet of Flowers with a Purse* (see fig.55), which are each less than two feet in width.[34] The latter painting depicts a dark blue porcelain coupe vase, populated by pink sweet peas, tiny pale purple violets and bluebells and thick roses, accompanied by a *portefeuille.* The drawstring bag, adorned with a thick gold trim around its mouth and a floral motif embroidered on its body, lies agape and oriented toward the viewer. Though its contents are not visible, we can assume that the bag contained potpourri or perfumed fabric, like those sold at Fargeon's shop. The bouquet of fresh flowers and the *portefeuille* represent a juxtaposition of flowers (real and embroidered) and scents (fresh and artificially concentrated).

These floral paintings in particular received ample praise in the contemporary press. A writer in the *Mercure de France* remarked, 'Mademoiselle Vallayer has again responded to the pleas of connoisseurs, with pictures representing fruits, vegetables, vases of flowers, [rendered with] free touches and grouped with all the intelligence possible in order to produce the best effect.'[35] In *Observations sur les ouvrages exposés au Sallon du Louvre*, the author acknowledged Vallayer-Coster's established reputation: 'Mademoiselle Vallayer [enjoys] a celebrity, justly acquired by excellent paintings . . . the table where we see a bust of Flora is also of the greatest beauty.'[36] The author of *La lanterne magique* hailed her flower paintings as 'Superb! Truly superb! Observe how very truthful and seductive!'[37] These critical excerpts do not refer explicitly to the sense of smell. Read together, however, it is clear that the authors are searching for ways to describe the 'seductive' quality of her paintings, which seems to exceed the visual beauty of her 'free touches' of color.

Perhaps because of the positive critical responses to her work at the Salon of 1775, Vallayer-Coster continued to paint flowers in greater numbers and in

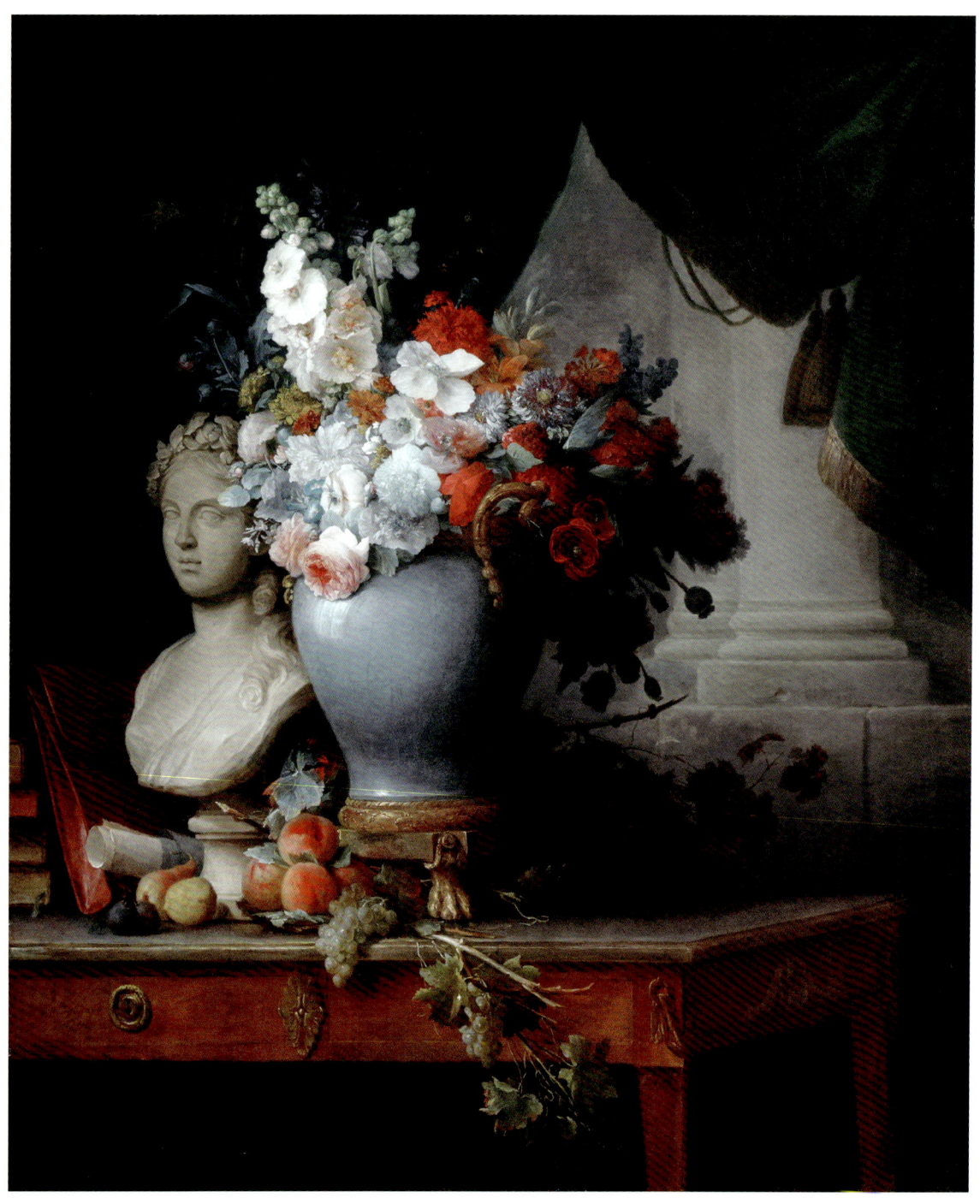

56 Anne Vallayer-Coster, *Vase of Flowers with a Bust of Flora*, 1774, oil on canvas, 154 × 130 cm (60 ⅝ × 51 ⅛ in),
Private collection

an increasingly 'free' style. At the subsequent Salon two years later, she showed five paintings in the genre, including two large floral pendants that now belong to the Dallas Museum of Art: *Bouquet of Flowers in a Blue Porcelain Vase* (fig.58) and *Bouquet of Flowers in a Terracotta Vase with Peaches and Grapes* (fig.59).[38] It was at this Salon, in response to the scale of her paintings (both measuring approximately four feet in height), as well as the visual and olfactory complexity of their arrangement, that the critic of *Lettres pittoresques* praised the brilliant 'freshness' of her flowers, that she treated on the scale of history painting.[39]

The Dallas pendants were lent to the Salon of 1777 by their owner, Jean-Baptiste-François de Montullé, an honorary member (*associé libre*) of the Académie who later took over the Gobelins manufactory. Despite his prestigious titles and royal connections, Montullé accumulated enormous debts. He was later forced to sell part of his collection in a 1783 sale, organized by Vigée Le Brun's art dealer husband. Montullé seems to have kept Vallayer-Coster's pendants until his death five years later, perhaps a sign of his personal attachment to those paintings. (He also owned a lobster painting by Vallayer-Coster; see Chapter 2 and fig.33.[40])

One of the Dallas pendants features a blue porcelain *jardinière* (planter) with gilt-bronze lion paw feet, which Sophie Mouquin and Christophe Huchet de Quénetain have likened to a neoclassical vase designed by Louis Félix de La Rue (1731–65).[41] The luxurious vessel is filled with familiar flowers (roses, daisies, violets, hydrangeas, poppies, carnations and hollyhocks), with two large additions: white lilies with fuzzy orange stamens and blue irises with yellow-striped petals. Singular stalks of purple, red and white chrysanthemum lie alongside the arrangement, as if waiting to fill a void in the bouquet.

This painting's pendant, *Bouquet of Flowers in a Terracotta Vase with Peaches and Grapes*, features flowers arranged in a clay vase carved with ornament: a thick floral garland draped above four frolicking putti who tug at a recalcitrant goat (fig.59). This

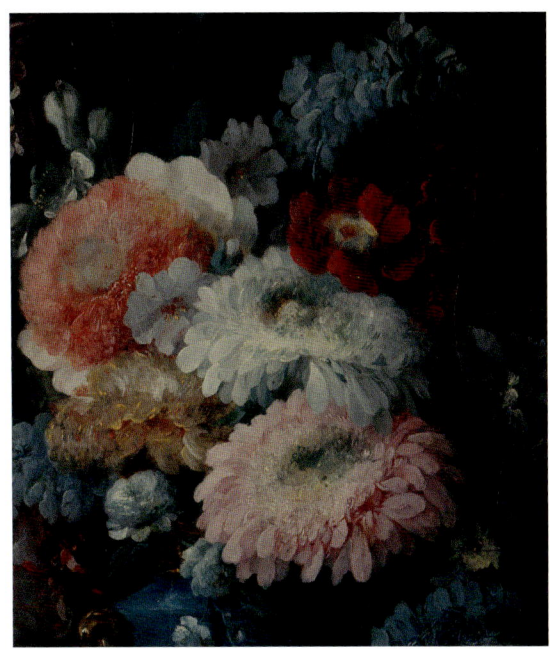

57 Anne Vallayer-Coster, detail of *Vase of Flowers with Shell*, 1780, oil on canvas, 50.2 × 38.1 cm (19 ¾ × 15 in), The Metropolitan Museum of Art, New York

Bacchanalian theme recalls the work of Vallayer-Coster's contemporary academician Claude Michel, called Clodion (1738–1814), who showed three similar terracotta vases at the Salon of 1772.[42] Some of these flowers (morning glories, violets, hydrangeas, hollyhocks) appeared in earlier paintings, but Vallayer-Coster reserved her loosest brushwork for the moist cruxes of two fantastic white poppies. The crush of pink and blue petals at their center is rendered with a flurry of haphazard, nearly abstract strokes.

In later works, Vallayer-Coster pushed this impressionistic effect even further. A trio of oval flower paintings exhibited at the Salon of 1781 likely included the Metropolitan Museum of Art's *Vase of Flowers with Shell* (fig.57; see also fig.45), which features a bouquet in

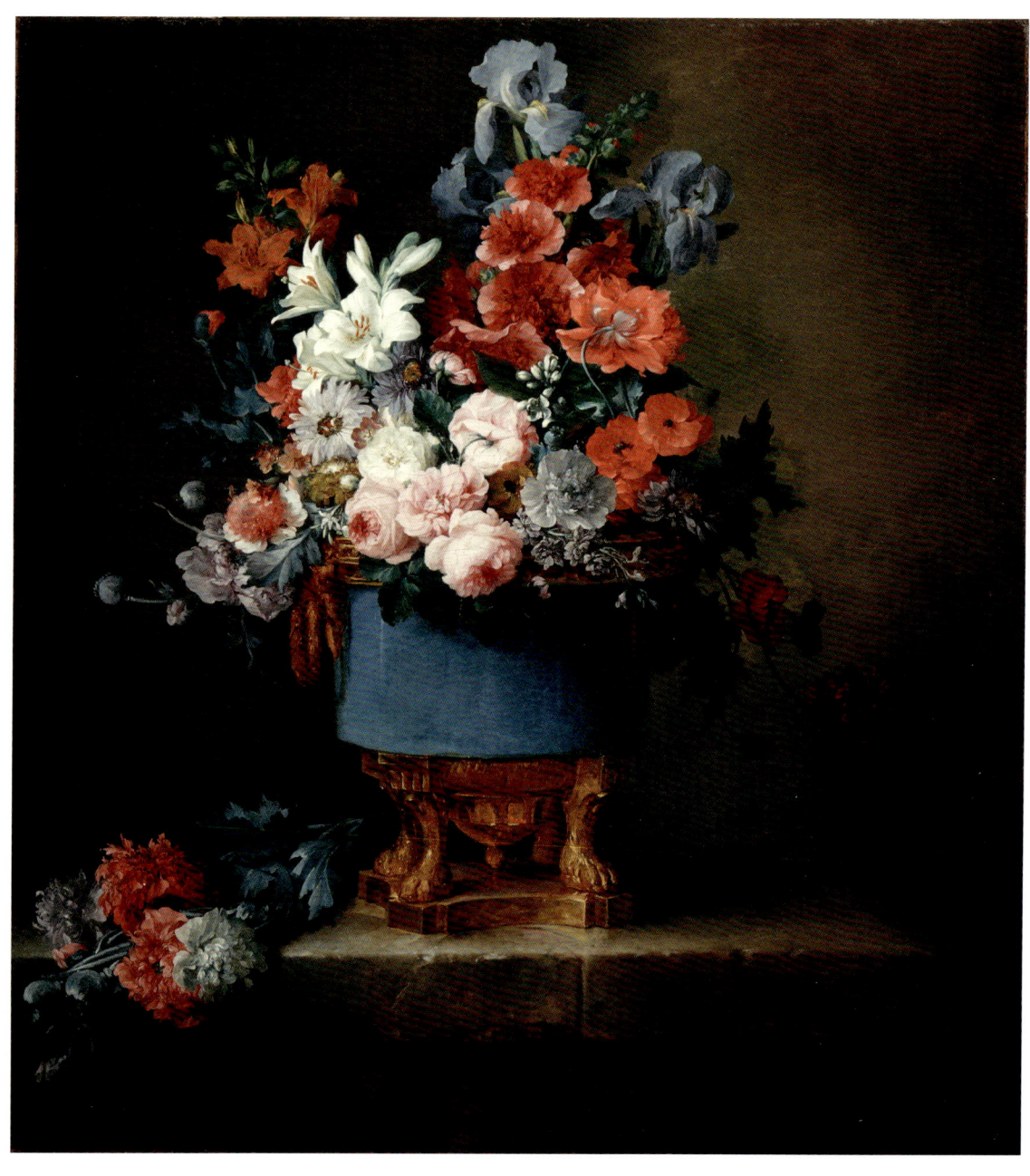

58   Anne Vallayer-Coster, *Bouquet of Flowers in a Blue Porcelain Vase*, 1776, oil on canvas, 122.2 × 113.4 cm (48 ⅛ × 44 ⅝ in),
Dallas Museum of Art, TX, Foundation for the Arts Collection, Mrs John B. O'Hara Fund and gift of Michael L.
Rosenberg, 1998.52.FA

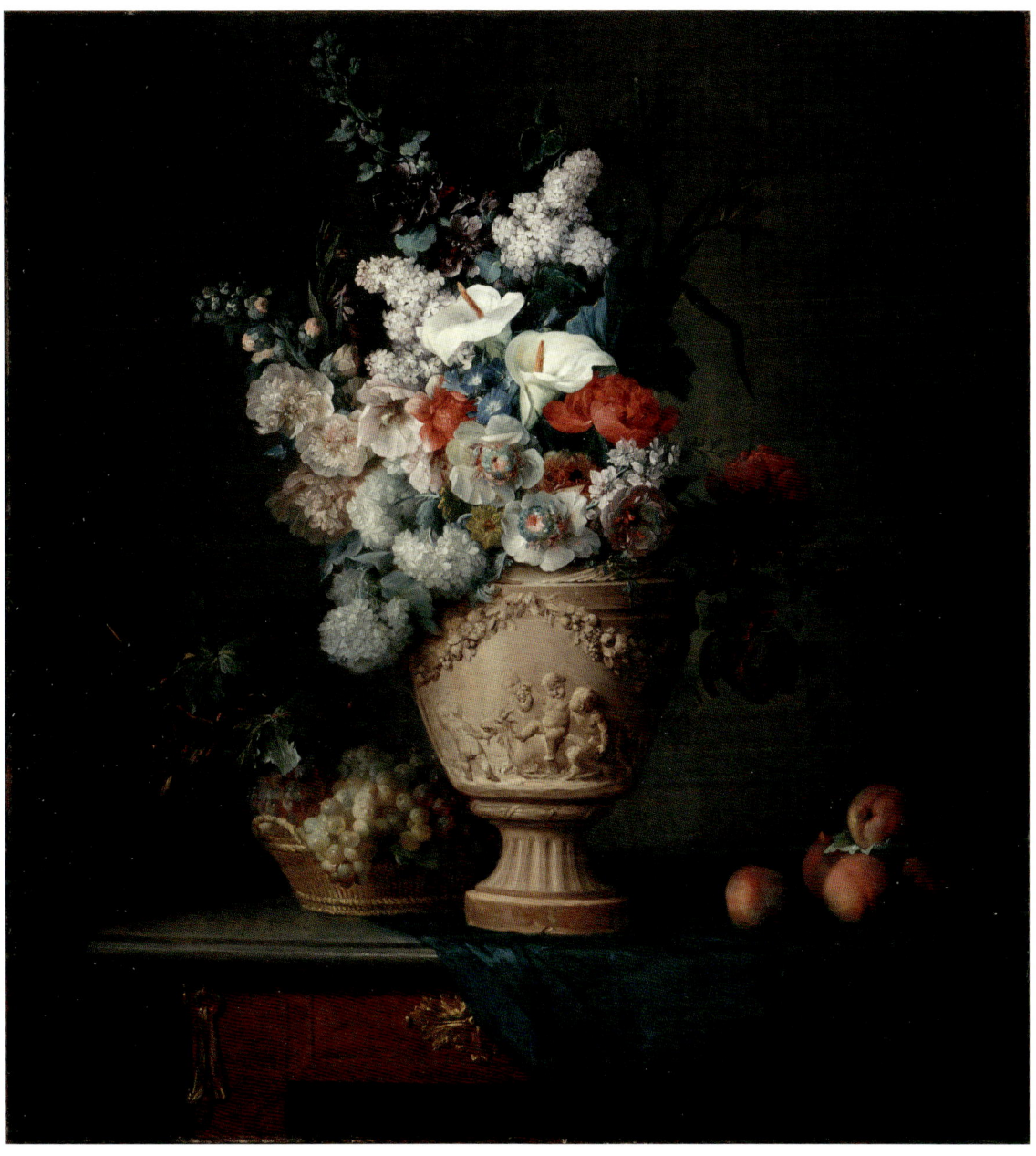

59 Anne Vallayer-Coster, *Bouquet of Flowers in a Terracotta Vase with Peaches and Grapes*, 1776, oil on canvas, 122.2 × 114 cm (48 ⅛ × 44 ⅞ in), Dallas Museum of Art, TX, Foundation for the Arts Collection, Mrs John B. O'Hara Fund and gift of Michael L. Rosenberg, 1998.51.FA

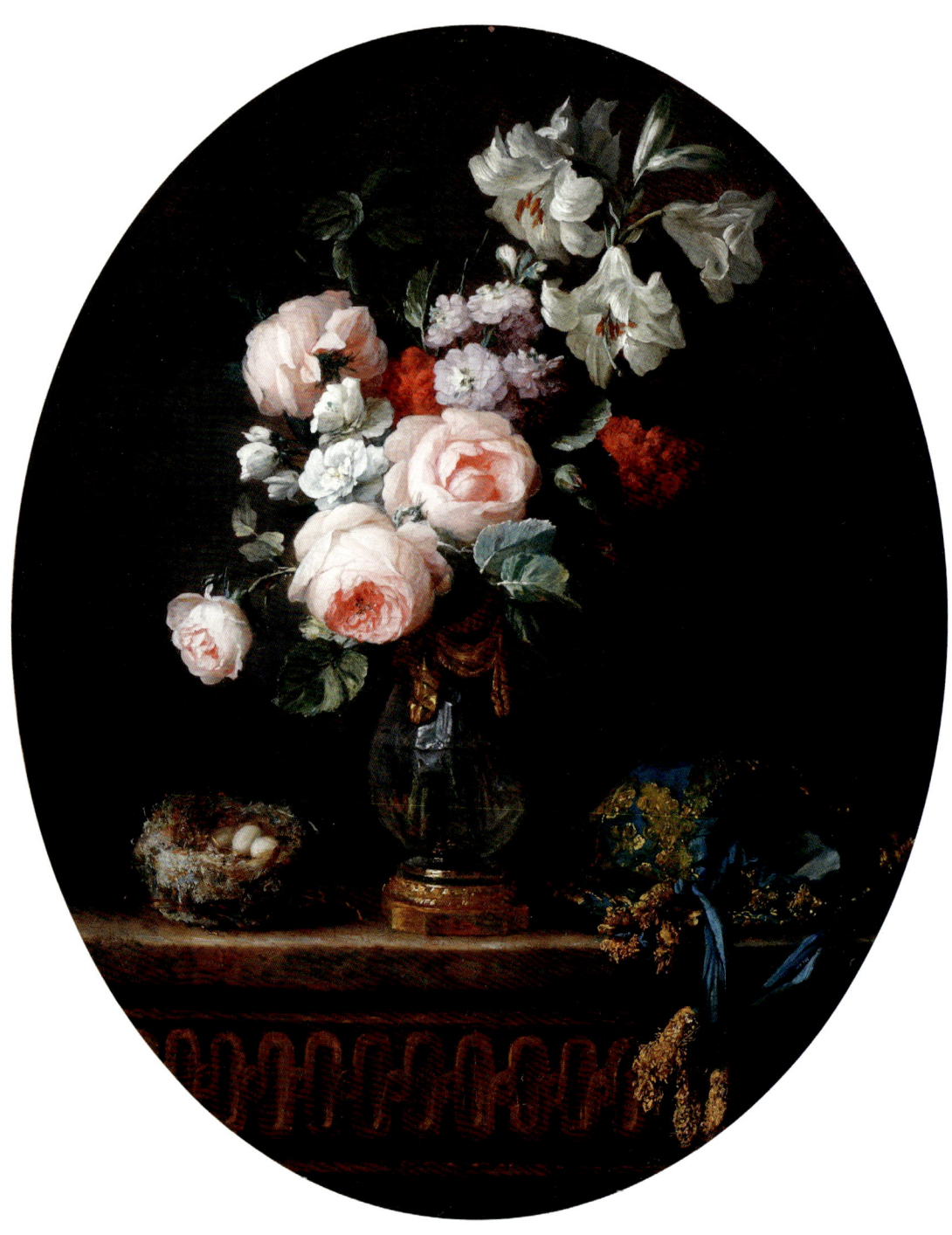

60 Anne Vallayer-Coster, *Vase of Flowers, Bird's Nest and Purse*, 1780–81, oil on canvas, 63 × 51.5 cm (24¾ × 20¼ in), The Horvitz Collection, Wilmington

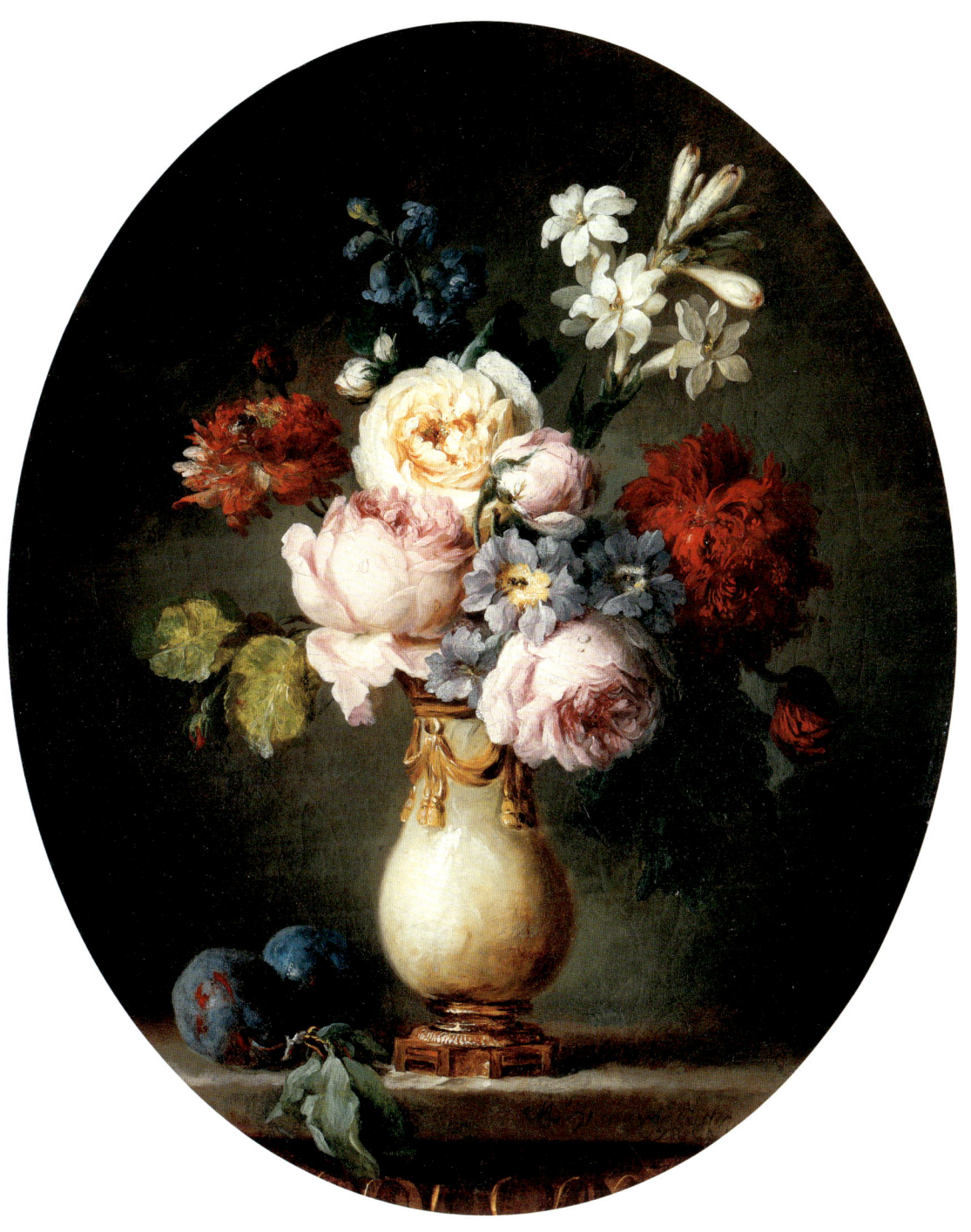

61 Anne Vallayer-Coster, *Vase of Flowers and Two Plums on a Marble Tabletop*, 1781, oil on canvas, 39.8 × 48 cm (15¾ × 18⅞ in),
Private collection

floral pictures offer striking material contrast between the flowers, vases and their small delicate accessories: a spindly conch shell, a ripe glaucous plum, and a bird's nest with two miniature eggs and a purse. The juxtaposition between the delicately woven bird's nest and the embroidered purse is a particularly compelling expression of feminine creativity, both avian and human. Vallayer-Coster manifests this metaphor by painting both twigs and metallic threads with the same wiry impasto.[47]

These audacious, loosely painted canvases from the 1770s and 1780s differ significantly from those of her contemporary, Spaendonck, who replaced Basseporte as the official painter of the Jardin du Roi after her death in 1780. Spaendonck operated within the meticulous, hyper-illusionistic mode of seventeenth-century Dutch flower painting (fig.62). His waxy striped tulip bulbs, roses and leaves are smoothly rendered and seem to be uniformly sealed with an antiperspirant glaze – in contrast to Vallayer-Coster's free, viscous touches of paint. Spaendonck's bouquets are no more capable of 'oozing' a scented fluid than were the polished porcelain flowers of Madame de Pompadour, who was known to douse her ceramic bouquets with perfume or 'plant' them with potpourri in order to enhance the multi-sensory experience of the objects.[48]

Several contemporary observers favorably compared Vallayer-Coster and Spaendonck's paintings. One critic observed that Vallayer-Coster 'sustains her reputation admirably, and even survives proximity to M. Van Spaendonck, the most famous of her rivals in the genre . . .'.[49] Another directly contrasted the painterly 'touch' of these two artists, suggesting that Vallayer-Coster's was 'the more precious touch, [his] the more virile' – an implicitly gendered characterization.[50] Diderot, meanwhile, who had been so complimentary of Vallayer-Coster's work in previous Salons, betrayed his own squeamishness in describing her loose handling. While admitting that there was a vague element of truth in her representations of flowers, he expressed

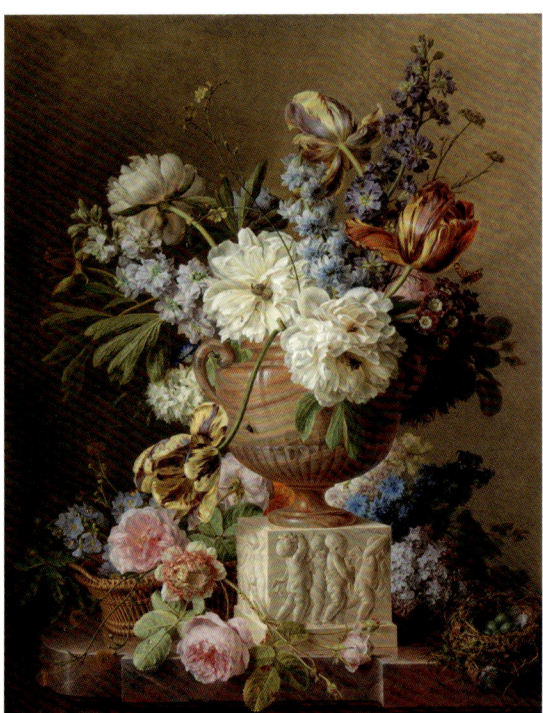

62 Gerard van Spaendonck, *Still Life of Flowers in Alabaster Vase*, 1783, oil on canvas, 80.5 × 64 cm (31¾ × 25¼ in), Rijksmuseum, Amsterdam

a cobalt-blue porcelain vase with gilt-bronze handles.[43] In this canvas, plentiful dabs of paint give form to individual petals of frilly chrysanthemum heads and hyacinth combs, while flecks of gold paint stand for the sweet secretions of the tubular honeysuckle. These relatively rare blooms are paired with another natural specimen: a miniature peach-colored conch shell.

The trio of works at the Salon of 1781 may have also included *Vase of Flowers, Bird's Nest and Purse* (fig.60)[44] and *Vase of Flowers and Two Plums on a Marble Tabletop* (fig.61).[45] These two paintings are both set upon a gilded marble desktop, each with vases of crystal and creamy porcelain, mounted with gilt-bronze *à la Grecque* (in the Greek style).[46] These

a distaste for what he described as her 'soft' touches, which for him indicated a lack of 'finesse' or control over her own fluid paints.[51]

AFTER THE REVOLUTION

Even if Diderot developed an aversion to her painting technique, other contemporaries praised Vallayer-Coster for excelling in the floral genre, while admonishing her for attempting to paint figurative subjects (see figs 52–3). As Bonnefoy de Bouyon wrote in 1787, 'Madame Vallayer-Coster is finally in her sphere, and the public applauds her . . . It is better to succeed in a pretty, minor genre than to stumble in a higher one.'[52]

As if taking her cue from this disparaging critic, Vallayer-Coster almost exclusively painted small-scale bouquets (with the occasional pile of fruit or dead game) in the 1790s and early 1800s. The reasons for her diminished productivity are potentially manifold, as other scholars have surmised. Her 1781 marriage to a successful lawyer may have eliminated the urgency of painting to support herself, although she certainly did not cease to paint or exhibit. Later, in the wake of the Revolution, Vallayer-Coster's former royal and aristocratic patrons were largely unable to commission large-scale paintings, which certainly threatened her practice.[53] Perhaps Vallayer-Coster continued to paint modestly sized florals precisely because of their perceived lack of political meaning – a form of self-preservation, particularly during the political instability and anti-royalist violence of the 1790s.

At the height of the Reign of Terror, the artist and her husband also briefly occupied another home in Villemomble-en-Montreuil. In this Parisian suburb, about 15 kilometers from the Louvre, she might have cultivated a flower garden of her own. She was completely absent from the Salons of 1791 and 1793, the first time that she declined to exhibit her work since she had been admitted to the Académie 20 years earlier. Importantly, 1791 also marked the death

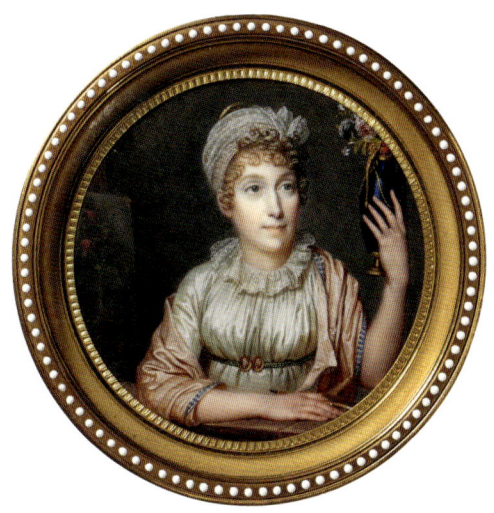

63 François Dumont, *Portrait of Anne Vallayer-Coster*, 1804, watercolor on ivory, diameter 7.6 cm (3 in), Cleveland Museum of Art, OH, The Edward B. Greene Collection 1943.639

of Vallayer-Coster's mother, Anne de la Fontaine. The artist's reasons for abstaining from those Salons may have been personal, rather than political.[54] She continued to participate, at irregular intervals, in the Salons of 1795 through 1817 (see Appendix).[55] This suggests that she considered herself a professional artist for the rest of her life, even after the execution of her most important patron, Queen Marie Antoinette, and the collapse of the Académie, in 1793.

Vallayer-Coster's reputation as a painter of flowers in this final phase of her career is perhaps best represented by a miniature portrait painted in 1804, the same year of Emperor Napoleon and Empress Josephine's coronation, by her friend and fellow academician, miniaturist François Dumont (fig.63).[56] The watercolor on ivory pictures the mature artist still at work, holding a *porte-crayon* in one hand and a blue porcelain vase filled with flowers in the other.

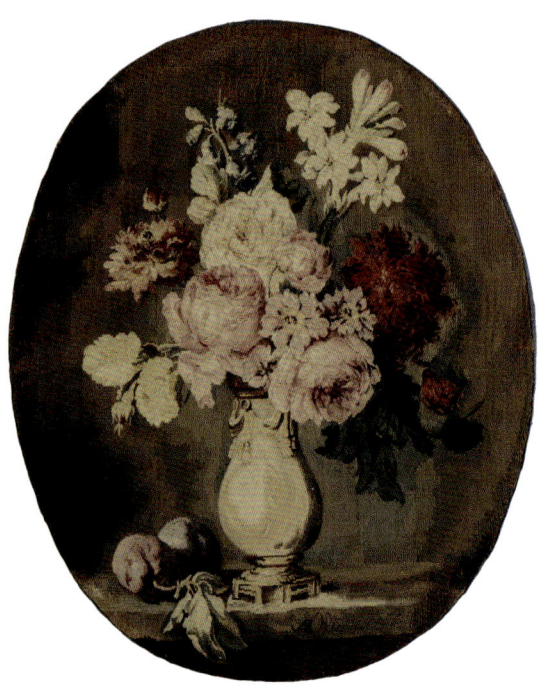

64 Deyrolle after Anne Vallayer-Coster, *Vase of Flowers and Two Plums on a Marble Tabletop*, 1800–4, wool and silk, 45.4 × 37.5 cm (17 ⅞ × 14 ¾ in), The Metropolitan Museum of Art, New York

The artist closely examines her subjects – and, if her sanguine and preternaturally youthful expression is any indication, smells them, as well. By then 60 years old, Vallayer-Coster is simply dressed: she wears a sheer, white lace wrapped around her natural auburn curls, and a loose, gauzy white dress – fashionable during the French Empire – is cinched under her breasts by a thin blue cord with gold medallions. Long gone are the corseted décolletage and elaborate updos pictured in the royal *académicienne* portraits of 1771 (see fig.1) and 1783 (see fig.4); she has adapted instead to the fashions of a new day.

Though her subject matter became somewhat redundant and the scale of her work was reduced in

this period, critics continued to respond to her floral works with sensual or liquid metaphors. In a review of the exhibition of 1804, for example, the editors of the *Journal des arts, de littérature et de commerce* wrote of Vallayer-Coster:

> Did Flora reveal her secrets to her? Did she instruct her to weave the crown of Spring? What truth, what freshness . . . Under Madame Vallayer's brush, it is just a simple flower gathered by a shepherdess; it is the small bouquet that the furtive hand of the lover will slip in the presence of a mother or a jealous rival.[57]

A few years later, Pierre-François Gueffier wrote of the artist at the Salon of 1810, 'It is impossible to pass by [her work] without admiring it; the best days of this *académicienne* were spent on flowers, she only had eyes for flowers, and they are born again under her fingers as under the dew of an eternal spring . . . sweet like the nectar of flowers'.[58] These quotes suggest that *ancien régime* ideas about the seductive powers of femininity, flowers and fragrant fluids lingered into the nineteenth century and continued to inform critical reactions to Vallayer-Coster's paintings.

EXPERIMENTS IN OTHER MEDIA

In this late phase of her career, Vallayer-Coster began to execute compositions for other media: tapestry, gouache, chalk and print. The Gobelins manufactory wove reproductions of several of Vallayer-Coster's still-life paintings. At least three wool and silk tapestries after her 1781 *Vase of Flowers and Two Plums on a Marble Tabletop* (see fig.61), for example, were woven by a designer named Deyrolle sometime between 1800 and 1804 (fig.64).[59] Many questions about these tapestries remain unanswered. Did Vallayer-Coster initiate their production? Had she maintained ties to the Gobelins manufactory through her late father, who was employed as a goldsmith there when she was a child – or perhaps through her patron Montullé,

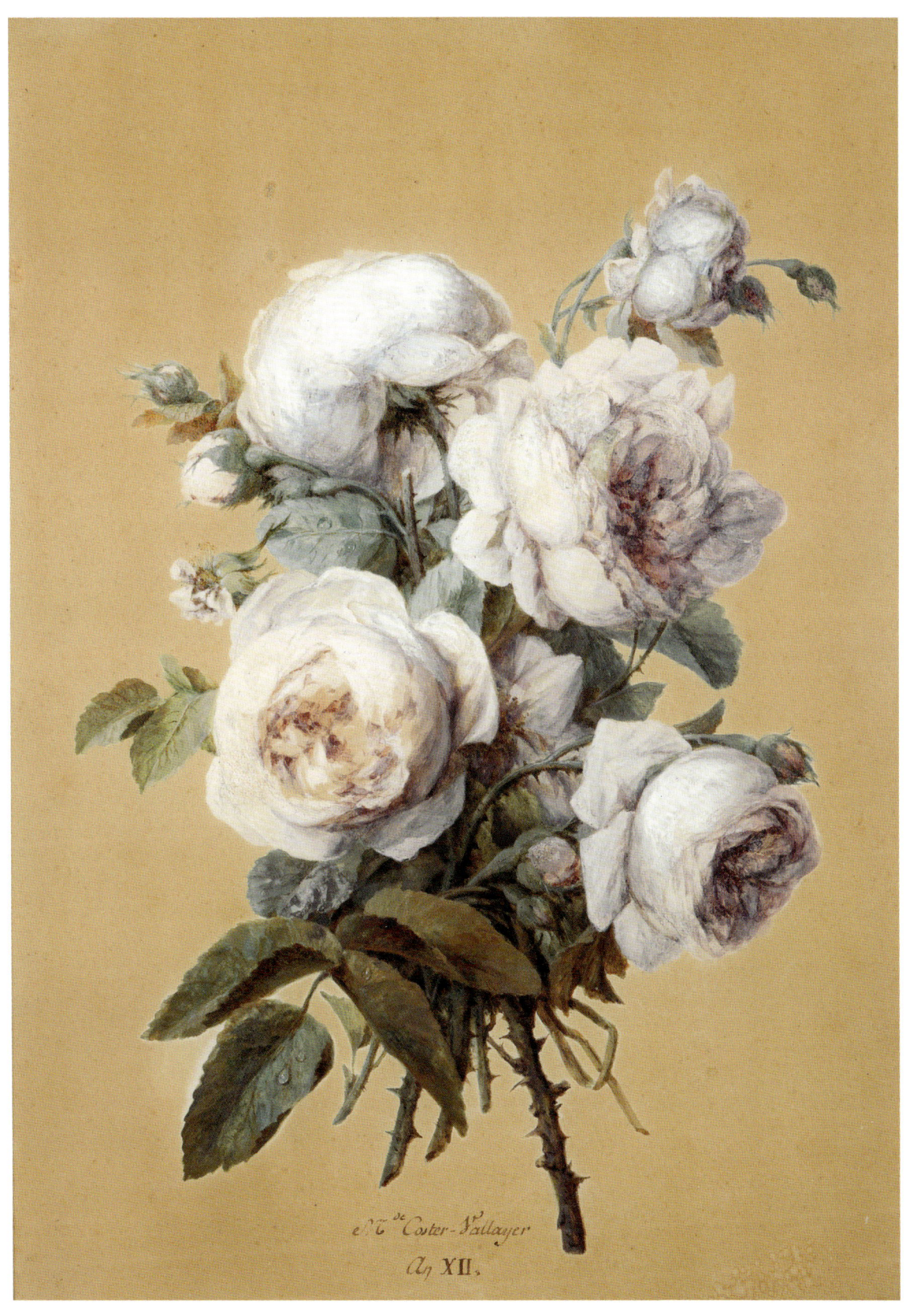

65 Anne Vallayer-Coster, *Bouquet of Roses*, 1804, gouache on brown paper, 35 × 25.5 cm (13 ¾ × 10 in), Chateaux de Malmaison et Bois-Preau/Reuil-Malmaison, France

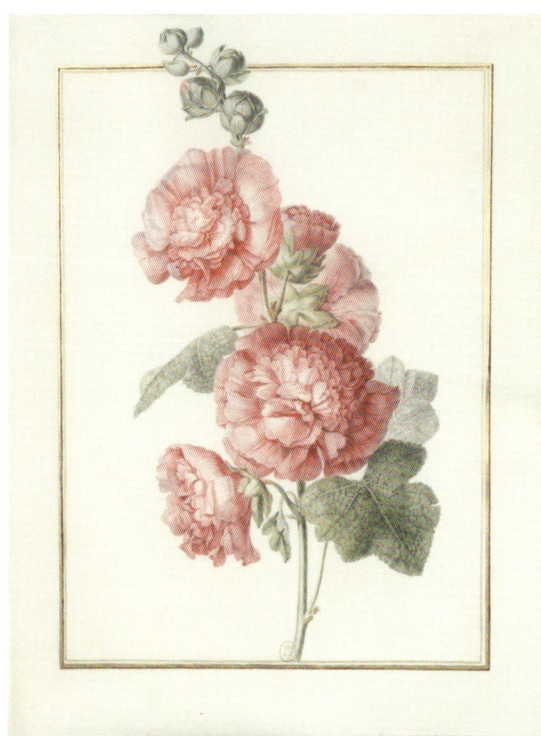

66 Madeleine Françoise Basseporte, *Rose* from *Recueil de dessins de fleurs*, c.1750, gouache on vellum, 40 × 31.1 cm (15 ¾ × 12 ¼ in), Bibliothèque nationale de France, Paris

who was the head of Gobelins until his death in 1787?[60] How many different designs were woven in total and how many sets produced? Were the ovular works intended to upholster the back of a chair or a fire screen – as in the example of two paintings exhibited at the Salons of 1798 and 1817?[61] Or were the tapestries intended to be framed and hung on a wall? The latter hypothesis is supported by the fact that the Metropolitan Museum of Art's *Vase of Flowers and Two Plums* tapestry has been tacked to a wooden stretcher, as an oil on canvas painting would be.

Vallayer-Coster's floral works on paper are less mysterious than the tapestries. She first exhibited this medium at the Salon of 1802: two drawings of flowers in black chalk.[62] At the Salon of 1804, she exhibited several floral studies, as well as two finished gouache paintings on paper, one depicting dahlias and the other, roses (fig.65), both of which belonged to the Empress Josephine.[63] On 27 Fructidor, Year XI (the twelfth month of the French Republican Calendar, corresponding to 14 September 1804), the Director of the Musée Napoléon (formerly the Louvre) wrote to the concierge of the Palais de Saint-Cloud, asking him to send these two sheets from the apartments of the Empress so that they might be exhibited at the Salon; afterwards, they were returned to her Château de Malmaison.[64] The impetus for this loan must have been the artist, another indication of her enduring desire for public recognition.

Empress Josephine, like her royal predecessor Queen Marie Antoinette, had a personal passion for flowers and gardening. In 1805, Josephine appointed Redouté as her official 'painter of flowers' – similar to the role he had performed for the Queen prior to the Revolution. Josephine commissioned from Redouté a series of watercolors depicting botanical specimens from the Malmaison gardens, which were later reproduced in a series of multi-volume reference books.[65] Vallayer-Coster's gouaches certainly adhere to the same compositional conventions of both Basseporte and Redouté: cut stems float, unmoored from the dirt, against blank backgrounds, highlighting the form of each specimen (fig.66). Even in her works on paper, Vallayer-Coster's painterly touch is undeniably thicker and looser than the crisp lines of Basseporte and Redouté.

Finally, Vallayer-Coster became involved in her own printmaking project during the first decade of the nineteenth century. Sometime after 1800, she began a series of grisaille drawings depicting small bunches of flowers, observed from two different perspectives, placed side by side on a single sheet. Around 1810, ten of those drawings were engraved by the printmaker Louis-Jean Allais (1762–1833). There is clear evidence

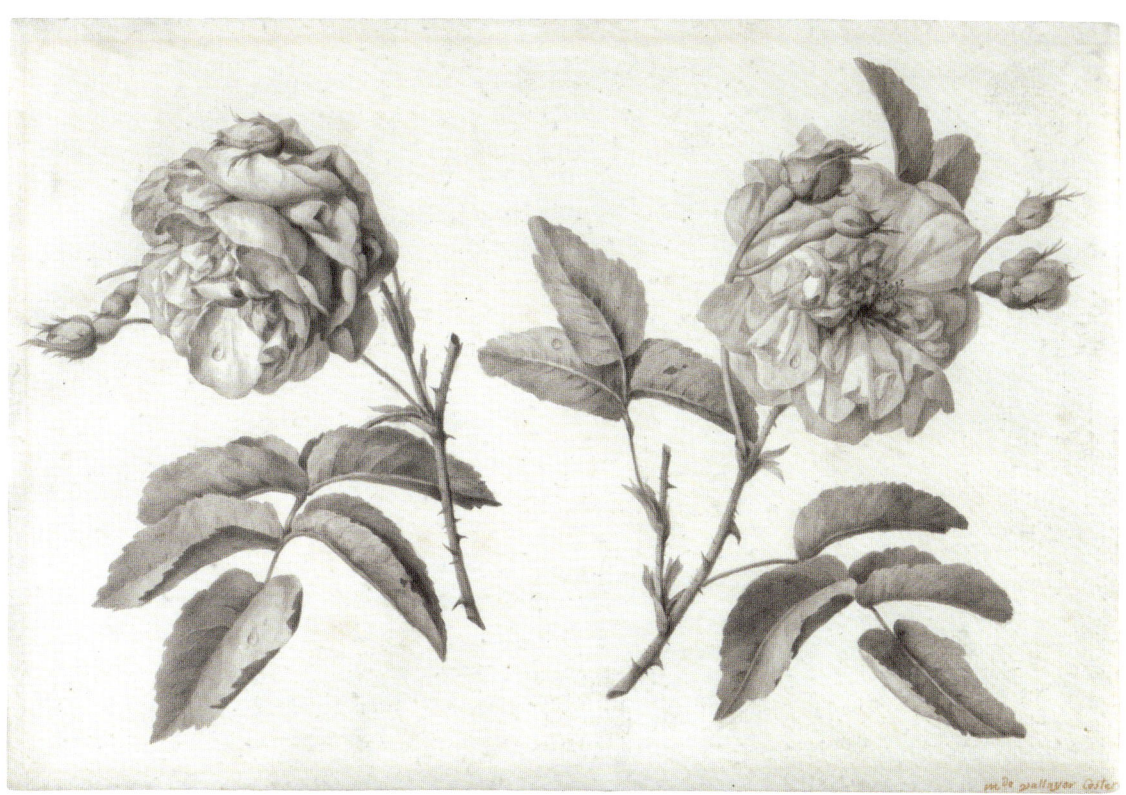

67 Anne Vallayer-Coster, *Two Roses*, c.1810, pen and gray ink, brush and gray wash over black chalk, 21 × 33.5 cm
   (8 ¼ × 13 ¼ in), The Metropolitan Museum of Art, New York

of Vallayer-Coster's participation in the speculative commission and sale of the resulting prints, which were advertised in the 10 April 1811 and 27 October 1811 issues of *Journal de l'Empire*. The April issue notes that the engravings are available for purchase in two locations in Paris: the artist's apartment on rue Neuve de Bons Enfants, as well as the shop of print dealer Jacques-Louis Bance (1761–1847) on the nearby rue Saint-Denis.[66] Later, the 1824 Coster sale catalogue indicates that the artist and her husband kept the original drawings, a few unsold prints and the ten copper plates used to produce the engravings.[67]

The precision of Vallayer-Coster's grisaille drawings suggest that they were prepared in anticipation of translation to print, though they still retain something of the soft and loose touches of her oil paintings. In the Metropolitan Museum of Art's *Two Roses*, for example, the thorns of the stem and the tendrils of rosebuds are rendered sharp with lines of pen with gray ink; delicate flourishes of gray wash applied with a brush represent the robust pleats of the rose, as well as the droplets of water that trickle down its petals and leaves (fig.67). The October issue of *Journal de l'Empire* also notes that a few of the prints for sale were retouched by the hand of the artist – that is, she applied color, likely gouache, to the engravings. Vallayer-Coster's painterly interventions suggest how highly she valued her own liquid touch

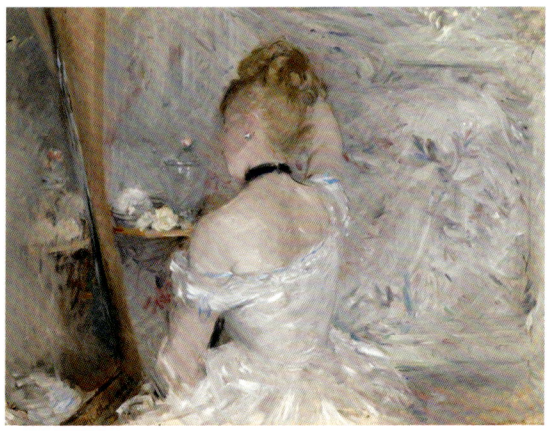

68 Berthe Morisot, *Woman at Her Toilette*, 1875–80, oil on
canvas, 60.3 × 80.4 cm (23 ¾ × 31 ⅝ in), The Art Institute
of Chicago, IL

and considered it her artistic signature, even with
printed reproductions of her work.

As the *Journal de l'Empire* descriptions make clear,
these prints were envisaged as collectable artworks as
well as artistic teaching tools, rather than scientific
botanical illustrations: 'A painter of flowers of merit,
such as Mad. Vallayer-Coster, was obliged to transmit
to her compatriots the lessons of an art that she has
brought to perfection . . . this work will also be useful
to manufacturers, to *pensionnaires*, to drawing schools,
to fathers who want to give their children the talent
of painting.'[68] While she is not known to have taught
any of her own students, as did Adélaïde Labille-
Guiard, Vallayer-Coster may have been motivated
to offer a new generation of female artists access
to the floral still-life tradition. After all, she had
benefited from the expertise of older female artists
like Basseporte or Reboul Vien – no doubt thanks to
the encouragement of her father, who wanted to give
his own child 'the talent of painting'.[69] The veritable
explosion of women artists after the Revolution
attests to the new professional possibilities in the

ever-shifting political landscape of Paris, long after
Vallayer-Coster's own academic debut.[70]

In Vallayer-Coster's lifetime and beyond, women
were closely associated with the delicate and ephemeral
beauty of flowers, as well as their intoxicating scents:
women smelled of flowers and flowers smelled of
women. Like women artists themselves, floral paintings
have long been dismissed as amateur and decorative,
and, therefore, vacant of serious meaning. Vallayer-
Coster's own late-career devotion to the subject has,
perhaps unfairly, come to define her entire oeuvre. Yet
her flower works were also the vehicles for some of her
most intriguing material innovations, including forays
into new media.

Still, it was the facture of her paintings – the 'soft'
and 'seductive' touches, so evocative of the smell of
flowers – that elicited the strongest, most sensorial
reactions from her contemporaries. Though many
flower painters followed in Vallayer-Coster's wake,
Impressionist Berthe Morisot (1841–95) is perhaps
the most significant heiress to her legacy. Though
we have no evidence that Morisot knew of Vallayer-
Coster's work, there are clear connections between
their painting techniques. In Morisot's canvas, *Woman
at Her Toilette*, for example, the floral wallpaper
is painted so loosely that the lavender, pink and
white petals seem to swirl off the wall, like a mist of
perfume or a cloud of scented powder (fig.68). As
the art critic Charles Ephrussi famously wrote of
Morisot, 'She grinds flower petals onto her palette, in
order to spread them later on her canvas.'[71] He invites
us to imagine that Morisot was painting with actual
flowers, employing their delicate color, shape, texture
and smell in order to seduce the viewer – as Vallayer-
Coster had done a century prior.

Conclusion

Much has been made of the quiet beauty of still-life paintings. Yet Vallayer-Coster's paintings are anything but silent; they speak directly to the textural and material facts of Parisian life. In this way, Vallayer-Coster's organoleptic still lifes 'seduce' the viewer, stimulating visceral memories of our own subjective experiences of the world and provoking our desires to touch, taste and smell. Her lush and evocative brushstrokes certainly appeal to the eye, but our fingers, tongues and noses cannot be indifferent to her work. This book endeavors to understand this corporeal aspect of Vallayer-Coster's paintings, and to understand them as they were seen in eighteenth-century France. Accordingly, Vallayer-Coster's paintings of paintbrushes, palettes, fruits, vegetables, meat, game, weapons, shells and flowers have been placed in dialogue with the Enlightenment discourse on the senses – as well as contemporary paintings, sculptures, prints, embroidery, metalwork and porcelain.

Several of Vallayer-Coster's works have appeared in the art market and been acquired by major museums within the past 20 years, including the British National Trust (see fig.11); Nationalmuseum, Stockholm (see fig.2); the Kimbell Art Museum in Fort Worth, Texas (see fig.30) and the Art Institute of Chicago (the 2025 gift of the Horvitz Collection; see

figs 41 and 60). Another important example is *Still Life with Flowers in an Alabaster Vase and Fruit*, which was sold at Christie's Paris to the National Gallery of Art in Washington, DC in 2023 (fig.69). This painting depicts a bountiful bouquet in a veiny alabaster vase with exquisitely carved ornament, including a thick garland and a young satyr perched on the handle. The floral arrangement is amplified by a panoply of fruits, including an upended pineapple with a spiky, armored body and serrated fronds.

Pineapples were grown in the French colonies in the Caribbean, and were later cultivated as rare botanical specimens and incorporated into elaborate desserts at the court of Versailles.[1] Symbolic of colonial power, exotic beauty, horticultural fascination and culinary delight, pineapples must have attracted Vallayer-Coster's royal and aristocratic patrons. Did the artist ever taste the stringy flesh and punchy, acidic sweetness of a pineapple herself? Or was she more intrigued by the unique bulbous shape, golden color and reptilian surface of the pineapple, which formed an intriguing textural contrast to the mossy peaches and juicy, translucent grapes?[2]

In any case, Vallayer-Coster exhibited this canvas at the Salon of 1783 and kept it all her life; it sold in her 1824 estate sale for 1100 francs, and was highlighted in that catalogue as 'the best of

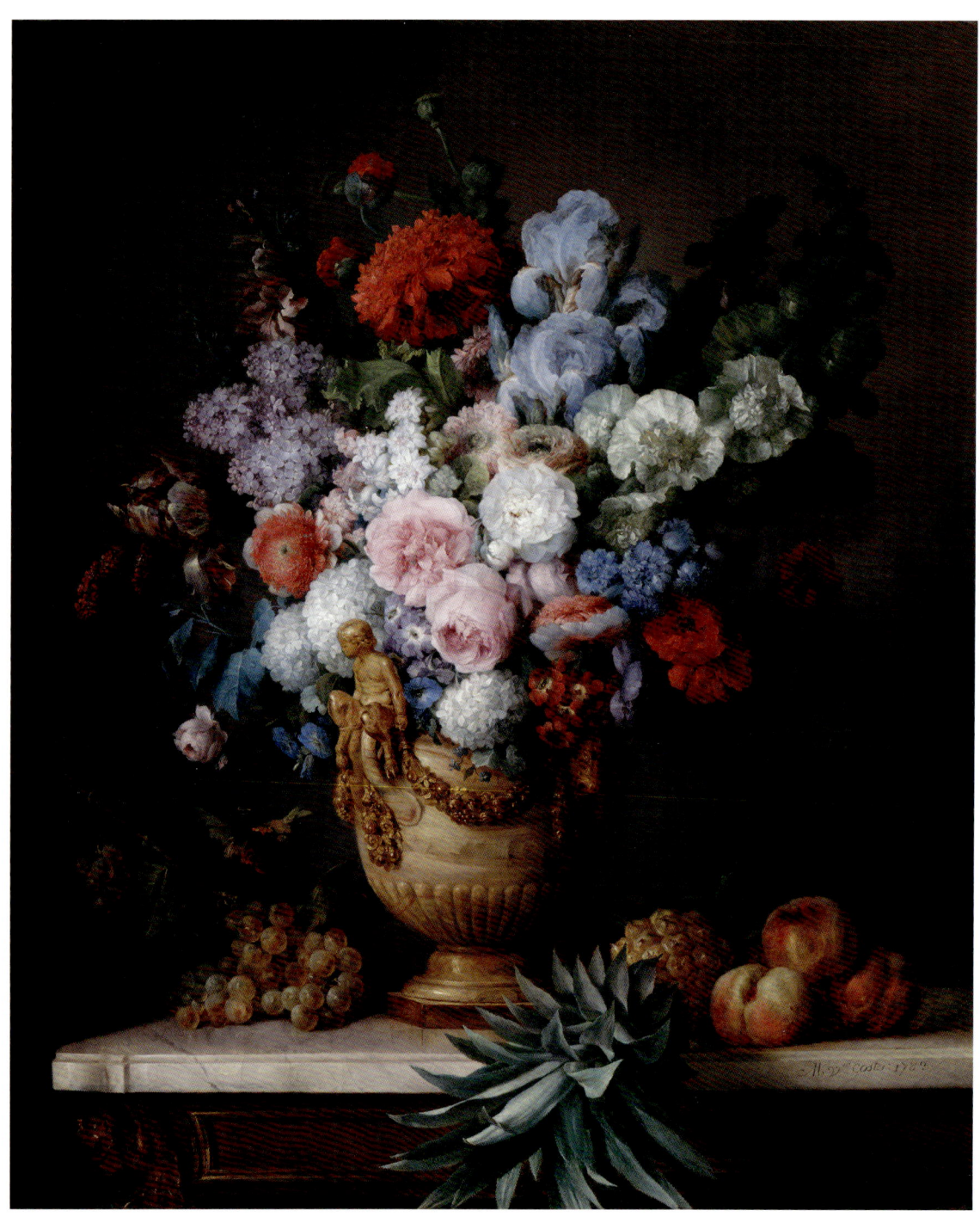

69 Anne Vallayer-Coster, *Still Life with Flowers in an Alabaster Vase and Fruit*, 1783, oil on canvas, 108.5 × 89.5 cm (42 ¾ × 35 ¼ in), National Gallery of Art, Washington, DC

her works'.[3] After disappearing from public view for nearly two centuries, this work achieved a new auction record for the artist in 2023 when it sold at Christie's and was acquired by the National Gallery of Art for €2.58 million (US $2.8 million).[4] This landmark acquisition will undoubtedly make Vallayer-Coster's paintings more accessible and her name more recognizable to a new generation of museum-goers – and buoy the contemporary market for her work. The Appendix that follows consolidates new information about many of her works, although a large number still remain untraced or in private collections. Future art historians may discover these works or reveal more information about Vallayer-Coster's extensive patronage network, or her political activities during and after the Revolution.

This study belongs to a growing tide of research into the roles of women in the visual, material and intellectual culture of Europe in the eighteenth century and beyond. Many of Vallayer-Coster's female peers within and outside of the Académie, for example, are the subject of recent and forthcoming publications and exhibitions by other feminist art historians and curators, all of which have greatly enriched the field.[5] For now, however, we remain frustrated by the dearth of documentation of many earlier *académiciennes*, to say nothing of those working outside of the official auspices of the Académie. Indeed, our work is far from finished.

Appendix

Vallayer-Coster at the Salon, 1771–1817

This Appendix provides an updated list of works shown by Vallayer-Coster at the Salon, the biannual public exhibition staged by the Académie at the Louvre in Paris (which was known by different names after the Revolution, including Musée central des Arts and the Musée Napoléon). This checklist is based on eighteenth- and nineteenth-century *livrets*, printed catalogues that included all of the works exhibited by the academicians at the Salon. The original *livrets* (with varying titles) have been digitized and made accessible to the public by the Bibliothèque nationale de France.[1]

The Appendix is also based upon the monumental research of the French scholar Marianne Roland Michel, who outlined the artist's oeuvre in a 1970 catalogue raisonné, and a 2002 monographic exhibition catalogue, referenced by their dates in the lists below.[2] Since Roland Michel's death in 2004, however, a number of Vallayer-Coster's paintings and works on paper have resurfaced on the art market. The Appendix notes the current or last known locations of these works, as well as the notable sales that have taken place after 2002.

KEY

Bold = Original *livret* descriptions
Italic = Author's notes

141. Military musical instruments
Painting of 5 feet by 4 feet
Current Location: Unknown (1970 no.259; 2002 no.13)

142. A young Arab woman, full-length
Painting of 5 feet by 3 feet 6 inches
Current Location: Unknown

143. A bowl
Painting of 2 feet 6 inches by 2 feet
Current Location: *The White Tureen*, Private collection (1970 no.222; 2002 no.14); fig.26

144. Fruits and vegetables
Painting of 2 feet 9 inches by 2 feet 2 inches
Current Location: Unknown

145. Two paintings representing diverse pieces of natural history
Each 4 feet by 3 feet
Current Location:
 – Unknown (1970 no.260)
 – *Still Life with Seashells and Coral*, Musée du Louvre, Paris (1970 no.261; 2002 no.11); fig.44

146. A *trompe l'oeil* bas-relief, children playing
Painting of 2 feet 2 inches by one foot 6 inches
Current Location: Possibly *Trompe l'oeil of a Terracotta Bas-relief
. . . Depicting Children and a Young Faun Gathering Grapes*,
Private collection; Sotheby's, New York, 29 January 2009,
lot 71 (1970 no.240)

147. A basket of plums
Painting of one foot 4 inches by 1 foot 1 inch
Current Location:
– Possibly *Basket of Plums*, Cleveland Museum of Art, OH;
fig.21
OR
– Private collection (1970 nos 52–9; 2002 no.7 or 117)
– see also Salon of 1773, no.143

148. A rabbit
Painting of 1 foot 8 inches by 1 foot 4 inches
Current Location: Unknown

149. Two paintings; one representing the attributes of
painting, sculpture & architecture; & the other, musical
instruments
These two paintings were her reception pieces to the
Académie
Current Location:
– *The Attributes of Painting, Sculpture and Architecture*,
Musée du Louvre, Paris (1970 no.257; 2002 no.6); fig.5
– *The Attributes of Music*, Musée du Louvre, Paris (1970
no.258; 2002 no.12); fig.6

Salon of 1773, Louvre
'Mlle Valayer [*sic*], *Académicienne*', p.29, nos 139–44

139. A desk with a marble figure and different attributes of
music and geography
Painting of 5 feet high by 4 feet wide
Current Location: Unknown

140. Portrait of Mme de [Bouhébent]
Current Location: Unknown (1970 no.309; 2002 no.21)

141. A basket of grapes. A basket of peaches
Oval paintings, 2 feet wide by 1 foot 8 inches high
Current Location:
– *Basket of Grapes*, Musée de Nissim de Camondo, Paris
(1970 no.132; 2002 no.15)
– Aguttes, Neuilly-sur-Seine, 20 December 2016, lot 59
(1970 nos 133 and 134; 2002 no.16)

142. A lunch. A bowl filled with apples
Paintings of 19 inches wide by 16 inches high
Current Location: Unknown (1970 nos 223 and 135; 2002 no.23)

143. A basket of plums
Painting of 17 inches wide by 14 inches high
Current Location:
– Possibly *Basket of Plums*, Cleveland Museum of Art, OH;
fig.21
OR
– Private collection (1970 nos 52–9; 2002 no.7 or 117)
– see also Salon of 1771, no.147

144. A small *trompe l'oeil* bas-relief after M. de la Rue
One foot wide by 8 inches high
Current Location: Private collection, England (1970 no.365;
2002 no.19)

Salon of 1775, Louvre
'Mlle VALLAYER, *Académicienne*', pp 18–19, nos 98–102

98. An urn, fruits and a lobster
This painting, 6 feet by 4, belongs to M. Montullé, free
associate of the Académie
Current Location: Possibly *Still Life with Lobster*, Musée du
Louvre, Paris (1970 no.151; 2002 no.99); fig.33
– see also Salon of 1817, no.737

99. A bust of Flora & a vase filled with flowers on a desk
4 feet 9 inches by 4 feet
Current Location: *Vase of Flowers with a Bust of Flora*, Private
collection; Sotheby's, New York, 27 January 2022, lot 49
(1970 no.1; 2002 no.30); fig.56

100. A bust of Ceres & attributes of the harvest, with different species of vegetables
4 feet 6 inches by 5 feet
Current Location: *The Attributes of Hunting and Gardening*, Basildon Park, Berkshire, National Trust (1970 no.283; 2002 no.24 as lost); fig.11

101. Portrait of M. L'Abbé le Monier
2 feet by one foot 7 inches
Current Location: Unknown

102. Several paintings of flowers and fruits under the same number
Current Location:
– *Bouquet of Flowers with a Purse*, Fondation Ephrussi de Rothschild, Saint-Jean Cap Ferrat (1970 no.63; 2002 no.26); fig.55
– *Bouquet of Flowers with Grapes and Apples*, Fondation Ephrussi de Rothschild, Saint-Jean Cap Ferrat (1970 no.77; 2002 no.31)

Salon of 1777, Louvre
'Mlle VALLAYER, *Académicienne*', pp 20–21, nos 100–7

100. Two paintings of flowers and fruits
4 feet by 3 feet and a half. They belong to M. de Montullé, Secretary of Commandments to the Queen [Marie Leszczyńska]
Current Location:
– *Bouquet of Flowers in a Blue Porcelain Vase*, Dallas Museum of Art, TX (1970 no.3; 2002 no.36); fig.58
– *Bouquet of Flowers in a Terracotta Vase with Peaches and Grapes*, Dallas Museum of Art, TX (1970 no.2; 2002 no.37); fig.59

101. Two paintings: one, a vase of Chinese porcelain with marine plants, shells and different species of minerals; the other, armor, a bust of Minerva, surrounded by military awards, united under a laurel crown
These paintings, 5 feet 5 inches by 4 feet 1 inch, belong to Madame Vissitier
Current Location:
– Private collection (1970 no.265; 2002 no.41)
– *Bust of Minerva with Military Attributes*, Private collection; Sotheby's, New York, 2 February 2018, lot 292 (1970 no.264; 2002 no.44); fig.13

102. Two round paintings, one of flowers in a crystal vase; the other of flowers in a lapis vase
18 inches
Current Location: Unknown (possibly 1970 nos 6 and 25; 2002 nos 39 and 38)

103. Another painting of flowers in a basket
The same shape and the same dimensions as the preceding works
Current Location: Unknown

104. Portrait of M. [Joseph-Charles] Roettiers, former engraver of coins
Oval painting, 2 feet by 1 foot 7 inches high
Current Location: *Portrait of M. [Joseph-Charles] Roettiers*, Musée national des châteaux de Versailles et de Trianon (1970 no.313; 2002 no.46)

105. Two small paintings: one, a young woman, with a child on her knee, who offers her flowers; the other, a young girl who has just received a letter
One foot by 9 inches
Current Location: Unknown

106. A young person showing a statue of Love to his girlfriend
Small oval painting, 13 inches by 9
Current Location: Unknown

107. Two small *trompe l'oeil* bas-reliefs of children: one, Winter; the other, Spring
Current Location: Both Private collection (1970 nos 243 and 244; 2002 nos 42 and 47)

Salon of 1779, Louvre
'Mlle Vallayer, *Académicienne*', pp 27–8, nos 102–8

102. A vestal crowned with roses and holding a bouquet of flowers
This small painting, oval-shaped, belongs to the Queen
 [Marie Antoinette]
Current Location: Private collection (1970 no.318; 2002 no.53)

103. Flowers in a lapis vase
This oval-shaped painting, 2 feet high by 18 inches wide,
 belongs to M. le Comte de Merle
Current Location: Unknown

104. Two small paintings; one of peaches and a silver goblet;
& the other, of pâté, liqueur and grapes
They are 15 inches wide by 12 high, & belong to M. Gérardon
 de Marigny [Jean Girardot de Marigny?]
Current Location: Unknown (1970 nos 139 and 140; 2002
 no.48)

105. A basket of plums, a lemon, & others
Oval painting, 13 inches high by 15 wide
Current Location: Possibly *Still Life with Plums and a Lemon*,
 Fine Arts Museum of San Francisco, CA (1970 no.138;
 2002 no.49); fig.23

106. Two fantasy figures
1 foot high by 10 inches wide
Current Location: Unknown

107. Flowers & grapes
15 inches high by 12 wide
Current Location: Unknown

108. Portrait of M. Le Comte de M. . .
Oval painting, 2 feet high by 1 foot 6 inches wide
Current Location: Possibly *Portrait of Comte de Mesnilglaise*
 Wearing a Medal of the Order of Saint Louis, Piasa, Paris,
 22 June 2007, lot 202

Salon of 1781, Louvre
'Mme. VALLAYER-COSTER', p.22, nos 104–7

104. Portrait of Madame Sophie de France in the interior of
her cabinet, holding a plan of the Abbey of Argentière
6 feet high by 5 feet 10 inches wide
Current Location: Unknown

105. Three small oval paintings, of flowers and fruits
Current Location:
 – Possibly *Vase of Flowers, Bird's Nest and Purse*, The Horvitz
  Collection, Wilmington; Sotheby's, Paris, 25 March 2014, lot 74
  (1970 no.71; 2002 no.62); fig.60
 – *Vase of Flowers with Shell*, The Metropolitan Museum of Art,
  New York (1970 no.67; 2002 no.61); fig.45
 – *Vase of Flowers and Two Plums on a Marble Tabletop*, Private
  collection; Christie's, New York, 26 January 2005, lot 50 (1970
  nos 429–31; 2002 no.67); fig.61

106. A basket of grapes
Current Location: Unknown

107. Portrait of Madame **, arranging flowers in a vase
3 feet 2 inches high, by 5 feet 10 inches wide
Current Location: Possibly related to *Portrait of Madame*
 Adélaide Auguié, Private collection; Sotheby's, London,
 8 July 2009, lot 41 (1970 no.333; 2002 no.123); fig.52
 [dimensions do not match *livret*]

Salon of 1783, Louvre
**'Mme. VALLAYER-COSTER, *Académicienne*', pp 19–20,
nos 75–81**

75. Portrait of M. L'Abbé ***
3 feet 9 inches high by 2 feet 3 inches wide
Current Location: Unknown

76. Painting of Game, with attributes of the hunt
2 feet 10 inches wide by 2 feet 4 inches high; it belongs to
 M. Gérardot de Marigny [Jean Girardot de Marigny]
Current Location: *Still Life with Game*, Toledo Museum of
 Art, OH (1970 no.286; 2002 no.69); fig.40

77. A painting representing an alabaster vase filled with flowers, on a table with several types of fruits, such as pineapples, peaches and grapes
3 feet 4 inches high by 2 feet 9 inches wide
Current Location: *Still Life with Flowers in an Alabaster Vase and Fruit*, National Gallery of Art, Washington, DC; Christie's, Paris, 15 June 2023, lot 42 (1970 no.4; 2002 p.61); fig.69

78. A child holding a pigeon in one hand and a cherry in the other
Oval painting of 1 ½ feet high by 13 inches wide
Current Location: Unknown

79. A young female cook flaying an eel
17 inches high by 12 wide
Current Location: Unknown

80. Two small oval paintings, one representing a woman selling fish, and the other a woman selling flowers
Current Location: Unknown

81. Another small oval representing two golden plovers [small birds] and a young rabbit
This painting, painted on copper, is 7 inches high by 6 wide
Current Location: Unknown

Salon of 1785, Louvre
'Mde. VALLAYER-COSTER, *Académicienne*', **pp 19–20, nos 56–61**

56. A full-length portrait of Madamoiselle de Coigny, gathering flowers in her garden
5 ½ feet high by 4 feet 5 inches wide
Current Location: Possibly *Portrait of a Woman Holding a Basket of Flowers*, Private collection; Christie's, Paris, 28 Oct 2022, lot 29; fig.53

57. Portrait of M. l'Evêque de ***
5 feet 4 inches high by 3 feet 6 inches wide
Current Location: Unknown

58. Portrait of Madame de Saint-Huberty in the guise of Dido
5 ½ feet high by 4 feet 5 inches wide
Current Location: *Madame de Saint-Huberty in the Role of Dido*, National Museum of Women in the Arts, Washington, DC (1970 no.345; 2002 no.74)

59. Painting of game, comprised of a duck, a teal-headed duck, a hare, etc.
3 feet 6 ½ inches high by 2 feet 8 inches wide, belonging to M. le chevalier de Roslin [Alexandre Roslin]
Current Location: Possibly Tajan, Paris, 20 June 2007, lot 30

60. A hunting dog with its paw on a hare; one can see a rifle, a game bag, a powder flask, hung from the trunk of a tree
This painting is 4 feet 1 inch high by 3 ½ feet wide
Current Location: Unknown

61. Small painting of flowers in a glass vase
1 ½ feet high by 1 foot 8 inches wide
Current Location: Unknown

Salon of 1787, Louvre
'Mde. VALLAYER-COSTER, *Académicienne*', **pp 15–16, nos 68–75**

68. A dog near a deer and other game, like a hare, pheasant, etc. in front of a landscape
4 ½ feet high by 3 ½ feet wide
Current Location: Unknown

69. Flowers in a porphyry vase adorned with gilt bronze
2 feet high by 1 foot 8 inches wide
Current Location: *Still Life with Flowers and Fruit*, Musées d'art et d'histoire, Ville de Genève (1970 no.82; 2002 no.81)

70. Two round paintings, one representing a basket of grapes, and the other an alabaster bowl adorned with gilt bronze and filled with peaches
Current Location: Both Private collection (1970 nos 147 and 148; 2002 nos 74 and 75)

71. Two paintings, one with two dead rabbits, a powder keg and other attributes of the hunt, and the other, a rooster and white chicken
Current Location:
  – Unknown (1970 no.293; 2002 no.84)
  – *A Rooster and a White Chicken on a Ledge*, Musée de Tessé, Le Mans (1970 no.294; 2002 no.80)

72. A silver vessel with glasses, mackerel, a cruet of oil, etc.
Current Location: *Still Life with Mackerel*, Kimbell Art Museum, Fort Worth, TX; Sotheby's, London, 6 July 2011, lot 7 (1970 no.227; 2002 no.83); fig.30

73. Oval portrait of M. ***
Current Location: Unknown

74. Another oval portrait
Current Location: Unknown

75. Two small oval paintings, one representing a duck and the other two red partridges painted on copper
Current Location:
  – *Still Life with Duck*, Musée des beaux-arts de Strasbourg (1970 no.291; 2002 no.82)
  – Private collection (1970 no.301; 2002 no.78)

Salon of 1789, Louvre
'Mde. VALLAYER-COSTER, *Académicienne*', pp 13–14, nos 48–51

48. A figurative model, in white marble, grouped with coral, shells & minerals
Height, 3 feet; width, 2 feet 8 inches
Current Location: Private collection (1970 no.266 or 267; 2002 no.87) [dimensions do not match *livret*]

49. A child making a house of cards
Oval painting, 3 feet by 2 feet 8 inches
Current Location: Unknown (1970 no.348; 2002 no.85 as lost)

50. Flowers in a crystal vase
2 feet square
Current Location: Unknown

51. Two small *trompe l'oeil* paintings of bronze bas-reliefs
Width, 1 foot 3 inches; height, 1 foot 1 inch
Current Location: Unknown

Salon of 1791, Louvre

None

Salon of 1793, Louvre

None

Salon of 1795, Museum au Louvre
'Citoyenne VALLAYER-COSTER, Galleries du Louvre', p.61, no.504

504. Several paintings of flowers and still lifes
Current Location: Unknown

Salon of 1796, Musée central des arts

None

Salon of 1798, Musée central des arts
'Cnne. COSTER (*née* Vallayer), galeries du Louvre',
pp 16–17, nos 95–8

95. Flowers in a porcelain vase with gilt bronze
This painting is intended to serve as a fire screen
Current Location: Unknown

96. Flowers in a crystal vase with fruits
Oval painting on copper
Current Location: Unknown

97. Two oval paintings of flowers, oil paint on silk taffeta;
same number.
Current Location: Unknown

98. Two round paintings forming the tops of [snuff?] boxes.
One of flowers and a bronze vase; the other with attributes of
the hunt and game
Oil paint on silk taffeta
Current Location: Unknown

Salon of 1799, Muséum central des arts

None

Salon of 1800, Muséum central des arts
'Mme VALAYER COSTER [*sic*]', p.63, nos 356–8

356. A painting representing game, a ham, etc.
Current Location: Unknown

357. Two paintings of flowers
Current Location: Unknown

358. A painting representing a small terracotta bas-relief
Current Location: Unknown

Salon of 1801, Muséum central des arts
'Mme. VALAYER COSTER, member of former *Académie*',
p.60. nos 339–40

339. Alabaster vase filled with flowers
Current Location: Private collection (1970 no.34 as lost; 2002
    no.92)

340. Crystal bowl filled with peaches and grapes
Current Location: Unknown

Salon of 1802, Muséum central des arts
'Mme. VALAYER-COSTER, of the former *Académie*',
p.59, nos 283–4

283. A painting representing a basket of peaches, grapes, and
a granite vase adorned with gilt bronze
Current Location: Private collection (1970 no.151; 2002 no.95)

284. Two black chalk drawings representing flowers
Current Location: Unknown

Salon of 1804, Musée Napoléon
'Mme. VALLAYER-COSTER', p.84, nos 480–85

480. Roses in a glass, next to a bunch of grapes
Current Location: Possibly *Still Life of Roses in a Glass Vase,
    with Grapes Beside*, Private collection; Sotheby's, New
    York, 26 January 2023, lot 136 (1970 nos 84 and 86; 2002
    no.96)

481. Dahlias
Gouache
Current Location: *Bouquet of Dahlias*, Napoleonmuseum
    Arenenberg, Salenstein, Switzerland (1970 no.393; 2002
    no.146)

482. Roses . . .
Same
Current Location: *Bouquet of Roses*, Chateaux de Malmaison et
  Bois-Preau; Artcurial, Paris, 28 March 2017, lot 131 (1970
  no.392); fig.65

483. Anemones and other flowers
Current Location: Unknown

484. A branch of lilac
Current Location: Unknown

485. Branch of hyacinth
Current Location: Unknown

Salon of 1806, Musée Napoléon

None

Salon of 1808, Musée Napoléon

None

Salon of 1810, Musée Napoléon
'Mad. VALLAYER COSTER, of the former *Académie*, rue
Neuve-des-Bons-Enfans, no.19', p.100, nos 796–8

796. Roses in a crystal vase
Current Location: Unknown

797. Anemones, daisies, etc.
Current Location: Unknown

798. Flowers and fruits, under the same number
Current Location: Unknown

Salon of 1812, Musée Napoléon

None

Salon of 1814, Musée royal des arts

None

Salon of 1817, Musée royal des arts
'VALLAYER-COSTER (Mme.)', pp 85–6, nos 736–7

736. Flowers in a Chinese porcelain vase, ornamented with
gilt bronze
For a fire screen
Current Location: Unknown

737. A table laden with a grand vase, a lobster, different fruits,
game, etc.
This painting belongs to the King [Louis XVIII]
Current Location: *Still Life with Lobster*, Musée du Louvre,
  Paris (1970 no.151; 2002 no.99); fig.33
  – see also Salon of 1775, no.98

Notes

For references to the eighteenth-century Salon catalogues, see the Appendix.

INTRODUCTION

1   Marianne Roland Michel, *Anne Vallayer-Coster (1744–1818)*, Comptoir International du Livre, Paris, 1970.

2   Laura Auricchio, *Adélaïde Labille-Guiard: Artist in the Age of Revolution*, Getty Publications, Los Angeles, CA, 2009; Mary D. Sheriff, *The Exceptional Woman: Elisabeth Vigée-Lebrun and the Cultural Politics of Art*, University of Chicago Press, Chicago, IL, 1996; Joseph Baillio, Katharine Baetjer and Paul Lang (eds), *Vigée Le Brun: Woman Artist in Revolutionary France*, exh.cat., The Metropolitan Museum of Art, New York, 2015.

3   Christian Michel, *The Académie Royale de Peinture et de Sculpture: The Birth of the French School, 1648–1793*, Getty Publications, Los Angeles, CA, 2018, p.xvi.

4   Colin B. Bailey, 'A Still-Life Painter and Her Patrons: Collecting Vallayer-Coster, 1770–1789', in Eik Kahng and Marianne Roland Michel (eds), *Anne Vallayer-Coster: Painter to the Court of Marie-Antoinette*, exh.cat., Dallas Museum of Art, Dallas, TX, 2002, pp 59–73, on p.62.

5   Pierre Rosenberg, *Chardin*, exh.cat., The Metropolitan Museum of Art, New York, 2000.

6   Kahng and Roland Michel (eds), *Vallayer-Coster*.

7   Sheriff, *The Exceptional Woman*.

8   See, among many others, Melissa Hyde, 'Marie-Thérèse Reboul (Madame Vien): More than a Footnote in Art History', in Mechthild Fend, Jennifer Germann and Melissa Hyde (eds), *Thinking Women and Eighteenth-Century Art: Strategic Reinterpretations*, Amsterdam University Press, Amsterdam, 2024, pp 239–80.

9   Paris Spies-Gans, *A Revolution on Canvas: The Rise of Women Artists in Britain and France, 1760–1830*, Yale University Press, New Haven, CT, and London, 2022.

10 Sarah R. Cohen, *Enlightened Animals in Eighteenth-Century Art: Sensation, Matter, and Knowledge*, Bloomsbury, London and New York, 2021; Ewa Lajer-Burcharth, *The Painter's Touch: Boucher, Chardin, Fragonard*, Princeton University Press, Princeton, NJ, 2018; among others.

11 John C. O'Neal, *The Authority of Experience: Sensationist Theory in the French Enlightenment*, Pennsylvania State University Press, University Park, PA, 1996.

12 Étienne Bonnot de Condillac, *Traité des sensations*, Chez de Bure l'aîné, London and Paris, 1754.

13 Rosenberg, *Chardin*, 2000, p.107.

14 Denis Diderot, *Lettres sur les sourds et les muets: à l'usage de ceux qui entendent & qui parlent*, Jean-Baptiste-Claude II Bauche, Paris, 1751, p.12.

15 Denis Diderot, *Oeuvres*, ed. André Billy, Gallimard, Paris, 1951, pp 949–58, on p.950.

16 Sheriff, *The Exceptional Woman*, p.21.

17 ibid.

18 Jean-Jacques Rousseau, *Emile, or, On Education: Includes Emile and Sophie, or, The Solitaries* (1762), trans. Allan Bloom, Basic Books, New York, 1979, p.326.

19 Nicholas Mirzoeff, 'Revolution, Representation, Equality: Gender, Genre, and Emulation in the Académie Royale de Peinture et Sculpture, 1785–93', *Eighteenth-Century Studies*, vol.31, no.2, Winter 1997/8, pp 153–74, on p.164.

20 ibid., p.162.

21 M. Guichard, 'Académie royal de peinture & sculpture', *Mercure de France*, September 1770, pp 174–6, on pp 175–6.

22 Marianne Roland Michel, 'Vallayer in Her Time', in Kahng and Roland Michel (eds), *Vallayer-Coster*, pp 13–37, on p.18.

23 ibid.

24 Pierre Rémy, *Catalogue de tableaux précieux . . . d'un cabinet distingue* [Madame du Barry], Chez M. Cattilan, Paris, 22 December 1775, p.15, no.34.

25 *La lanterne magique aux Champs-Elysées, ou Entretien des grands peintres sur le Sallon de 1775*, Paris, 1775, p.28.

26 Roland Michel, 'Vallayer in Her Time', p.33.

27 Mario Naves, 'Subtle Pleasures of Still Life Blossom in Specialist Show', *The New York Observer*, 17 February 2003, http://observer.com/2003/02/subtle-pleasures-of-still-life-blossom-in-specialist-show/.

28 Blake Gopnik, 'Sensual Still Lifes: Built to Lust?', *The Washington Post*, 15 September 2002, https://www.washingtonpost.com/archive/lifestyle/style/2002/09/15/sensual-still-lifes-built-to-lust/5c7e540d-7cf6-41c2-98bf-4d97f4201800/?noredirect=on&utm_term=.08dcfd526909.

29 Amy Freund, 'Good Dog! Jean-Baptiste Oudry and the Politics of Animal Painting', in Heather MacDonald (ed.), *French Art of the Eighteenth Century: The Michael L. Rosenberg Lecture Series at the Dallas Museum of Art*, Yale University Press, New Haven, CT, and London, 2016, pp 67–80; Amy Freund, 'Men and Hunting Guns', in Jennifer G. Germann and Heidi A. Strobel (eds), *Materializing Gender in Eighteenth-Century Europe*, Routledge, New York, 2016, pp 17–34; Cohen, *Enlightened Animals*.

30 Roland Michel, *Vallayer-Coster*, p.214, no.327; Kahng and Roland Michel (eds), *Vallayer-Coster*, pp 205–6, nos 55, 59 and 60.

31 Roland Michel, *Vallayer-Coster*, pp 222–4, no.345; Kahng and Roland Michel (eds), *Vallayer-Coster*, pp 208–9, no.74, pl.35.

32 Roland Michel, *Vallayer-Coster*, p.208, no.310; Kahng and Roland Michel (eds), *Vallayer-Coster*, p.200, no.22, pl.10; Magnus Olausson, 'Anne Vallayer-Coster, *Portrait of a Violinist*', *Art Bulletin of Nationalmuseum Stockholm*, vol.22, 2015, pp 17–20.

33 *Journal de Paris*, no.258, 15 September 1785, p.1064; 'Exposition des peintures, sculptures & gravures de MM. de l'Académie royale, dans le Sallon du Louvre, depuis de 25 août jusqu'au dernier septembre 1785', *Mercure de France*, October 1785, pp 18–44, on pp 28–9.

1 VALLAYER-COSTER, ACADÉMICIENNE / CITOYENNE

1 Marianne Roland Michel, *Anne Vallayer-Coster (1744–1818)*, Comptoir International du Livre, Paris, 1970, pp 13–15; Marianne Roland Michel, 'Vallayer in Her Time', in Eik Kahng and Marianne Roland Michel (eds), *Anne Vallayer-Coster: Painter to the Court of Marie-Antoinette*, exh.cat., Dallas Museum of Art, Dallas, TX, 2002, pp 13–37, on pp 13–14.

2 Roland Michel, 'Vallayer in Her Time', p.15; see also Londa Schiebinger, *The Mind Has No Sex? Women in the Origins of Modern Science*, Harvard University Press, Cambridge, MA, 1991; and Nina Rattner Gelbart, *Minerva's French Sisters: Women of Science in Enlightenment France*, Yale University Press, New Haven, CT, and London, 2021.

3 Roland Michel, *Vallayer-Coster*, p.15; Roland Michel, 'Vallayer in Her Time', pp 14–15.

4 *Catalogue de la vente Coster: notice des tableaux des fleurs peints par Mme Vallayer-Coster . . . provenant du cabinet de feu M. et Mad. Coster*, 21 June and the following days, 1824, British Library, London, lots 48 and 52–6; Roland Michel, *Vallayer-Coster*, pp 274–6.

5 Melissa Hyde, 'Marie-Thérèse Reboul (Madame Vien): More than a Footnote in Art History', in

Mechthild Fend, Jennifer Germann and Melissa Hyde (eds), *Thinking Women and Eighteenth-Century Art: Strategic Reinterpretations*, Amsterdam University Press, Amsterdam, 2024, pp 239–80.

6   Roland Michel, *Vallayer-Coster*, p.258.

7   Anatole Montaiglon (ed.), *Procès-verbaux de l'Académie royale de peinture et de sculpture*, J. Baur and Charavay frères, Paris, 10 vols, 1875–92, vol.8, p.48; Roland Michel, 'Vallayer in Her Time', p.14.

8   Hannah Williams, *Académie Royale: A History in Portraits*, Ashgate, Farnham, 2015, pp 94–6.

9   ibid.

10 Mary D. Sheriff, *The Exceptional Woman: Elisabeth Vigée-Lebrun and the Cultural Politics of Art*, University of Chicago Press, Chicago, IL, 1996, p.78; Angela Oberer, *Rosalba Carriera*, Getty Publications, Los Angeles, CA, 2022, pp 77–82; Walter Liedtke, *Dutch Paintings in the Metropolitan Museum of Art*, The Metropolitan Museum of Art and Yale University Press, New York, New Haven, CT, and London, 2007, pp 308–10.

11 Tori E. Champion, 'Le pinceau à la main: The Intertwined Lives and Careers of Madeleine Françoise Basseporte and Marie-Thérèse Reboul Vien', Master's Thesis, University of Washington, Seattle, WA, 2021; Hyde, 'Marie-Thérèse Reboul (Madame Vien)'; Christina Lindeman, *The Art of Anna Dorothea Therbusch (1721–1782)*, Amsterdam University Press, Amsterdam, 2024.

12 Neil Jeffares, 'ROSLIN, Mme Alexander, née Jeanne-Suzanne Giroust (Paris 1734–1772)', *Dictionary of Pastellists before 1800*, online edn, 2022, http://www.pastellists.com/Articles/RoslinMS.pdf; See also Melissa Hyde's forthcoming book, *Painted by Herself: Marie-Suzanne Giroust: Madame Roslin, the Forgotten Académicienne*.

13 Sheriff, *The Exceptional Woman*, pp 73–104.

14 ibid., pp 80–81; Williams, *Académie Royale*, pp 94–6.

15 Pierre Rosenberg, *Chardin*, Flammarion, Paris, 1999, pp 40–41.

16 *Journal de Paris*, no.203, 22 July 1781, p.817; *Mercure de France*, 4 August 1781, p.47; Roland Michel, *Vallayer-Coster*, p.58, no.334; Kahng and Roland Michel (eds), *Vallayer-Coster*, p.222, no.156, pl.86.

17 Sheriff, *The Exceptional Woman*, p.79.

18 *Adresse à l'Assemblée nationale, par la presque totalité des officiers de l'Académie royale de peinture et de sculpture auxquels se sont joints quelques académiciens*, Veuve Hérissant, Paris, 1790, pp 6–7.

19 Montaiglon (ed.), *Procès-verbaux*, vols 8–10.

20 Letter from Vallayer-Coster to M. Dumont, Saturday, 16 July [no year], Morgan Library & Museum, New York, 106479; 16 July fell on a Saturday in 1785 and 1791.

21 See Roland Michel, 'Vallayer in Her Time', p.18, fig.4, for Dumont's (now lost) 1769 portrait of Vallayer-Coster.

22 Williams, *Académie Royale*, p.162.

23 Laura Auricchio, *Adélaïde Labille-Guiard: Artist in the Age of Revolution*, Getty Publications, Los Angeles, CA, 2009, p.35.

24 ibid., p.36; Sheriff, *The Exceptional Woman*, pp 101–3.

25 Élisabeth Vigée Le Brun, *Souvenirs de Madame Vigée Le Brun*, Charpentier et cie, Paris, 1869, p.57.

26 Neil Jeffares, 'Vigée Le Brun's Petitioners', *Pastels & Pastellists*, 2022, http://www.pastellists.com/Essays/VigeeLeBrunPetition.pdf.

27 Roland Michel, *Vallayer-Coster*, pp 260–62; Roland Michel, 'Vallayer in Her Time', p.19.

28 Brébion to d'Angiviller, 12 April 1779, quoted in Katie Scott, 'Lantern', in Katie Scott and Hannah Williams (eds), *Artists' Things: Rediscovering Lost Property from Eighteenth-Century France*, Getty Research Institute, Los Angeles, CA, 2024, https://www.getty.edu/publications/artists-things/.

29 Roland Michel, *Vallayer-Coster*, pp 260–62; Roland Michel, 'Vallayer in Her Time', p.19.

30 Laurent d'Houry (ed.), *Almanach royale*, Paris, 1781, p.507; Roland Michel, 'Vallayer in Her Time', p.19; Katie Scott, 'Bath', in Scott and Williams (eds), *Artists' Things*.

31 Emmanuelle Philippe and Séverine Sofio, 'I Was Born in this Palace: Emotional Bonds in the Artistic Community of the Louvre (1750–1800)', in Susan Broomhall (ed.), *Emotions in the Household, 1200–1900*, Palgrave Macmillan, New York, 2007, pp 234–51, on p.246.

32 Auricchio, *Labille-Guiard*, pp 14 and 50.

33 Salon of 1783, p.14, no.39; Roland Michel, *Vallayer-Coster*, p.25; Kahng and Roland Michel (eds),

Vallayer-Coster, p.225, F, pl.87; Magnus Olausson and Xavier Salmon, *Alexandre Roslin (1718–1793): un portraitise pour l'Europe*, exh.cat., Réunion des musées nationaux, Paris, 2008, p.106, no.14.

34 Roland Michel, *Vallayer-Coster*, pp 32–3 and 264–7; Roland Michel, 'Vallayer in Her Time', pp 19–20.

35 Roland Michel, *Vallayer-Coster*, pp 36 and 259; Auricchio, *Labille-Guiard*, pp 93 and 119, n.249; Joseph Baillio, Katharine Baetjer and Paul Lang (eds), *Vigée Le Brun: Woman Artist in Revolutionary France*, exh.cat., The Metropolitan Museum of Art, New York, 2015, pp 131–3, 237 and 242.

36 Auricchio, *Labille-Guiard*, pp 58–83.

37 Roland Michel, *Vallayer-Coster*, p.216, no.329; Roland Michel, 'Vallayer in Her Time', pp 19 and 219, no.140, pl.63; Versailles Enchères, 4 October 2009, lot 122.

38 Jeanne Louise Henriette Campan, *Mémoires de Madame Campan, première femme de chambre de Marie Antoinette*, ed. Jean Chalon and Carlos de Augulo, Gallimard, Paris, 1988, p.342; Roland Michel, *Vallayer-Coster*, pp 34–5; Roland Michel, 'Vallayer in Her Time', p.21.

39 Roland Michel, *Vallayer-Coster*, pp 36–8 and 259–60; Anne Higonnet, 'Through a Louvre Window', *Journal18*, vol.2, Fall 2016, http://www.journal18.org/1057.

40 *Catalogue de la vente Coster*; Roland Michel, *Vallayer-Coster*, pp 274–6; Roland Michel, *Vallayer-Coster*, p.22.

2 ALLEGORIES

1 Salon of 1771, p.28, no.149; Marianne Roland Michel, *Anne Vallayer-Coster (1744–1818)*, Comptoir International du Livre, Paris, 1970, p.184, no.257; Eik Kahng and Marianne Roland Michel (eds), *Anne Vallayer-Coster: Painter to the Court of Marie-Antoinette*, exh.cat., Dallas Museum of Art, Dallas, TX, 2002, pp 196–7, no.6.

2 Salon of 1771, p.28, no.149; Roland Michel, *Vallayer-Coster*, p.185, no.258; Kahng and Roland Michel (eds), *Vallayer-Coster*, p.198, no.12, pl.5.

3 Roger de Piles, *Cours de peinture par principes avec un balance de peintres*, Chez Jacques Estienne, Paris, 1708, p.44.

4 Salon of 1775, p.19, no.100; Roland Michel, *Vallayer-Coster*, p.195, no.283 (as lost); Kahng and Roland Michel (eds), *Vallayer-Coster*, p.200, no.24 (as lost).

5 Salon of 1777, p.20, no 101; Roland Michel, *Vallayer-Coster*, pp 187–8, no.264; Kahng and Roland Michel (eds), *Vallayer-Coster*, p.203, no.44.

6 Hannah Williams, *Académie Royale: A History in Portraits*, Ashgate, Farnham, 2015, p.65.

7 Pierre Rosenberg, *Chardin*, Flammarion, Paris, 1999, pp 141–50; Pierre Rosenberg, *Chardin*, exh.cat., The Metropolitan Museum of Art, New York, 2000, pp 302–9.

8 Williams, *Académie Royale*, pp 31–3, 42 and 100; Christian Michel, *The Académie Royale de Peinture et de Sculpture: The Birth of the French School, 1648–1793*, Getty Publications, Los Angeles, CA, 2018, pp 219–21 and 270–71.

9 Rosenberg, *Chardin*, 1999, p.146.

10 Williams, *Académie Royale*, p.49.

11 Henry Millon, 'The French Academy of Architecture: Foundation and Program', in June Hargrove (ed.), *The French Academy: Classicism and Its Antagonists*, University of Delaware Press, Newark, DE, 1990, pp 68–77.

12 Katie Scott, 'Porte-Crayon', in Katie Scott and Hannah Williams (eds), *Artists' Things: Rediscovering Lost Property from Eighteenth-Century France*, Getty Research Institute, Los Angeles, CA, 2024, https://www.getty.edu/publications/artists-things/.

13 Claire Barry, 'The Painting Technique of Anne Vallayer-Coster: Searching for the Origins of Style', in Kahng and Roland Michel (eds), *Vallayer-Coster*, pp 95–113, on p.101. See Chapter 6 for Vallayer-Coster's known works on paper.

14 Hannah Williams, 'Palette', in Scott and Williams (eds), *Artists' Things*.

15 Roger de Piles, *Dialogue sur le coloris*, Chez Nicholas Langlois, Paris, 1699.

16 Michael Levey, 'The Pose of Pigalle's *Mercury*', *The Burlington Magazine*, vol.106, no.739, October 1964, pp 460–63.

17 Williams, *Académie Royale*, p.44.

18 Helena Taylor, 'The Quarrel of the Ancients and Moderns', *French Studies: A Quarterly Review*, vol.74, no.4, 2020, pp 605–20.

19 Marianne Roland Michel, 'Vallayer in Her Time', in Kahng and Roland Michel (eds), *Vallayer-Coster*, pp 13–37, on p.16.

20 Anatole Montaiglon and Jules Guiffrey (eds), *Correspondance des directeurs de l'Académie de France à Rome avec les surintendants des bâtiments*, Charavay frères, Paris, 18 vols, 1887–1912, vol.1, p.129.

21 Francis Haskell and Nicholas Penny, *Taste and the Antique: The Lure of Classical Sculpture 1500–1900*, Yale University Press, New Haven, CT, and London, 1981, p.37.

22 Linda Nochlin, 'Why Have There Been No Great Women Artists?' (1971), in *Women, Art, and Power and Other Essays*, Harper & Row, New York, 1988, pp 159–60.

23 Anatole Montaiglon (ed.), *Procès-verbaux de l'Académie royale de peinture et de sculpture*, J. Baur and Charavay frères, Paris, 10 vols, 1875–92, vol.9, p.157; Mary D. Sheriff, *The Exceptional Woman: Elisabeth Vigée-Lebrun and the Cultural Politics of Art*, University of Chicago Press, Chicago, IL, 1996, pp 105–6.

24 *Catalogue de la vente Coster: notice des tableaux des fleurs peints par Mme Vallayer-Coster . . . Provenant du cabinet de feu M. et Mad. Coster*, 21 June and the following days, 1824, British Library, London, lot 58; Roland Michel, *Vallayer-Coster*, pp 274–6.

25 See Chapter 1 and Margaret A. Oppenheimer, '"The Charming Spectacle of a Cadaver": Anatomical and Life Study by Women Artists in Paris, 1775–1815', *Nineteenth-Century Art Worldwide*, vol.6, no.1, Spring 2007.

26 Rozsika Parker and Griselda Pollock, *Old Mistresses: Women, Art and Ideology*, Routledge, London, 1981, pp 87–90; Paris Spies-Gans, *A Revolution on Canvas: The Rise of Women Artists in Britain and France, 1760–1830*, Yale University Press, New Haven, CT, and London, 2022, pp 19–20.

27 Wendy Wassyng Roworth, 'Anatomy as Destiny: Regarding the Body in the Art of Angelica Kauffman', in Gill Perry and Michael Rossington (eds), *Femininity and Masculinity in Eighteenth-Century Art and Culture*, Manchester University Press, Manchester, 1994, pp 41–62; Spies-Gans, *A Revolution on Canvas*, pp 89–92.

28 Roland Michel, *Vallayer-Coster*, p.42.

29 ibid., p.65.

30 Parker and Pollock, *Old Mistresses*, p.96.

31 Antoine-Joseph Dezallier d'Argenville, *Description sommaire des ouvrages de peinture, sculpture et gravure exposés dans les salles de l'Académie royale*, Chez de Bure l'aîné, Paris, 1781, p.76.

32 Salon of 1775, p.19, no.99; Roland Michel, *Vallayer-Coster*, pp 102–3, no.1; Kahng and Roland Michel (eds), *Vallayer-Coster*, p.201, no.30.

33 Colin B. Bailey, 'The abbé Terray: An Enlightened Patron of Modern Sculpture', *The Burlington Magazine*, vol.135, no.1079, February 1993, pp 121–32.

34 Montaiglon (ed.), *Procès-verbaux de l'Académie royale*, vol.8, pp 134–5.

35 Bailey, 'The abbé Terray', p.123; Colin B. Bailey, 'A Still-Life Painter and Her Patrons: Collecting Vallayer-Coster, 1770–1789', in Kahng and Roland Michel (eds), *Vallayer-Coster*, pp 59–73, on pp 65–6.

36 Colin B. Bailey, *Patriotic Taste: Collecting Modern Art in Pre-Revolutionary Paris*, Yale University Press, New Haven, CT, and London, 2002, p.94.

37 *Catalogue d'une belle collection . . . provenant de la succession du feu M. l'abbé Terray*, François-Charles Joullain fils, Paris, 1778 [20 January 1779], lots 12 and 13.

38 Salon of 1775, p.29, no.179.

39 Stuart W. Pyhrr, *Of Arms and Men: Arms and Armor at the Metropolitan, 1912–2012*, The Metropolitan Museum of Art, New York, 2012, pp 44–5.

40 Everett Fahy, *The Wrightsman Pictures*, Yale University Press and The Metropolitan Museum of Art, New Haven, CT, and New York, 2005, pp 167–9, no.47.

41 Isabelle Deflers, 'The Difficult Reform of Military Discipline in the Latter Half of the Eighteenth-Century', in Susan Richter, Thomas Maissen and Manuela Albertone, *Languages of Reform in the Eighteenth Century: When Europe Lost Its Fear of Change*, Routledge, New York, 2020, pp 323–43.

42 *Journal de politique et de littérature*, no.61, 5 November 1777, p.348.

43 Deflers, 'The Difficult Reform of Military Discipline'.

44 Robert Werlich, *Orders and Decorations of All Nations*, Quaker Press, Washington, DC, 1974, p.166.

45 Salon of 1779, p.22, no.108; Piasa, Paris, 22 June 2007, lot 202.

46 Andrew McClellan, *Inventing the Louvre: Art, Politics, and the Origins of the Modern Museum*, University of California Press, Berkeley and Los Angeles, CA, 1999, p.52.

47 Andrew McClellan, 'Musée du Louvre, Paris: Palace of the People, Art for All', in Carole Paul (ed.), *The First Modern Museums of Art: The Birth of an Institution in 18th- and Early 19th-Century Europe*, Getty Publications, Los Angeles, CA, 2012, pp 213–36, on pp 216–17.

48 McClellan, *Inventing the Louvre*, p.49.

49 McClellan, 'Musée du Louvre, Paris', p.216.

50 Louis Petit de Bachaumont, *Lettres sur les peintures, sculptures et gravures de mrs. de l'Académie royale, exposés au sallon du Louvre depuis* MDCCLXVII *jusqu'en* MDCCLXXIX, John Adamson, London, 1780, p.263.

51 Roland Michel, 'Vallayer in Her Time', p.14; Andaleeb Badiee Banta and Alexa Greist, with Theresa Kutasz Christensen (eds), *Making Her Mark: A History of Women Artists in Europe, 1400–1800*, exh.cat., Art Gallery of Ontario, Toronto, and Baltimore Museum of Art, Baltimore, MD, 2023, pp 239–41.

52 Salon of 1777, no.101.

53 Michel Faré, *Le grand siècle de la nature morte en France, Le* XVIIe *siècle*, Société Française du Livre, Paris, 1974, pp 245–9; Renaud Serrette, 'De Versailles à Rambouillet: quatre dessus-de-porte de Madeleine Boullogne retrouvés', *Versalia*, no.19, 2016, pp 87–92.

54 Bailey, 'A Still-Life Painter and Her Patrons', p.68.

55 Mary D. Sheriff, 'The Naked Truth? The Allegorical Frontispiece and Woman's Ambition in Eighteenth-Century France', in Cristelle Baskins and Lisa Rosenthal (eds), *Early Modern Visual Allegory: Embodying Meaning*, Ashgate, Aldershot and Burlington, VT, 2007, pp 243–64.

56 Marina Warner, *Monuments and Maidens: The Allegory of the Female Form*, University of California Press, Berkeley and Los Angeles, CA, 2000, pp 238–9.

57 I thank Susan Sidlauskas for this suggestion. See J.L. Carr, 'Pygmalion and the Philosophes: The Animated Statue in Eighteenth-Century France', *Journal of the Warburg and Courtauld Institutes*, vol.23, nos 3/4, July–December 1960, pp 239–55; Sheriff, 'The Naked Truth?'.

3 FOOD

1 Jean Anthelme Brillat-Savarin, *Physiologie du goût, ou Méditations de gastronomie transcendante* … Boulé, Paris, 1850 p.35; Viktoria Von Hoffman, *From Gluttony to Enlightenment: The World of Taste in Early Modern Europe*, University of Illinois Press, Champaign, IL, 2016, p.86.

2 François-Marie Arouet de Voltaire and Charles-Louis de Secondat, baron de La Brède et de Montesquieu, 'Taste', trans. Nelly S. Hoyt and Thomas Cassirer, in Denis Diderot and Jean d'Alembert, *The Encyclopedia of Diderot & d'Alembert Collaborative Translation Project*, Michigan Publishing, University of Michigan Library, Ann Arbor, MI, 2003–16, http://hdl.handle.net/2027/spo.did2222.0000.168.

3 ibid.

4 Chevalier Louis de Jaucourt, 'Cuisine', trans. Sean Takats, in *The Encyclopedia of Diderot & d'Alembert*, http://hdl.handle.net/2027/spo.did2222.0000.075.

5 Susan Pinkard, *A Revolution in Taste: The Rise of French Cuisine, 1650–1800*, Cambridge University Press, Cambridge, 2009, pp 60–61.

6 ibid., p.138.

7 ibid., pp 108 and 196.

8 Melissa Hyde, *Making Up the Rococo: Boucher and His Critics*, Getty Publications, Los Angeles, CA, 2006, pp 3–5.

9 Charlotte Guichard, Anne-Solenn Le Hô and Hannah Williams, 'Prussian Blue: Chemistry, Commerce, and Colour in Eighteenth-Century Paris', *Art History*, vol.46, no.1, February 2023, pp 154–186, https://doi.org/10.1111/1467-8365.12695.

10 Pinkard, *A Revolution in Taste*, p.156.

11 Louis-Sébastien Mercier, *Panorama of Paris: Selections from Tableau de Paris* (1781), trans. Jeremy Popkin, Pennsylvania State University Press, Philadelphia, PA, 2010, pp 44–5, 96.

12 Sean Takats, *The Expert Cook in Enlightenment France*, Johns Hopkins University Press, Baltimore, MD, 2011, p.16.

13 Pinkard, *A Revolution in Taste*, p.178.

14 Marianne Roland Michel, *Anne Vallayer-Coster (1744–1818)*, Comptoir International du Livre, Paris, 1970, pp 260–61.

15   Salon of 1783, p.19, no.79.

16   ibid.

17   'Kitchen Garden', trans. Ann-Marie Thornton, in *The Encyclopedia of Diderot & d'Alembert*, http://hdl.handle.net/2027/spo.did2222.0000.229; Pinkard, *A Revolution in Taste*, p.73.

18   Pinkard, *A Revolution in Taste*, pp 128, 275–6, 335–6.

19   Antoine-Joseph Dezallier d'Argenville, 'Fruit Picking', trans. Ann-Marie Thornton, in *The Encyclopedia of Diderot & d'Alembert*, http://hdl.handle.net/2027/spo.did2222.0001.897.

20   Brillat-Savarin, *Physiologie du goût*, p.171.

21   'Plum' and 'Plum Tree', trans. Ann-Marie Thornton, in *The Encyclopedia of Diderot & d'Alembert*, http://hdl.handle.net/2027/spo.did2222.0002.317, http://hdl.handle.net/2027/spo.did2222.0002.321.

22   Possibly Salon of 1771, p.28, no.147 or Salon of 1773, p.29, no.143; Roland Michel, *Vallayer-Coster*, p.155, no.183, fig. 155; Marianne Roland Michel and Ursula Korneitchouk, 'A Basket of Plums', *The Bulletin of the Cleveland Museum of Art*, vol.60, no.2, 1973, pp 52–9; Eik Kahng and Marianne Roland Michel (eds), *Anne Vallayer-Coster: Painter to the Court of Marie-Antoinette*, exh.cat., Dallas Museum of Art, Dallas, TX, 2002, p.197, no.7, pl.2.

23   Pierre Rosenberg, *Chardin*, exh.cat., The Metropolitan Museum of Art, New York, 2000, pp 298–9.

24   Probably Salon of 1779, p.22, no.105; Roland Michel, *Vallayer-Coster*, pp 144–5, no.138, fig.144; Kahng and Roland Michel (eds), *Vallayer-Coster*, p.204, no.49, pl.24.

25   Joseph Menon, *Les soupers de la cour, ou L'art de travailler toutes sortes d'alimens, pour servir les meilleures tables, suivant les quatre saisons*, Chez Guillyn, Paris, 1755, p.232.

26   Roland Michel, *Vallayer-Coster*, p.167 and 169, no.224; Kahng and Roland Michel (eds), *Vallayer-Coster*, p.202, no.34, pl.18.

27   Alan Davidson, *The Oxford Companion to Food*, Oxford University Press, Oxford, 2006, pp 110–11.

28   Rosenberg, *Chardin*, 2000, pp 294–5.

29   Silvia Malaguzzi, *Food and Feasting in Art*, Getty Publications, Los Angeles, CA, 2008, p.264.

30   Jean-Jacques Rousseau, *Confessions de J.-J.Rousseau* (1767), Ménard et Desenne fils, Paris, 1827, pp 221–2.

31   Barbara Ketcham Wheaton, *Savoring the Past: The French Kitchen and Table from 1300 to 1789*, Simon and Schuster, New York, 2011, p.101.

32   Denis Diderot, 'Baker', trans. Malcolm Eden, in *The Encyclopedia of Diderot & d'Alembert*, http://hdl.handle.net/2027/spo.did2222.0000.845.

33   Salon of 1771, p.27, no.143; Roland Michel, *Vallayer-Coster*, pp 165 and 171, no.222; Kahng and Roland Michel (eds), *Vallayer-Coster*, p.198, no.12, pl.6.

34   Brillat-Savarin, *Physiologie du goût*, p.171.

35   Denis Diderot, *Salons*, ed. Jean Seznec and Jean Adhémar, Clarendon Press, Oxford, 4 vols, 1957–68, vol.4, p.202.

36   ibid., vol.2, p.114.

37   Colin B. Bailey, *Patriotic Taste: Collecting Modern Art in Pre-Revolutionary Paris*, Yale University Press, New Haven, CT, and London, 2002, p.79; Kahng and Roland Michel (eds), *Vallayer-Coster*, p.198.

38   Roland Michel, *Vallayer-Coster*, no.221, fig.83; Kahng and Roland Michel (eds), *Vallayer-Coster*, p.196, no.4, pl.1.

39   Roland Michel, *Vallayer-Coster*, no.281, fig.202; Kahng and Roland Michel (eds), *Vallayer-Coster*, p.197, no.8.

40   Mercier, *Panorama of Paris*, p.228.

41   Thomas Edward Brennan, *Public Drinking and Popular Culture in Eighteenth-Century Paris*, Princeton University Press, Princeton, NJ, 2014, pp 95 and 99.

42   Chevalier Louis de Jaucourt, 'Cuisine', in *The Encyclopedia of Diderot & d'Alembert*.

43   Sydney Watts, *Meat Matters: Butchers, Politics, and Market Culture in Eighteenth-Century Paris*, University of Rochester Press, Rochester, NY, 2006, pp 1–3.

44   Sydney Watts, 'Enlightened Fasting: Religious Conviction, Scientific Inquiry, and Medical Knowledge in Early Modern France', in Ken Albala and Trudy Eden (eds), *Food & Faith in Christian Culture*, Columbia University Press, New York, 2011, pp 105–24.

45   Brillat-Savarin, *Physiologie du goût*, p.172.

46   Colin B. Bailey with Philip Conisbee and Thomas W. Gaehtgens (eds), *The Age of Watteau, Chardin,*

and Fragonard: Masterpieces of French Genre Painting,
exh.cat., Yale University Press, New Haven, CT, and
London, 2003, pp 146–7.

47   Wheaton, *Savoring the Past*, p.266.

48   Salon of 1787, p.16, no.72; Roland Michel, *Vallayer-Coster*, no.227; Kahng and Roland Michel (eds),
Vallayer-Coster, p.211, no.83, pl.41.

49   *Catalogue de la vente Coster: notice des tableaux des fleurs peints par Mme Vallayer-Coster . . . Provenant du cabinet de feu M. et Mad. Coster*, 21 June and the following days, 1824, British Library, London 1824, lot 31; Kahng and Roland Michel (eds), *Vallayer-Coster*, p.211.

50   Rosenberg, *Chardin*, 2000, pp 206–7.

51   Fernand Braudel, *Civilization and Capitalism, 15th–18th Century: The Wheels of Commerce*, University of California Press, Oakland, CA, 1982, p.38.

52   Mercier, *Panorama of Paris*, p.45.

53   Alain Corbin, *The Foul and the Fragrant: Odor and the French Social Imagination*, Harvard University Press, Cambridge, MA, 1986, p.58.

54   Carla Hesse, *The Other Enlightenment: How French Women Became Modern*, Princeton University Press, Princeton, NJ, 2001, p.3.

55   Julia V. Douthwaite, 'From Fish Seller to Suffragist: The Women's March on Versailles', in *The Frankenstein of 1790 and Other Lost Chapters from Revolutionary France*, University of Chicago Press, Chicago, IL, 2012, pp 17–58, on p.31.

56   Salon of 1783, p.19, no.80.

57   Roland Michel, *Vallayer-Coster*, p.168, no.226; Kahng and Roland Michel (eds), *Vallayer-Coster*, p.207, no.65, pl.33.

58   Salon of 1817, no.747; Roland Michel, *Vallayer-Coster*, pp 169–70, no.228; Kahng and Roland Michel (eds), *Vallayer-Coster*, p.213, no.99, pl.45.

59   Arie Wallert (ed.), *Still Lifes: Techniques and Styles: An Examination of Paintings from the Rijksmuseum*, Rijksmuseum and Waanders Publishers, Amsterdam and Zwolle, 1999, pp 66–8.

60   Donna R. Barnes and Peter G. Rose, *Matters of Taste: Food and Drink in Seventeenth-Century Dutch Art and Life*, Syracuse University Press, Syracuse, NY, 2002, p.140.

61   Miriam Hospodar, 'Aphrodisiac Foods: Bringing Heaven to Earth', *Gastronomica*, vol.4, no.4, 2004, pp 82–93, on p.85.

62   ibid.

63   Blanche C. Hardy, *Princess Lamballe: A Biography*, A. Constable, London, 1908, p.75.

64   Andaleeb Badiee Banta and Alexa Greist, with Theresa Kutasz Christensen (eds), *Making Her Mark: A History of Women Artists in Europe, 1400–1800*, exh.cat., Art Gallery of Ontario, Toronto, and Baltimore Museum of Art, Baltimore, MD, 2023, p.212.

65   Bailey, *Patriotic Taste*, pp 160, 240–41, 288.

66   Pahin de la Blancherie, *Essai d'un tableau historique des peintres de l'école francoise depuis Jean Cousin en 1550 jusqu'en 1783 inclusivement*, Bureau de la Correspondance, Paris, 1783, p.31, no.146; Roland Michel, *Vallayer-Coster*, p.168, no.226; Bailey, *Patriotic Taste*, pp 155, 160 and 289.

67   Martin Wrede and Christine Weil, 'Le portrait du roi restauré, ou la fabrication de Louis XVIII', *Revue d'histoire moderne et contemporaine*, vol.53, no.2, April–June 2006, pp 112–38.

68   Sophie Mouquin and Christophe Huchet de Quénetain, 'Essai', in *Anne Vallayer-Coster: Protégée de Marie-Antoinette*, exh.cat., Galerie Eric Coatalem, Paris, 2023, pp 66–91, on p.82; Colin B. Bailey, 'A Still-Life Painter and Her Patrons: Collecting Vallayer-Coster, 1770–1789', in Kahng and Roland Michel (eds), *Vallayer-Coster*, pp 59–73, on pp 66–7.

69   Jan van Huysum (1682–1749), *Basket of Flowers with Butterfly*, Musée du Louvre, Paris, INV 1385.

70   Marianne Roland Michel, 'Vallayer in Her Time', in Kahng and Roland Michel (eds), *Vallayer-Coster*, pp 13–37, on p.22.

71   Jennifer J. Davis, 'To Make a Revolutionary Cuisine: Gender and Politics in French Kitchens, 1789–1815', *Gender & History*, vol.23, no.2, August 2011, pp 301–20.

4 GUNS AND GAME

1   An earlier version of this chapter was published in *The Rutgers Art Review*, vol.36, 2020.

2   See Georges de Lastic and Pierre Jacky, *Desportes*, Monelle Hayot, Saint-Rémy-en-l'Eau, 2010; and Hal

Opperman, *J.-B. Oudry*, Kimbell Art Museum, Fort Worth, TX, 1983.

3   Amy Freund, 'Good Dog! Jean-Baptiste Oudry and the Politics of Animal Painting', in Heather MacDonald (ed.), *French Art of the Eighteenth Century: The Michael L. Rosenberg Lecture Series at the Dallas Museum of Art*, Yale University Press, New Haven, CT, and London, 2016, pp 67–80, on p.72.

4   Hannah Williams, *Académie Royale: A History in Portraits*, Ashgate, Farnham, 2015, p.131.

5   ibid., p.83.

6   Antoine Trémolières de St Saturnin, *L'art de la chasse, pour le divertissement de la noblesse, et de tous ceux qui aiment cet exercice* (1724), Société des lettres, sciences et arts de l'Aveyron, Rodez, 1996.

7   Freund, 'Good Dog!', p.79, n.10.

8   Rosamond Hooper-Hamersley, *The Hunt after Jeanne-Antoinette de Pompadour: Patronage, Politics, Art, and the French Enlightenment*, Lexington Books, Lanham, MD, 2011, pp 72–5.

9   ibid., p.234.

10 Xavier Salmon (ed.), *Jean-Marc Nattier, 1685–1766*, exh.cat., Réunion des musées nationaux, Paris, 1999, pp 184, 266–70, no.76.

11 Amy Freund, 'Men and Hunting Guns', in Jennifer G. Germann and Heidi A. Strobel (eds), *Materializing Gender in Eighteenth-Century Europe*, Routledge, New York, 2016, pp 17–34, on p.18.

12 Robert L. Wilson, *Silk and Steel: Women at Arms*, Skyhorse Publishing, New York, 2015, pp 59–61.

13 Élisabeth Caude, Jérôme de La Gorce and Béatrix Saule (eds), *Fêtes & divertissements à la cour*, exh.cat., Musée national des châteaux de Versailles et de Trianon, Versailles, 2016, p.47, no.9.

14 Pierre de Saintes, flintlock rifle of Maria Theresa of Austria, *c.*1780, Musée de la chasse et de la nature, Paris, PO 962.

15 Freund, 'Men and Hunting Guns', p.32.

16 Jacob D. Melish, 'The Power of Wives: Managing Money and Men in the Family Businesses of Old Regime Paris', in Daryl M. Hafter and Nina Kushner (eds), *Women and Work in Eighteenth-Century France*, Louisiana State University Press, Baton Rouge, LA, 2015, pp 77–90.

17 Freund, 'Men and Hunting Guns', p.26.

18 Linda Zerilli, '"Une Maitresse Imperieuse": Woman in Rousseau's Semiotic Republic', in Lynda Lange (ed.), *Feminist Interpretations of Jean-Jacques Rousseau*, Pennsylvania State University Press, University Park, PA, 2010, pp 277–314, on p.294.

19 Jean-Jacques Rousseau, *A Discourse on Inequality* (1754), Open Road Media, New York, 2016.

20 Darlene Levy, Harriet Applewhite and Mary Durham Johnson (eds), *Women in Revolutionary Paris, 1789–1795*, University of Illinois Press, Urbana, IL, 1997, p.215.

21 Another anonymous huntress is depicted in Étienne Maurice Falconet's biscuit porcelain sculpture, *Rest from the Hunt* of 1763; thank you to Melissa Hyde for this comparison.

22 Guillaume Glorieux, *A l'enseigne de Gersaint: Edme-François Gersaint, marchand d'art sur le Pont Notre-Dame, 1694–1750*, Editions Champ Vallon, Seyssel, 2002, pp 96–7.

23 *Mercure de France*, December 1727, vol.1, p.2677.

24 Jean-Jacques Rousseau, *Emile, or, On Education: Includes Emile and Sophie, or, The Solitaries* (1762), trans. Allan Bloom, Basic Books, New York, 1979, p.353.

25 Jade Higa, 'Charlotte Charke's Gun: Queering Material Culture and Gender Performance', *ABO: Interactive Journal for Women in the Arts, 1640–1830*, vol.7, no.1, 2017, http://scholarcommons.usf.edu/abo/vol7/iss1/2.

26 Balázs Németh, *Early Military Rifles: 1740–1850*, Bloomsbury, London and New York, 2020, pp 6–8.

27 Freund, 'Men and Hunting Guns', p.20; Clive Ponting, *Gunpowder*, Chatto & Windus, London, 2005, pp 152–3.

28 Freund, 'Men and Hunting Guns', p.32.

29 Marianne Roland Michel, *Anne Vallayer-Coster (1744–1818)*, Comptoir International du Livre, Paris, 1970, p.194, no.280; Eik Kahng and Marianne Roland Michel (eds), *Anne Vallayer-Coster: Painter to the Court of Marie-Antoinette*, exh.cat., Dallas Museum of Art, Dallas, TX, 2002, p.197, no.10, pl.3.

30 I thank Melissa Hyde for this suggestion. See Michael Shrubb, *Feasting, Fowling and Feathers: A History of the Exploitation of Wild Birds*, Bloomsbury, London, 2013.

31 Rousseau, *Emile*, p.352.

32 Freund, 'Men and Hunting Guns', p.26.

33 Sarah R. Cohen, *Enlightened Animals in Eighteenth-Century Art: Sensation, Matter, and Knowledge*, Bloomsbury, London and New York, 2021, p.71.

34 Jennifer Milam, 'Rococo Representations of Interspecies Sensuality and the Pursuit of Volupté', *The Art Bulletin*, vol.97, no.2, June 2015, pp 192–209.

35 Salon of 1783, no.76; Roland Michel, *Vallayer-Coster*, p.196, no.286; Kahng and Roland Michel (eds), *Vallayer-Coster*, p.208, no.69, pl.34; Colin B. Bailey, *Patriotic Taste: Collecting Modern Art in Pre-Revolutionary Paris*, Yale University Press, New Haven, CT, and London, 2002, pp 131–62.

36 Walt Harrington, 'Cleaning Rabbits', *The American Scholar*, vol.71, no.4, Autumn 2002, pp 69–74.

37 Roland Michel, *Vallayer-Coster*, p.195, no.284 (as lost); Kahng and Roland Michel (eds), *Vallayer-Coster*, p.201, no.28.

38 Roland Michel, *Vallayer-Coster*, p.196, no.288; Kahng and Roland Michel (eds), *Vallayer-Coster*, p.208, no.71; Sotheby's, Paris, 26 June 2014, lot 58.

39 Salon of 1785, p.20, no.60; Salon of 1787, p.15, no.68; Roland Michel, *Vallayer-Coster*, pp 196–8, nos 288 and 292.

40 Freund, 'Good Dog!', pp 72–3.

41 James M. Saslow, '"Disagreeably Hidden": Construction and Constriction of the Lesbian Body in Rosa Bonheur's Horse Fair', in Norma Broude and Mary D. Garrard (eds), *The Expanding Discourse: Feminism and Art History*, Harper Collins, New York, 1992, pp 187–206.

5 SHELLS

1 Part of this text was published in Arlene Leis and Kacie L. Wills (eds), *Women and the Art and Science of Collecting in Eighteenth-Century Europe*, 2020. Reproduced by permission of Taylor and Francis Group, LLC, a division of Informa plc.

2 Salon of 1777, pp 20–21, no.101; Marianne Roland Michel, *Anne Vallayer-Coster (1744–1818)*, Comptoir International du Livre, Paris, 1970, p.188, no.265 (as lost); Eik Kahng and Marianne Roland Michel (eds), *Anne Vallayer-Coster: Painter to the Court of Marie-Antoinette*, exh.cat., Dallas Museum of Art, Dallas, TX, 2002, p.203, no.41, pl.22.

3 Salon of 1781, p.22, no.105, Roland Michel, *Vallayer-Coster*, pp 121 and 125, no.67; Kahng and Roland Michel (eds), *Vallayer-Coster*, pp 206–7, no.61; Katharine Baetjer, *French Paintings in The Metropolitan Museum of Art from the Early Eighteenth Century through the Revolution*, The Metropolitan Museum of Art, New York, 2019, pp 299–301, no.100.

4 Salon of 1789, pp 13–14, no.48; Roland Michel, *Vallayer-Coster*, pp 179 and 188, no.266 or 267; Kahng and Roland Michel (eds), *Vallayer-Coster*, p.211, no.87.

5 Salon of 1771, p.27, no.145; Pierre Rémy, *Catalogue d'une riche collection de tableaux des maitres les plus celebres des trois écoles . . . qui composent le Cabinet de feu son Altesse Sérénissime Monseigneur le Prince de Conti, prince du sang et Grand Prieur de France*, Chez Muzier, Paris, 8 April–6 June 1777, lot 775; Roland Michel, *Vallayer-Coster*, pp 181, 186–7, no.260, fig.181; Jacques Foucart et al., *Musée du Louvre: nouvelles acquisitions du department des peintre, 1991–1995*, Réunion des musées nationaux, Paris, 1996, p.147; Kahng and Roland Michel (eds), *Vallayer-Coster*, pp 197–8, no.11, pl.4.

6 Madeleine Pinault-Sorensen and Marie-Catherine Sahut, 'Panaches de mer, Lithophytes et Coquilles (1769), un tableau d'histoire naturelle par Anne Vallayer-Coster', *Revue du Louvre: la revue des musées de France*, vol.XLVII, February 1998, pp 49–50.

7 'Exposition des peintures, sculptures, gravures de MM. de l'Académie royale', *Mercure de France*, October 1771, pp 174–201, on p.193.

8 Denis Diderot, *Oeuvres complètes de Diderot*, ed. J. Assézat and Maurice Tourneux, Garnier frères, Paris, 20 vols, 1876, vol.11, p.512, no.154.

9 Colin B. Bailey, 'A Still-Life Painter and Her Patrons: Collecting Vallayer-Coster, 1770–1789', in Kahng and Roland Michel (eds), *Vallayer-Coster*, pp 59–73, on p.61.

10 Pierre Rémy, *Catalogue de tableaux précieux . . . d'un cabinet distingue* [Madame du Barry], Chez M. Cattilan, Paris, 22 December 1775.

11 Foucart et al., *Musée du Louvre: nouvelles acquisitions*, p.146.

12   Colin B. Bailey, 'Conventions of the Eighteenth-Century *Cabinet de tableaux*: Blondel d'Azincourt's *La première idée de la curiosité*', *The Art Bulletin*, vol.69, no.3, September 1987, pp 431–47.

13   Frédéric Chappey, *Les tresors des princes de Bourbon Conti*, Musée d'art et d'histoire Louis Senlecq, L'Isle Adam, 2000, p.38.

14   Bailey, 'A Still-Life Painter and Her Patrons', p.63; Chappey, *Les tresors des princes de Bourbon Conti*, pp 42 and 163.

15   Bailey, 'Conventions of the Eighteenth-Century *Cabinet de tableaux*'.

16   Natasha Shoory, 'Review: Women and the Art and Science of Collecting in Eighteenth-Century Europe', *The Society for the History of Collecting*, 19 April 2021, https://societyhistorycollecting.org/reviews/review-women-and-the-art-and-science-of-collecting-in-eighteenth-century-europe/.

17   JoLynn Edwards, 'The Conti Sales of 1777 and 1779 and their Impact on the Parisian Art Market', *Studies in the Eighteenth-Century Culture*, vol.39, 2010, pp 77–110.

18   ibid., p.77; Roland Michel, *Vallayer-Coster*, pp 179 and 188, no.266 or 267; Kahng and Roland Michel (eds), *Vallayer-Coster*, p.211, no.87; Bailey, 'A Still-Life Painter and Her Patrons', p.64, fig.4.

19   Londa Schiebinger, *The Mind Has No Sex? Women in the Origins of Modern Science*, Harvard University Press, Cambridge, MA, 1991, p.28.

20   Michel Adanson, *Histoire naturelle du Sénégal: coquillages, avec la relation abrégée d'un voyage fait en ce pays, pendant les années 1749, 50, 51, 52 & 53*, Bauche, Paris, 1757; Tori E. Champion, 'Le pinceau à la main: The Intertwined Lives and Careers of Madeleine Françoise Basseporte and Marie-Thérèse Reboul Vien', Master's Thesis, University of Washington, Seattle, WA, 2021, pp 54 and 94.

21   Krzysztof Pomian, *Collectors and Curiosities: Paris and Venice, 1500–1800*, trans. Elizabeth Wiles-Portier, Polity Press, Cambridge, 1990, p.122.

22   Edmé-François Gersaint, *Catalogue d'une collection considérable de curiosites de différent genres*, Chez Prault fils, Paris, 2 December 1737; Edmé-François Gersaint, *Catalogue raisonné d'une collection considérable de diverses curiosités en tous genres contenues dans les cabinets de feu Monsieur Bonnier de la Mosson, Bailly et Captaine des Chasses de la Varenne des Thuilleries & ancien Colonel du Regiment Dauphin par E.F. Gersaint*, J. Barois, Paris, 1744.

23   Pierre Rémy, *Catalogue raisonné . . . de feu Monsieur Dezallier d'Argenville*, Chez Didot l'aîné, Paris, 3 March 1766; Pierre Rémy, *Catalogue raisonné des curiosités qui composoient le cabinet de feu Mme Dubois-Jourdain*, Chez Didot l'aîné, Paris, 12 May 1766.

24   Jessica S. Priebe, *François Boucher and the Art of Collecting in Eighteenth-Century France*, Routledge, New York, 2022, pp 175–202.

25   Antoine-Joseph Dezallier d'Argenville, *L'Histoire naturelle éclaircie dans deux de ses parties principales, la lithologie et la conchyliologie*, Chez de Bure l'aîné, Paris, 1742; Priebe, *François Boucher and the Art of Collecting*, p.72.

26   Claudia Swan, 'The Nature of Exotic Shells', in Marisa Anne Bass, Anne Goldgar, Hanneke Grootenboer and Claudia Swan (eds), *Conchophilia: Shells, Art, and Curiosity in Early Modern Europe*, Princeton University Press, Princeton, NJ, 2021, pp 21–47.

27   Dezallier d'Argenville, *L'Histoire naturelle éclaircie*, pp 116–17.

28   Bettina Dietz, 'Mobile Objects: The Space of Shells in Eighteenth-Century France,' *British Society for the History of Science*, vol.39, no.3, September 2006, pp 363–82, on p.373.

29   ibid., p.374.

30   Charlotte Guichard, 'Taste Communities: The Rise of the Amateur in Eighteenth-Century Paris', *Eighteenth-Century Studies*, vol.45, no.4, Summer 2016, pp 519–47, on p.535.

31   Kristel Smentek, *Rococo Exotic: French Mounted Porcelains and the Allure of the East*, exh.cat., The Frick Collection, New York, 2007, p.21.

32   Nina Rattner Gelbart, *Minerva's French Sisters: Women of Science in Enlightenment France*, Yale University Press, New Haven, CT, and London, 2021, p.118.

33   Carl Linnaeus, *Systema Naturae*, 10th edn, Laurentii Salvii, Stockholm, 1758; Beth Fowkes Tobin, *The Duchess's Shells: Natural History Collecting in the Age of Cook's Voyages*, Yale University Press, New Haven, CT, and London, 2014, pp 101–2.

34 Tobin, *The Duchess's Shells*, p.104.

35 Gelbart, *Minerva's French Sisters*, pp 118, 151, 165, 170–71, 210.

36 ibid., pp 172–3, 184–5, 188, 209.

37 ibid., pp 176–7, 182–3.

38 Louis Petit de Bachaumont, *Mémoires secrets pour servir à l'histoire de la République, des lettres en France depuis 1762 jusqu'à nos jours*, John Adamson, London, 36 vols, 1777–89, vol.1 (1777), p.324; Gelbart, *Minerva's French Sisters*, p.180; Adeline Gargam, 'Marie-Marguerite Biheron et son cabinet d'anatomie: une femme de science et une pédagogue', in Isabelle Brouard-Arends and Marie-Emmanuelle Plagnol-Diéval (eds), *Femmes éducatrices au siècle des Lumières*, Presses universitaires de Rennes, 2007, pp 147–56, https://doi.org/10.4000/books.pur.39353.

39 Schiebinger, *The Mind Has No Sex?*, p.28.

40 ibid.

41 Mary D. Sheriff, *The Exceptional Woman: Elisabeth Vigée-Lebrun and the Cultural Politics of Art*, University of Chicago Press, Chicago, IL, 1996, p.13.

42 Gelbart, *Minerva's French Sisters*, pp 202–3.

43 Imperial Roman IV fresco in the House of Venus at Pompeii, *c.* first century CE, Museo Archeologico Nazionale di Napoli; Sandro Botticelli, *Birth of Venus*, 1486, Uffizi, Florence; François Boucher, *The Triumph of Venus*, 1740, Nationalmuseum, Stockholm.

44 Michael Bycroft, 'Style and Substance in Rococo Science', *The Journal of Interdisciplinary History*, vol.48, no.3, 2018, pp 359–84.

45 Danielle Bleichmar, 'Learning to Look: Visual Expertise Across Art and Science in Eighteenth-Century France', *Eighteenth-Century Studies*, vol.46, no.1, Fall 2012, pp 85–111; Anna Grasskamp, 'Shells, Bodies, and the Collector's Cabinet', in Bass et al. (eds), *Conchophilia*, pp 49–71.

46 Chevalier Louis de Jaucourt, 'Painting', trans. Nelly S. Hoyt and Thomas Cassirer, in Denis Diderot and Jean d'Alembert, *The Encyclopedia of Diderot & d'Alembert Collaborative Translation Project*, Michigan Publishing, University of Michigan Library, Ann Arbor, MI, 2003–16, http://hdl.handle.net/2027/spo.did2222.0000.163.

47 Claire Barry, 'The Painting Technique of Anne Vallayer-Coster: Searching for the Origins of Style', in Kahng and Roland Michel (eds), *Vallayer-Coster*, pp 95–113, on p.100.

48 Daudé de Jossan, *Lettres de M. Raphael le jeune, eleve des ecoles gratuites de dessin, neveu de feu M. Raphael, peintre de l'Académie de St Luc, a un de ses amis, architecte à Rome: sur les peintures, sculptures & gravures qui sont exposées cette année au Louvre*, Paris, 1771, p.18.

49 Étienne Bonnot de Condillac, *Traité des sensations*, Chez de Bure l'aîné, London and Paris, 1754; John C. O'Neal, *The Authority of Experience: Sensationist Theory in the French Enlightenment*, Pennsylvania State University Press, University Park, PA, 1996, p.21.

50 Denis Diderot, *Lettres sur les sourds et les muets: à l'usage de ceux qui entendent & qui parlent*, Jean-Baptiste-Claude II Bauche, Paris, 1751, p.12.

51 Denis Diderot, 'Le Rêve de d'Alembert' (1769), in *Oeuvres complètes de Diderot*, vol.2, p.146.

52 Michel Foucault, *The Order of Things: An Archaeology of the Human Sciences*, Pantheon Books, New York, 1970, pp 127–49.

53 Nicole Garnier-Pelle, *Carmontelle (1717–1806), ou Le temps de la douceur de vivre: collection les Carnets de Chantilly*, Éditions Faton, Dijon, 2020, pp 84–5, nos 42 and 43.

54 Salon of 1777, pp 20–21, no.101; Roland Michel, *Vallayer-Coster*, p.188, no.265 (as lost); Kahng and Roland Michel (eds), *Vallayer-Coster*, p.203, no.41, pl.22.

55 Salon of 1781, p.22, no.105, Roland Michel, *Vallayer-Coster*, pp 121 and 125, no.67; Kahng and Roland Michel (eds), *Vallayer-Coster*, pp 206–7, no.61; Baetjer, *French Paintings in The Metropolitan Museum of Art*, pp 299–301, no.100.

56 Salon of 1789, pp 13–14, no.48; Roland Michel, *Vallayer-Coster*, pp 179 and 188, no.266 or 267; Kahng and Roland Michel (eds), *Vallayer-Coster*, p.211, no.87.

6 FLOWERS

1 *Lettres pittoresques à l'occasion des tableaux exposés au Sallon en 1777*, Paris, 1777, p.56; Marianne Roland Michel, 'Vallayer in Her Time', in Eik Kahng and Marianne Roland Michel (eds), *Anne Vallayer-Coster:*

Painter to the Court of Marie-Antoinette, exh.cat., Dallas Museum of Art, Dallas, TX, 2002, pp 13–37, on pp 33 and 37, n.115.

2 An exception to this rule can be found in a German-born *académicienne*; see Christina Lindeman, *The Art of Anna Dorothea Therbusch (1721–1782)*, Amsterdam University Press, Amsterdam, 2024, pp 20 and 51–60.

3 *Catalogue de la vente Coster: notice des tableaux des fleurs peints par Mme Vallayer-Coster . . . Provenant du cabinet de feu M. et Mad. Coster*, 21 June and the following days, 1824, British Library, London; Roland Michel, 'Vallayer in Her Time', p.36.

4 Élisabeth Vigée Le Brun, *Souvenirs de Madame Vigée Le Brun*, Charpentier et cie, Paris, 1869, p.57.

5 Nira Tessler, 'The Flower Motif and the Feminine Representation in the History of Art', in *Flowers and Towers: Politics of Identity in the Art of the American 'New Woman'*, Cambridge Scholars Publishing, Newcastle upon Tyne, 2015, pp 8–39.

6 Marianne Roland Michel et al. (eds), *The Floral Art of Pierre-Joseph Redouté*, exh.cat., Bruce Museum of Arts & Science and Kimbell Art Museum, Greenwich, CT, and Fort Worth, TX, 2002; Pierre Rosenberg, *Chardin*, exh.cat., The Metropolitan Museum of Art, New York, 2000, pp 40–41, fig.4, and 272–3, no.72.

7 Caroline Weber, *Queen of Fashion: What Marie Antoinette Wore to the Revolution*, Macmillan, New York, 2006, p.131.

8 Susan Taylor-Leduc, *Marie-Antoinette's Legacy: The Politics of French Garden Patronage and Picturesque Design, 1775–1867*, Amsterdam University Press, Amsterdam, 2022, pp 63–125.

9 ibid., p.86.

10 Christian Cajus Lorenz Hirschfeld, *Théorie de l'art des jardins*, Chez les heritiers de M.G. Weidmann et Reich, Leipzig, 1779, p.171.

11 Elisabeth de Feydeau, *A Scented Palace: The Secret History of Marie Antoinette's Perfumer*, trans. Jane Lizop, I.B. Tauris & Co., London and New York, 2007, p.22, n.18.

12 Possibly Salon of 1781, p.22, no.107; Marianne Roland Michel, *Anne Vallayer-Coster (1744–1818)*, Comptoir International du Livre, Paris, 1970, pp 217–18, no.333; Kahng and Roland Michel (eds), *Vallayer-Coster*, p.216, no.123.

13 Possibly Salon of 1785, p.19, no.56; Roland Michel, *Vallayer-Coster*, p.221, no.343 (as lost); Christie's, Paris, 28 October 2022, lot 29.

14 Louis-Sébastien Mercier, *Panorama of Paris: Selections from Tableau de Paris* (1781), trans. Jeremy Popkin, Pennsylvania State University Press, Philadelphia, PA, 2010, pp 127–8.

15 Salon of 1783, p.19, no.80.

16 Mercier, *Panorama of Paris*, pp 41, 127–8.

17 Alain Corbin, *The Foul and the Fragrant: Odor and the French Social Imagination*, Harvard University Press, Cambridge, MA, 1986, pp 74–5; Clare Brant, 'Fume and Perfume: Some Eighteenth-Century Uses of Smell', *Journal of British Studies*, vol.43, no.4, October 2004, pp 444–63.

18 Pierre-Joseph Buc'hoz, *Toilette de flore, ou Essai sur les plantes et les fleurs qui peuvent servir d'ornement aux dames*, Chez Valade, Paris, 1771.

19 Jean-Louis Fargeon, *L'art du parfumeur ou Traité complet de la preparation des parfums, cosmétiques, pomades, pastilles, odeurs, huiles antiques, essences, bains aromatiques et gants de senteur*, Delalain fils, Paris, 1801, pp 4–6.

20 Eugénie Briot, 'Jean-Louis Fargeon, fournisseur de la cour de France: art et techniques d'un parfumeur du XVIIIe siècle', *Artefact*, vol.1, 2014, pp 167–77, on pp 167–8.

21 Corbin, *The Foul and the Fragrant*, p.76; Feydeau, *A Scented Palace*, pp 25–6 and 59.

22 Denis Diderot, *Lettres sur les sourds et les muets: à l'usage de ceux qui entendent & qui parlent*, Jean-Baptiste-Claude II Bauche, Paris, 1751, p.23.

23 Corbin, *The Foul and the Fragrant*, pp 82–3.

24 Jean-Jacques Rousseau, *Emile, or, On Education: Includes Emile and Sophie, or, The Solitaries* (1762), trans. Allan Bloom, Basic Books, New York, 1979, p.300.

25 Hirschfeld, *Théorie de l'art des jardins*, p.66.

26 Chevalier Louis de Jaucourt, 'Polianthes tuberosa, tuberose', trans. Ann-Marie Thornton, in Denis Diderot and Jean d'Alembert, *The Encyclopedia of Diderot & d'Alembert Collaborative Translation Project*, Michigan Publishing, University of Michigan Library, Ann Arbor, MI, 2003–16, http://hdl.handle.net/2027/spo.did2222.0002.474.

27 Colin B. Bailey, *Fragonard's Progress of Love at The Frick Collection*, D. Giles, London, 2011, pp 32–3.

28 Ariane van Suchtelen and Lizzie Marx, *Fleeting: Scents in Colour*, exh.cat., Mauritshuis, The Hague, 2021; Christina Bradstreet, *Scented Visions: Smell in Art, 1850–1914*, Pennsylvania State University Press, University Park, PA, and London, 2022.

29 Corbin, *The Foul and the Fragrant*, p.55.

30 Nina Rattner Gelbart, *Minerva's French Sisters: Women of Science in Enlightenment France*, Yale University Press, New Haven, CT, and London, 2021, p.117.

31 Salon of 1775, p.19, no.99; Roland Michel, *Vallayer-Coster*, pp 102–3, no.1; Kahng and Roland Michel (eds), *Vallayer-Coster*, p.201, no.30.

32 Sophie Mouquin and Christophe Huchet de Quénetain, 'Essai', in *Anne Vallayer-Coster: Protégée de Marie-Antoinette*, exh.cat., Galerie Eric Coatalem, Paris, 2023, pp 66–91, on pp 81–2.

33 Arie Wallert (ed.), *Still Lifes: Techniques and Styles: An Examination of Paintings from the Rijksmuseum*, Rijksmuseum and Waanders Publishers, Amsterdam and Zwolle, 1999, p.51.

34 Salon of 1775, p.19, no.102; Roland Michel, *Vallayer-Coster*, pp 123 and 129, nos 63 and 77; Kahng and Roland Michel (eds), *Vallayer-Coster*, pp 200–1, nos 26 and 31; Mouquin and Huchet de Quénetain, 'Essai', p.81.

35 'Exposition au Salon du Louvre des peintures, sculptures & gravures de MM. de l'Académie royale', *Mercure de France*, October 1775, pp 176–202, on p.193.

36 Jean-François-Gille Colson, *Observations sur les ouvrages exposés au Sallon du Louvre, ou Lettre à M. le Comte de . . .* L'Imprimerie de Didot, Paris, 1775, pp 44–5.

37 *La lanterne magique aux Champs-Elysées, ou Entretien des grands peintres sur le Sallon de 1775*, Paris, 1775, p.28.

38 Salon of 1777, p.20, no.100; Roland Michel, *Vallayer-Coster*, pp 102–3, nos 2 and 3 (as lost); Kahng and Roland Michel (eds), *Vallayer-Coster*, p.202, nos 36 and 37, pls 19 and 20.

39 *Lettres pittoresques*, p.56.

40 Bailey, 'A Still-Life Painter and Her Patrons', pp 66–7.

41 Mouquin and Huchet de Quénetain, 'Essai', pp 80–81.

42 Anne L. Poulet, 'Neoclassical Vase by Clodion', *Art Institute of Chicago Museum Studies*, vol.15, no.2. 1989, pp 138–53.

43 Salon of 1781, p.22, no.105, Roland Michel, *Vallayer-Coster*, pp 121 and 125, no.67; Kahng and Roland Michel (eds), *Vallayer-Coster*, pp 206–7, no.61; Katharine Baetjer, *French Paintings in The Metropolitan Museum of Art from the Early Eighteenth Century through the Revolution*, The Metropolitan Museum of Art, New York, 2019, pp 299–301, no.100; Mouquin and Huchet de Quénetain, 'Essai', pp 80–81.

44 Roland Michel, *Vallayer-Coster*, p.127, no.71; Kahng and Roland Michel (eds), *Vallayer-Coster*, p.207, no.62.

45 Kahng and Roland Michel (eds), *Vallayer-Coster*, p.207, no.67; Philip Conisbee, 'Michael L. Rosenberg's Eighteenth Century', in Heather MacDonald (ed.), *French Art of the Eighteenth Century: The Michael L. Rosenberg Lecture Series at the Dallas Museum of Art*, Yale University Press, New Haven, CT, and London, 2016, pp 11–23, on pp 20–23.

46 Mouquin and Huchet de Quénetain, 'Essai', p.78.

47 Another nest appears in Vallayer-Coster's *Bouquet of Flowers in a Gilt-Bronze Mounted Vase*, 1776; Roland Michel, *Anne Vallayer-Coster*, p.124, no.65; Kahng and Roland Michel (eds), *Vallayer-Coster*, p.203, no.43; Christie's, New York, 31 October 2017, lot 31.

48 Mimi Hellman, 'The Nature of Artifice: French Porcelain Flowers and the Rhetoric of the Garnish', in Alden Cavanaugh and Michael E. Yonan (eds), *The Cultural Aesthetics of Eighteenth-Century Porcelain*, Ashgate, Farnham, 2010, pp 39–64.

49 Roland Michel, 'Vallayer in Her Time', p.23.

50 ibid., p.36, n.87.

51 Denis Diderot, 'Salon de 1781', in *Salons*, ed. Jean Seznec and Jean Adhémar, Clarendon Press, Oxford, 4 vols, 1957–68, vol.4, p.365.

52 *Lanlaire au Salon académique de peinture par M. L.B . . . de plusieurs academies*, Gattières, Paris, 1787, p.21.

53 Roland Michel, 'Vallayer in Her Time', p.19.

54 Roland Michel, *Vallayer-Coster*, pp 274–6; Roland Michel, 'Vallayer in Her Time', p.22.

55 Roland Michel, *Vallayer-Coster*, pp 36 and 259.

56 Possibly Salon of 1804, p.27, no.155; Kahng and Roland Michel (eds), *Vallayer-Coster*, p.224, C.

57 'Exposition de l'an XII', *Journal des arts, de littérature et de commerce*, vol.394, 10 January 1805, pp 73–81, on p.81.

58 Pierre-François Gueffier, *Entretiens sur les ouvrages de peinture, sculpture et gravure, exposés au Musée Napoléon en 1810 . . .*, C.F. Patris, Paris, 1811, p.74.

59 Marianne Roland Michel, 'Tapestries on Designs by Anne Vallayer-Coster', *The Burlington Magazine*, vol.102, no.692, November 1960, pp i–ii; Mouquin and Huchet de Quénetain, 'Essai', pp 80 and 91.

60 Bailey, 'A Still Life Painter and Her Patrons', pp 66–7.

61 I thank Perrin Stein for these suggestions. Salon of 1817, p.85, no.736; Roland Michel, 'Vallayer in Her Time', p.32.

62 Salon of 1802, p.59, no.284.

63 Salon of 1804, p.84, nos 481 and 482; Kahng and Roland Michel (eds), *Vallayer-Coster*, p.220, no.146, pl.56.

64 Roland Michel, 'Vallayer in Her Time', p.22.

65 Eleanor P. DeLorme (ed.), *Joséphine and the Arts of the Empire*, Getty Publications, Los Angeles, CA, 2005, pp 91–102.

66 *Journal de l'Empire*, 10 April 1811, p.4, and 27 October 1811, pp 3–4.

67 *Catalogue de la vente Coster*, lots 39, 40, 42.

68 *Journal de l'Empire*, 10 April 1811, p.4.

69 Laura Auricchio, *Adélaïde Labille-Guiard: Artist in the Age of Revolution*, Getty Publications, Los Angeles, CA, 2009, pp 40, 42–7, 49, 53–5, 105–6, 114.

70 Paris Spies-Gans, *A Revolution on Canvas: The Rise of Women Artists in Britain and France, 1760–1830*, Yale University Press, New Haven, CT, and London, 2022, pp 37–49.

71 Charles Ephrussi, 'Exposition des artistes indépendantes', *Gazette des Beaux-Arts*, 1 May 1880, p.487.

CONCLUSION

1 Kaori O'Connor, *Pineapple: A Global History*, Reaktion Books, London, 2013, pp 27–33.

2 Madeleine Françoise Basseporte likely painted pineapples too; see Nina Rattner Gelbart, 'Mlle Basseporte's *Jardin*, Mlle Biheron's *Cabinet*: Artist-Scientists and Their Spheres of Sociability', in

Mechthild Fend, Jennifer Germann and Melissa Hyde (eds), *Thinking Women and Eighteenth-Century Art: Strategic Reinterpretations*, Amsterdam University Press, Amsterdam, 2024, pp 281–300, on p.289.

3 *Catalogue de la vente Coster: notice des tableaux des fleurs peints par Mme Vallayer-Coster . . . Provenant du cabinet de feu M. et Mad. Coster*, 21 June and the following days, 1824, British Library, London, lot 1; Marianne Roland Michel, *Anne Vallayer-Coster (1744–1818)*, Comptoir International du Livre, Paris, 1970, p.274.

4 Salon of 1783, p.19, no.77; Roland Michel, *Vallayer-Coster*, p.103, no.4; Colin B. Bailey, 'A Still-Life Painter and Her Patrons: Collecting Vallayer-Coster, 1770–1789', in Eik Kahng and Marianne Roland Michel (eds), *Anne Vallayer-Coster: Painter to the Court of Marie-Antoinette*, exh.cat., Dallas Museum of Art, Dallas, TX, 2002, pp 59–73, on p.61; Christie's, Paris, 15 June 2023, lot 42.

5 See, for example, Melissa Hyde's forthcoming book, *Painted by Herself: Marie-Suzanne Giroust: Madame Roslin, the Forgotten Académicienne*; and Tori Champion's forthcoming dissertation, 'Marie-Thérèse Reboul Vien and the Emergence of Neoclassicism'.

APPENDIX

1 For Vallayer-Coster's work at the Salon, see the digitized *livrets*: *Explications des ouvrages de peinture, sculpture . . .* Bibliothèque nationale de France, Paris, 1771–1817, https://gallica.bnf.fr/ark:/12148/cb327720223/date&rk=150215;2. For more on the Salon catalogues, see Yuriko Jackall, 'The "Livrets" of the Salon, 1673–1800', in John Hagood (ed.), *Documenting the Salon: Paris Salon Catalogs, 1673–1945*, exh.cat., The National Gallery of Art, Washington, DC, 2016, pp 11–43.

2 Marianne Roland Michel, *Anne Vallayer-Coster (1744–1818)*, Comptoir International du Livre, Paris, 1970; Eik Kahng and Marianne Roland Michel (eds), *Anne Vallayer-Coster: Painter to the Court of Marie-Antoinette*, exh.cat., Dallas Museum of Art, Dallas, TX, 2002.

Select Bibliography

Adanson, Michel, *Histoire naturelle du Sénégal: coquillages, avec la relation abrégée d'un voyage fait en ce pays, pendant les années 1749, 50, 51, 52 & 53*, Bauche, Paris, 1757.

Adresse à l'Assemblée nationale, par la presque totalité des officiers de l'Académie royale de peinture et de sculpture auxquels se sont joints quelques académiciens, Veuve Hérissant, Paris, 1790.

Auricchio, Laura, *Adélaïde Labille-Guiard: Artist in the Age of Revolution*, Getty Publications, Los Angeles, CA, 2009.

Bachaumont, Louis Petit de, *Mémoires secrets pour servir à l'histoire de la République, des lettres en France depuis 1762 jusqu'à nos jours*, John Adamson, London, 36 vols, 1777–89.

—, *Lettres sur les peintures, sculptures et gravures de mrs. de l'Académie royale, exposés au sallon du Louvre depuis MDCCLXVII jusqu'en MDCCLXXIX*, John Adamson, London, 1780.

Baetjer, Katharine, *French Paintings in The Metropolitan Museum of Art from the Early Eighteenth Century through the Revolution*, The Metropolitan Museum of Art, New York, 2019.

Bailey, Colin B., 'Conventions of the Eighteenth-Century *Cabinet de tableaux:* Blondel d'Azincourt's *La première idée de la curiosité*', *The Art Bulletin*, vol.69, no.3, September 1987, pp 431–47.

—, 'The abbé Terray: An Enlightened Patron of Modern Sculpture', *The Burlington Magazine*, vol.135, no.1079, February 1993, pp 121–32.

—, 'A Still-Life Painter and Her Patrons: Collecting Vallayer-Coster, 1770–1789', in Kahng and Roland Michel (eds), *Vallayer-Coster*, pp 59–73.

—, *Patriotic Taste: Collecting Modern Art in Pre-Revolutionary Paris*, Yale University Press, New Haven, CT, and London, 2002.

—, *Fragonard's Progress of Love at The Frick Collection*, D. Giles, London, 2011.

Bailey, Colin B., with Philip Conisbee and Thomas W. Gaehtgens (eds), *The Age of Watteau, Chardin, and Fragonard: Masterpieces of French Genre Painting*, exh.cat., Yale University Press, New Haven, CT, and London, 2003.

Baillio, Joseph, Katharine Baetjer and Paul Lang (eds), *Vigée Le Brun: Woman Artist in Revolutionary France*, exh.cat., The Metropolitan Museum of Art, New York, 2015.

Banta, Andaleeb Badiee, and Alexa Greist, with Theresa Kutasz Christensen (eds), *Making Her Mark: A History of Women Artists in Europe, 1400–1800*, exh.cat., Art Gallery of Ontario, Toronto, and Baltimore Museum of Art, Baltimore, MD, 2023.

Barnes, Donna R., and Peter G. Rose, *Matters of Taste: Food and Drink in Seventeenth-Century Dutch Art and Life*, Syracuse University Press, Syracuse, NY, 2002.

Barry, Claire, 'The Painting Technique of Anne Vallayer-Coster: Searching for the Origins of Style', in Kahng and Roland Michel (eds), *Vallayer-Coster*, pp 95–113.

Bass, Marisa Anne, Anne Goldgar, Hanneke Grootenboer and Claudia Swan (eds), *Conchophilia: Shells, Art, and Curiosity in Early Modern Europe*, Princeton University Press, Princeton, NJ, 2021.

Bleichmar, Danielle, 'Learning to Look: Visual Expertise across Art and Science in Eighteenth-Century France', *Eighteenth-Century Studies*, vol.46, no.1, Fall 2012, pp 85–111.

Bradstreet, Christina, *Scented Visions: Smell in Art, 1850–1914*, Pennsylvania State University Press, University Park, PA, and London, 2022.

Brant, Clare, 'Fume and Perfume: Some Eighteenth-Century Uses of Smell', *Journal of British Studies*, vol.43, no.4, October 2004, pp 444–63.

Braudel, Fernand, *Civilization and Capitalism, 15th–18th Century: The Wheels of Commerce*, University of California Press, Oakland, CA, 1982.

Brennan, Thomas Edward, *Public Drinking and Popular Culture in Eighteenth-Century Paris*, Princeton University Press, Princeton, NJ, 2014.

Brillat-Savarin, Jean Anthelme, *Physiologie du goût, ou Méditations de gastronomie transcendante . . .* Boulé, Paris, 1850.

Briot, Eugénie, 'Jean-Louis Fargeon, fournisseur de la cour de France: art et techniques d'un parfumeur du XVIIIe siècle', *Artefact*, vol.1, 2014, pp 167–77.

Buc'hoz, Pierre-Joseph, *Toilette de flore, ou Essai sur les plantes et les fleurs qui peuvent servir d'ornement aux dames*, Chez Valade, Paris, 1771.

Bycroft, Michael, 'Style and Substance in Rococo Science', *The Journal of Interdisciplinary History*, vol.48, no.3, 2018, pp 359–84.

Campan, Jeanne Louise Henriette, *Mémoires de Madame Campan, première femme de chambre de Marie Antoinette*, ed. Jean Chalon and Carlos de Augulo, Gallimard, Paris, 1988.

Carr, J.L., 'Pygmalion and the Philosophes: The Animated Statue in Eighteenth-Century France', *Journal of the Warburg and Courtauld Institutes*, vol.23, nos 3/4, July–December 1960, pp 239–55.

Catalogue d'une belle collection . . . provenant de la succession du feu M. l'abbé Terray, François-Charles Joullain fils, Paris, 1778.

Catalogue de la vente Coster: notice des tableaux des fleurs peints par Mme Vallayer-Coster . . . provenant du cabinet de feu M. et Mad. Coster, 21 June and the following days, 1824, British Library, London.

Caude, Élisabeth, Jérôme de La Gorce and Béatrix Saule (eds), *Fêtes & divertissements à la cour*, exh.cat., Musée national des châteaux de Versailles et de Trianon, Versailles, 2016.

Champion, Tori E., 'Le pinceau à la main: The Intertwined Lives and Careers of Madeleine Françoise Basseporte and Marie-Thérèse Reboul Vien', Master's Thesis, University of Washington, Seattle, WA, 2021.

Chappey, Frédéric, *Les tresors des princes de Bourbon Conti*, Musée d'art et d'histoire Louis Senlecq, L'Isle Adam, 2000.

Cohen, Sarah R., *Enlightened Animals in Eighteenth-Century Art: Sensation, Matter, and Knowledge*, Bloomsbury, London and New York, 2021.

Colson, Jean-François-Gille, *Observations sur les ouvrages exposés au Sallon du Louvre, ou Lettre à M. le Comte de . . .* L'Imprimerie de Didot, Paris, 1775.

Condillac, Étienne Bonnot de, *Traité des sensations*, Chez de Bure l'ainé, London and Paris, 1754.

Conisbee, Philip, 'Michael L. Rosenberg's Eighteenth Century', in MacDonald (ed.), *French Art of the Eighteenth Century*, pp 11–23.

Corbin, Alain, *The Foul and the Fragrant: Odor and the French Social Imagination*, Harvard University Press, Cambridge, MA, 1986.

Davidson, Alan, *The Oxford Companion to Food*, Oxford University Press, Oxford, 2006.

Davis, Jennifer J., 'To Make a Revolutionary Cuisine: Gender and Politics in French Kitchens, 1789–1815', *Gender & History*, vol.23, no.2, August 2011, pp 301–20.

—, *Defining Culinary Authority: The Transformation of Cooking in France, 1650–1830*, Louisiana State University Press, Baton Rouge, LA, 2013.

Deflers, Isabelle, 'The Difficult Reform of Military Discipline in the Latter Half of the Eighteenth-Century', in Susan Richter, Thomas Maissen and Manuela Albertone (eds), *Languages of Reform in the Eighteenth Century: When Europe Lost Its Fear of Change*, Routledge, New York, 2020, pp 323–43.

DeLorme, Eleanor P. (ed.), *Joséphine and the Arts of the Empire*, Getty Publications, Los Angeles, CA, 2005.

De Piles, Roger, *Dialogue sur le coloris*, Chez Nicholas Langlois, Paris, 1699.

—, *Cours de peinture par principes avec un balance de peintres*, Chez Jacques Estienne, Paris, 1708.

Dezallier d'Argenville, Antoine-Joseph, *L'Histoire naturelle éclaircie dans deux de ses parties principales, la Lithologie et la Conchyliologie*, Chez de Bure l'aîné, Paris, 1742.

—, *Description sommaire des ouvrages de peinture, sculpture et gravure exposés dans les salles de l'Académie royale*, Chez de Bure l'aîné, Paris, 1781.

D'Houry, Laurent (ed.), *Almanach royale*, Paris, 1781.

Diderot, Denis, *Lettres sur les sourds et les muets: à l'usage de ceux qui entendent & qui parlent*, Jean-Baptiste-Claude II Bauche, Paris, 1751.

—, *Oeuvres complètes de Diderot*, ed. J. Assézat and Maurice Tourneux, Garnier frères, Paris, 20 vols, 1876.

—, *Oeuvres*, ed. André Billy, Gallimard, Paris, 1951.

—, *Salons*, ed. Jean Seznec and Jean Adhémar, Clarendon Press, Oxford, 4 vols, 1957–68.

—, *Diderot on Art: The Salon of 1765 and Notes on Painting*, trans. John Goodman, Yale University Press, New Haven, CT, 2 vols, 1995.

Diderot, Denis, and Jean d'Alembert, *The Encyclopedia of Diderot & d'Alembert Collaborative Translation Project*, Michigan Publishing, University of Michigan Library, Ann Arbor, MI, 2003–16, https://quod.lib.umich.edu/d/did/.

Dietz, Bettina, 'Mobile Objects: The Space of Shells in Eighteenth-Century France,' *British Society for the History of Science*, vol.39, no.3, September 2006, pp 363–82.

Douthwaite, Julia V., 'From Fish Seller to Suffragist: The Women's March on Versailles', in *The Frankenstein of 1790 and Other Lost Chapters from Revolutionary France*, University of Chicago Press, Chicago, IL, 2012, pp 17–58.

Edwards, JoLynn, 'The Conti Sales of 1777 and 1779 and their Impact on the Parisian Art Market', *Studies in the Eighteenth-Century Culture*, vol.39, 2010, pp 77–110.

Ephrussi, Charles, 'Exposition des artistes indépendantes', *Gazette des Beaux-Arts*, 1 May 1880, p.487.

Explications des ouvrages de peinture, sculpture . . . Bibliothèque nationale de France, Paris, 1771–1817, https://gallica.bnf.fr/ark:/12148/cb327720223/date&rk=150215;2.

'Exposition de l'an XII', *Journal des arts, de littérature et de commerce*, vol.394, 10 January 1805, pp 73–81.

'Exposition des peintures, sculptures, gravures de MM. de l'Académie royale', *Mercure de France*, October 1771, pp 174–201.

'Exposition au salon du Louvre des peintures, sculptures & gravures de MM. de l'Académie royale', *Mercure de France*, October 1775, pp 176–202.

'Exposition des peintures, sculptures & gravures de MM. de l'Académie royale, dans le Sallon du Louvre, depuis de 25 août jusqu'au dernier septembre 1785', *Mercure de France*, October 1785, pp 18–44.

Fahy, Everett, *The Wrightsman Pictures*, Yale University Press and The Metropolitan Museum of Art, New Haven, CT, and New York, 2005.

Faré, Michel, *Le grand siècle de la nature morte en France, Le XVIIe siècle*, Société Française du Livre, Paris, 1974.

Fargeon, Jean-Louis, *L'art du parfumeur ou Traité complet de la preparation des parfums, cosmétiques, pomades, pastilles, odeurs, huiles antiques, essences, bains aromatiques et gants de senteur*, Delalain fils, Paris, 1801.

Fend, Mechthild, Jennifer Germann and Melissa Hyde (eds), *Thinking Women and Eighteenth-Century Art: Strategic Reinterpretations*, Amsterdam University Press, Amsterdam, 2024.

Feydeau, Elisabeth de, *A Scented Palace: The Secret History of Marie Antoinette's Perfumer*, trans. Jane Lizop, I.B. Tauris & Co., London and New York, 2007.

Foucart, Jacques, et al., *Musée du Louvre: nouvelles acquisitions du department des peintre, 1991–1995*, Réunion des musées nationaux, Paris, 1996.

Foucault, Michel, *The Order of Things: An Archaeology of the Human Sciences*, Pantheon Books, New York, 1970.

Freund, Amy, 'Good Dog! Jean-Baptiste Oudry and the Politics of Animal Painting', in MacDonald (ed.), *French Art of the Eighteenth Century*, pp 67–80.

—, 'Men and Hunting Guns', in Jennifer G. Germann and Heidi A. Strobel (eds), *Materializing Gender in Eighteenth-Century Europe*, Routledge, New York, 2016, pp 17–34.

Gargam, Adeline, 'Marie-Marguerite Biheron et son cabinet d'anatomie: une femme de science et une pédagogue', in Isabelle Brouard-Arends and Marie-Emmanuelle Plagnol-Diéval (eds), *Femmes éducatrices au siècle des Lumières*, Presses universitaires de Rennes, 2007, pp 147–56, https://doi.org/10.4000/books.pur.39353.

Garnier-Pelle, Nicole, *Carmontelle (1717–1806), ou Le temps de la douceur de vivre: collection les Carnets de Chantilly*, Éditions Faton, Dijon, 2020.

Gelbart, Nina Rattner, *Minerva's French Sisters: Women of Science in Enlightenment France*, Yale University Press, New Haven, CT, and London, 2021.

—, 'Mlle Basseporte's *Jardin*, Mlle Biheron's *Cabinet*: Artist-Scientists and Their Spheres of Sociability', in Fend et al. (eds), *Thinking Women and Eighteenth-Century Art*, pp 281–300.

Gersaint, Edmé-François, *Catalogue d'une collection considérable de curiosités de différent genres*, Chez Prault fils, Paris, 2 December 1737.

—, *Catalogue raisonné d'une collection considérable de diverses curiosités en tous genres contenues dans les cabinets de feu Monsieur Bonnier de la Mosson, Bailly et Captaine des Chasses de la Varenne des Thuilleries & ancien Colonel du Regiment Dauphin par E.F. Gersaint*, J. Barois, Paris, 1744.

Glorieux, Guillaume, *A l'enseigne de Gersaint: Edme-François Gersaint, marchand d'art sur le Pont Notre-Dame, 1694–1750*, Editions Champ Vallon, Seyssel, 2002.

Gopnik, Blake, 'Sensual Still Lifes: Built to Lust?', *The Washington Post*, 15 September 2002, https://www.washingtonpost.com/archive/lifestyle/style/2002/09/15/sensual-still-lifes-built-to-lust/5c7e540d-7cf6-41c2-98bf-4d97f4201800/?noredirect=on&utm_term=.08dcfd526909.

Grasskamp, Anna, 'Shells, Bodies, and the Collector's Cabinet', in Bass et al. (eds), *Conchophilia*, pp 49–71.

Gueffier, Pierre-François, *Entretiens sur les ouvrages de peinture, sculpture et gravure, exposés au Musée Napoléon en 1810 . . .*, C.F. Patris, Paris, 1811.

Guichard, Charlotte, 'Taste Communities: The Rise of the Amateur in Eighteenth-Century Paris', *Eighteenth-Century Studies*, vol.45, no.4, Summer 2016, pp 519–47.

Guichard, Charlotte, Anne-Solenn Le Hô and Hannah Williams, 'Prussian Blue: Chemistry, Commerce, and Colour in Eighteenth-Century Paris', *Art History*, vol.46, no.1, February 2023, pp 154–86, https://doi.org/10.1111/1467-8365.12695.

Guichard, M., 'Académie royal de peinture & sculpture', *Mercure de France*, September 1770, pp 174–6.

Hardy, Blanche C., *Princess Lamballe: A Biography*, A. Constable, London, 1908.

Harrington, Walt, 'Cleaning Rabbits', *The American Scholar*, vol.71, no.4, Autumn 2002, pp 69–74.

Haskell, Francis, and Nicholas Penny, *Taste and the Antique: The Lure of Classical Sculpture 1500–1900*, Yale University Press, New Haven, CT, and London, 1981.

Hellman, Mimi, 'The Nature of Artifice: French Porcelain Flowers and the Rhetoric of the Garnish', in Alden Cavanaugh and Michael E. Yonan (eds), *The Cultural Aesthetics of Eighteenth-Century Porcelain*, Ashgate, Farnham, 2010, pp 39–64.

Hesse, Carla, *The Other Enlightenment: How French Women Became Modern*, Princeton University Press, Princeton, NJ, 2001.

Higa, Jade, 'Charlotte Charke's Gun: Queering Material Culture and Gender Performance', *ABO: Interactive Journal for Women in the Arts, 1640–1830*, vol.7, no.1, 2017, http://scholarcommons.usf.edu/abo/vol7/iss1/2.

Higonnet, Anne, 'Through a Louvre Window', *Journal18*, vol.2, Fall 2016, http://www.journal18.org/1057.

Hirschfeld, Christian Cajus Lorenz, *Théorie de l'art des jardins*, Chez les heritiers de M.G. Weidmann et Reich, Leipzig, 1779.

Hooper-Hamersley, Rosamond, *The Hunt after Jeanne-Antoinette de Pompadour: Patronage, Politics, Art, and the French Enlightenment*, Lexington Books, Lanham, MD, 2011.

Hospodar, Miriam, 'Aphrodisiac Foods: Bringing Heaven to Earth', *Gastronomica*, vol.4, no.4, 2004, pp 82–93.

Hyde, Melissa, *Making Up the Rococo: Boucher and His Critics*, Getty Publications, Los Angeles, CA, 2006.

—, 'Looking Elsewhere: Women and the Parisian Art World in the Eighteenth-Century', in Jordana Pomeroy (ed.), *Royalists to Romantics: Women Artists from the Louvre, Versailles, and other French National Collections*, exh.cat., National Museum of Women in the Arts, Washington, DC, 2012, pp 33–41.

—, 'Peinte par elle-même?', *Arts et Savoirs*, vol.6, 12 July 2016, http://journals.openedition.org/aes/794.

—, 'Marie-Thérèse Reboul (Madame Vien): More than a Footnote in Art History', in Fend et al. (eds), *Thinking Women and Eighteenth-Century Art*, pp 239–80.

Jackall, Yuriko, 'The "Livrets" of the Salon, 1673–1800', in John Hagood (ed.), *Documenting the Salon: Paris*

Salon Catalogs, 1673–1945, exh.cat., The National Gallery of Art, Washington, DC, 2016, pp 11–43.

Jeffares, Neil, 'ROSLIN, Mme Alexander, née Jeanne-Suzanne Giroust (Paris 1734–1772)', *Dictionary of Pastellists before 1800*, online edn, 2022, http://www.pastellists.com/Articles/RoslinMS.pdf.

—, 'Vigée Le Brun's Petitioners', *Pastels & Pastellists*, 2022, http://www.pastellists.com/Essays/VigeeLeBrunPetition.pdf.

Jossan, Daudé de, *Lettres de M. Raphael le jeune, eleve des ecoles gratuites de dessin, neveu de feu M. Raphael, peintre de l'Académie de St Luc, a un de ses amis, architecte à Rome: sur les peintures, sculptures & gravures qui sont exposées cette année au Louvre*, Paris, 1771.

Journal de l'Empire, 10 April 1811.

Journal de l'Empire, 27 October 1811.

Journal de Paris, no.203, 22 July 1781.

Journal de Paris, no.258, 15 September 1785.

Journal de politique et de littérature, no.61, 5 November 1777.

Kahng, Eik, and Marianne Roland Michel (eds), *Anne Vallayer-Coster: Painter to the Court of Marie-Antoinette*, exh.cat., Dallas Museum of Art, Dallas, TX, 2002.

Lajer-Burcharth, Ewa, *The Painter's Touch: Boucher, Chardin, Fragonard*, Princeton University Press, Princeton, NJ, 2018.

La lanterne magique aux Champs-Elysées, ou Entretien des grands peintres sur le Sallon de 1775, Paris, 1775.

Lanlaire au Salon académique de peinture par M. L.B . . . de plusieurs academies, Gattières, Paris, 1787.

Lastic, Georges de, and Pierre Jacky, *Desportes*, Monelle Hayot, Saint-Rémy-en-l'Eau, 2010.

Lettres pittoresques à l'occasion des tableaux exposés au Sallon en 1777, Paris, 1777.

Levey, Michael, 'The Pose of Pigalle's *Mercury*', *The Burlington Magazine*, vol.106, no.739, October 1964, pp 460–63.

Levy, Darlene, Harriet Applewhite and Mary Durham Johnson (eds), *Women in Revolutionary Paris, 1789–1795*, University of Illinois Press, Urbana, IL, 1997.

Liedtke, Walter, *Dutch Paintings in the Metropolitan Museum of Art*, The Metropolitan Museum of Art and Yale University Press, New York, New Haven, CT, and London, 2007.

Lindeman, Christina, *The Art of Anna Dorothea Therbusch (1721–1782)*, Amsterdam University Press, Amsterdam, 2024.

Linnaeus, Carl, *Systema Naturae*, 10th edn, Laurentii Salvii, Stockholm, 1758.

McClellan, Andrew, *Inventing the Louvre: Art, Politics, and the Origins of the Modern Museum*, University of California Press, Berkeley and Los Angeles, CA, 1999.

—, 'Musée du Louvre, Paris: Palace of the People, Art for All', in Carole Paul (ed.), *The First Modern Museums of Art: The Birth of an Institution in 18th- and early 19th-Century Europe*, Getty Publications, Los Angeles, CA, 2012, pp 213–36.

MacDonald, Heather (ed.), *French Art of the Eighteenth Century: The Michael L. Rosenberg Lecture Series at the Dallas Museum of Art*, Yale University Press, New Haven, CT, and London, 2016.

Malaguzzi, Silvia, *Food and Feasting in Art*, Getty Publications, Los Angeles, CA, 2008.

Melish, Jacob D., 'The Power of Wives: Managing Money and Men in the Family Businesses of Old Regime Paris', in Daryl M. Hafter and Nina Kushner (eds), *Women and Work in Eighteenth-Century France*, Louisiana State University Press, Baton Rouge, LA, 2015, pp 77–90.

Menon, Joseph, *Les soupers de la cour, ou L'art de travailler toutes sortes d'alimens, pour servir les meilleures tables, suivant les quatre saisons*, Chez Guillyn, Paris, 1755.

Mercier, Louis-Sébastien, *Panorama of Paris: Selections from Tableau de Paris (1781)*, trans. Jeremy Popkin, Pennsylvania State University Press, Philadelphia, PA, 2010.

Mercure de France, December 1727.

Mercure de France, 4 August 1781.

Michel, Christian, *The Académie Royale de Peinture et de Sculpture: The Birth of the French School, 1648–1793*, Getty Publications, Los Angeles, CA, 2018.

Milam, Jennifer, 'Rococo Representations of Interspecies Sensuality and the Pursuit of Volupté', *The Art Bulletin*, vol.97, no.2, June 2015, pp 192–209.

Millon, Henry, 'The French Academy of Architecture: Foundation and Program', in June Hargrove (ed.), *The French Academy: Classicism and Its Antagonists*, University of Delaware Press, Newark, DE, 1990, pp 68–77.

Mirzoeff, Nicholas, 'Revolution, Representation, Equality: Gender, Genre, and Emulation in the Académie Royale de Peinture et Sculpture, 1785–93', *Eighteenth-Century Studies*, vol.31, no.2, Winter, 1997/8, pp 153–74.

Montaiglon, Anatole (ed.), *Procès-verbaux de l'Académie royale de peinture et de sculpture*, J. Baur and Charavay frères, Paris, 10 vols, 1875–92.

Montaiglon, Anatole, and Jules Guiffrey (eds), *Correspondance des directeurs de l'Académie de France à Rome avec les surintendants des bâtiments*, Charavay frères, Paris, 18 vols, 1887–1912.

Mouquin, Sophie, and Christophe Huchet de Quénetain, 'Essai', in *Anne Vallayer-Coster: Protégée de Marie-Antoinette*, exh.cat., Galerie Eric Coatalem, Paris, 2023, pp 66–91.

Naves, Mario, 'Subtle Pleasures of Still Life Blossom in Specialist Show', *The New York Observer*, 17 February 2003, http://observer.com/2003/02/subtle-pleasures-of-still-life-blossom-in-specialist-show/.

Németh, Balázs, *Early Military Rifles: 1740–1850*, Bloomsbury, London and New York, 2020.

Nochlin, Linda, *Women, Art, and Power and Other Essays*, Harper & Row, New York, 1988.

Oberer, Angela, *Rosalba Carriera*, Getty Publications, Los Angeles, CA, 2022.

O'Connor, Kaori, *Pineapple: A Global History*, Reaktion Books, London, 2013.

Olausson, Magnus, 'Anne Vallayer-Coster, *Portrait of a Violinist*', *Art Bulletin of Nationalmuseum Stockholm*, vol.22, 2015, pp 17–20.

Olausson, Magnus, and Xavier Salmon, *Alexandre Roslin (1718–1793): un portraitise pour l'Europe*, exh.cat., Réunion des musées nationaux, Paris, 2008.

O'Neal, John C., *The Authority of Experience: Sensationist Theory in the French Enlightenment*, Pennsylvania State University Press, University Park, PA, 1996.

Oppenheimer, Margaret A., '"The Charming Spectacle of a Cadaver": Anatomical and Life Study by Women Artists in Paris, 1775–1815', *Nineteenth-Century Art Worldwide*, vol.6, no.1, Spring 2007.

Opperman, Hal, *J.-B. Oudry*, Kimbell Art Museum, Fort Worth, TX, 1983.

Pahin de la Blancherie, *Essai d'un tableau historique des peintres de l'école françoise depuis Jean Cousin en 1550 jusqu'en 1783 inclusivement*, Bureau de la Correspondance, Paris, 1783.

Parker, Rozsika, and Griselda Pollock, *Old Mistresses: Women, Art and Ideology*, Routledge, London, 1981.

Philippe, Emmanuelle, and Séverine Sofio, 'I Was Born in this Palace: Emotional Bonds in the Artistic Community of the Louvre (1750–1800)', in Susan Broomhall (ed.), *Emotions in the Household, 1200–1900*, Palgrave Macmillan, New York, 2007, pp 234–51.

Pinault-Sorensen, Madeleine, and Marie-Catherine Sahut, '*Panaches de mer, Lithophytes et Coquilles* (1769), un tableau d'histoire naturelle par Anne Vallayer-Coster', *Revue du Louvre: la revue des musées de France*, vol.XLVII, February 1998, pp 49–50.

Pinkard, Susan, *A Revolution in Taste: The Rise of French Cuisine, 1650–1800*, Cambridge University Press, Cambridge, 2009.

Pomian, Krzysztof, *Collectors and Curiosities: Paris and Venice, 1500–1800*, trans. Elizabeth Wiles-Portier, Polity Press, Cambridge, 1990.

Ponting, Clive, *Gunpowder*, Chatto & Windus, London, 2005.

Poulet, Anne L., 'Neoclassical Vase by Clodion', *Art Institute of Chicago Museum Studies*, vol.15, no.2. 1989, pp 138–53.

Priebe, Jessica S., *François Boucher and the Art of Collecting in Eighteenth-Century France*, Routledge, New York, 2022.

Pyhrr, Stuart W., *Of Arms and Men: Arms and Armor at the Metropolitan, 1912–2012*, The Metropolitan Museum of Art, New York, 2012.

Rémy, Pierre, *Catalogue raisonné . . . de feu Monsieur Dezallier d'Argenville*, Chez Didot l'aîné, Paris, 3 March 1766.

—, *Catalogue raisonné des curiousités qui composoient le cabinet de feu Mme Dubois-Jourdain*, Chez Didot l'aîné, Paris, 12 May 1766.

—, *Catalogue de tableaux précieux . . . d'un cabinet distingue* [Madame du Barry], Chez M. Cattilan, Paris, 22 December 1775.

—, *Catalogue d'une riche collection de tableaux des maîtres les plus celebres des trois écoles . . . qui composent le cabinet de feu son Altesse Sérénissime Monseigneur le Prince de Conti, prince du sang et Grand Prieur de France*, Chez Muzier, Paris, 8 April–6 June 1777.

Roland Michel, Marianne, 'Tapestries on Designs by Anne Vallayer-Coster', *The Burlington Magazine*, vol.102, no.692, November 1960, pp i–ii.

—, 'Of Women and Flowers', *The Burlington Magazine*, vol.108, no.760, July 1966, pp i–v.

—, *Anne Vallayer-Coster (1744–1818)*, Comptoir International du Livre, Paris, 1970.

—, 'Vallayer in Her Time', in Kahng and Roland Michel (eds), *Vallayer-Coster*, pp 13–37.

Roland Michel, Marianne, and Ursula Korneitchouk, 'A Basket of Plums', *The Bulletin of the Cleveland Museum of Art*, vol.60, no.2, 1973, pp 52–9.

Roland Michel, Marianne, et al. (eds), *The Floral Art of Pierre-Joseph Redouté*, exh.cat., Bruce Museum of Arts & Science and Kimbell Art Museum, Greenwich, CT, and Fort Worth, TX, 2002.

Rosenberg, Pierre, *Chardin*, Flammarion, Paris, 1999.

—, *Chardin*, exh.cat., The Metropolitan Museum of Art, New York, 2000.

Rousseau, Jean-Jacques, *Confessions de J.-J. Rousseau* (1767), Ménard et Desenne fils, Paris, 1827.

—, *Emile, or, On Education: Includes Emile and Sophie, or, The Solitaries* (1762), trans. Allan Bloom, Basic Books, New York, 1979.

—, *A Discourse on Inequality* (1754), Open Road Media, New York, 2016.

Roworth, Wendy Wassyng, 'Anatomy as Destiny: Regarding the Body in the Art of Angelica Kauffman', in Gill Perry and Michael Rossington (eds), *Femininity and Masculinity in Eighteenth-Century Art and Culture*, Manchester University Press, Manchester, 1994, pp 41–62.

Salmon, Xavier (ed.), *Jean-Marc Nattier, 1685–1766*, exh.cat., Réunion des musées nationaux, Paris, 1999.

Saslow, James M., '"Disagreeably Hidden": Construction and Constriction of the Lesbian Body in Rosa Bonheur's Horse Fair', in Norma Broude and Mary D. Garrard (eds), *The Expanding Discourse: Feminism and Art History*, Harper Collins, New York, 1992, pp 187–206.

Schiebinger, Londa, *The Mind Has No Sex? Women in the Origins of Modern Science*, Harvard University Press, Cambridge, MA, 1991.

Scott, Katie, and Hannah Williams (eds), *Artists' Things: Rediscovering Lost Property from Eighteenth-Century France*, Getty Research Institute, Los Angeles, CA, 2024, https://www.getty.edu/publications/artists-things/.

Serrette, Renaud, 'De Versailles à Rambouillet: quatre dessus-de-porte de Madeleine Boullogne retrouvés', *Versalia*, no.19, 2016, pp 87–92.

Sheriff, Mary D., *The Exceptional Woman: Elisabeth Vigée-Lebrun and the Cultural Politics of Art*, University of Chicago Press, Chicago, IL, 1996.

—, 'The Naked Truth? The Allegorical Frontispiece and Woman's Ambition in Eighteenth-Century France', in Cristelle Baskins and Lisa Rosenthal (eds), *Early Modern Visual Allegory: Embodying Meaning*, Ashgate, Aldershot and Burlington, VT, 2007, pp 243–64.

Shoory, Natasha, 'Review: Women and the Art and Science of Collecting in Eighteenth-Century Europe', *The Society for the History of Collecting*, 19 April 2021, https://societyhistorycollecting.org/reviews/review-women-and-the-art-and-science-of-collecting-in-eighteenth-century-europe/.

Shrubb, Michael, *Feasting, Fowling and Feathers: A History of the Exploitation of Wild Birds*, Bloomsbury, London, 2013.

Smentek, Kristel, *Rococo Exotic: French Mounted Porcelains and the Allure of the East*, exh.cat., The Frick Collection, New York, 2007.

Spies-Gans, Paris, *A Revolution on Canvas: The Rise of Women Artists in Britain and France, 1760–1830*, Yale University Press, New Haven, CT, and London, 2022.

Suchtelen, Ariane van, and Lizzie Marx, *Fleeting: Scents in Colour*, exh.cat., Mauritshuis, The Hague, 2021.

Swan, Claudia, 'The Nature of Exotic Shells', in Bass et al. (eds), *Conchophilia*, pp 21–47.

Takats, Sean, *The Expert Cook in Enlightenment France*, Johns Hopkins University Press, Baltimore, MD, 2011.

Taylor, Helena, 'The Quarrel of the Ancients and Moderns', *French Studies: A Quarterly Review*, vol.74, no.4, 2020, pp 605–20.

Taylor-Leduc, Susan, *Marie-Antoinette's Legacy: The Politics of French Garden Patronage and Picturesque Design, 1775–1867*, Amsterdam University Press, Amsterdam, 2022.

Tessler, Nira, 'The Flower Motif and the Feminine Representation in the History of Art', in *Flowers and*

Towers: Politics of Identity in the Art of the American 'New Woman', Cambridge Scholars Publishing, Newcastle upon Tyne, 2015, pp 8–39.

Tobin, Beth Fowkes, *The Duchess's Shells: Natural History Collecting in the Age of Cook's Voyages*, Yale University Press, New Haven, CT, and London, 2014.

Trémolières de St Saturnin, Antoine, *L'art de la chasse, pour le divertissement de la noblesse, et de tous ceux qui aiment cet exercice* (1724), Société des lettres, sciences et arts de l'Aveyron, Rodez, 1996.

Vigée Le Brun, Elisabeth, *Souvenirs de Madame Vigée Le Brun*, Charpentier et cie, Paris, 1869.

Von Hoffman, Viktoria, *From Gluttony to Enlightenment: The World of Taste in Early Modern Europe*, University of Illinois Press, Champaign, IL, 2016.

Wallert, Arie (ed.), *Still Lifes: Techniques and Styles: An Examination of Paintings from the Rijksmuseum*, Rijksmuseum and Waanders Publishers, Amsterdam and Zwolle, 1999.

Warner, Marina, *Monuments and Maidens: The Allegory of the Female Form*, University of California Press, Berkeley and Los Angeles, CA, 2000.

Watts, Sydney, *Meat Matters: Butchers, Politics, and Market Culture in Eighteenth-Century Paris*, University of Rochester Press, Rochester, NY, 2006.

—, 'Enlightened Fasting: Religious Conviction, Scientific Inquiry, and Medical Knowledge in Early Modern France', in Ken Albala and Trudy Eden (eds), *Food & Faith in Christian Culture*, Columbia University Press, New York, 2011, pp 105–24.

Weber, Caroline, *Queen of Fashion: What Marie Antoinette Wore to the Revolution*, Macmillan, New York, 2006.

Werlich, Robert, *Orders and Decorations of All Nations*, Quaker Press, Washington, DC, 1974.

Wheaton, Barbara Ketcham, *Savoring the Past: The French Kitchen and Table from 1300 to 1789*, Simon and Schuster, New York, 2011.

Williams, Hannah, *Académie Royale: A History in Portraits*, Ashgate, Farnham, 2015.

Wilson, Robert L., *Silk and Steel: Women at Arms*, Skyhorse Publishing, New York, 2015.

Wrede, Martin, and Christine Weil, 'Le portrait du roi restauré, ou la fabrication de Louis XVIII', *Revue d'histoire moderne et contemporaine*, vol.53, no.2, April–June 2006, pp 112–38.

Zerilli, Linda, '"Une Maitresse Imperieuse": Woman in Rousseau's Semiotic Republic', in Lynda Lange (ed.), *Feminist Interpretations of Jean-Jacques Rousseau*, Pennsylvania State University Press, University Park, PA, 2010, pp 277–314.

Image Credits

Index